THE PYRAMIDS OF EGYPT

THE PYRAMIDS
OF EGYPT

I. E. S. EDWARDS

A Studio Book **The Viking Press** New York

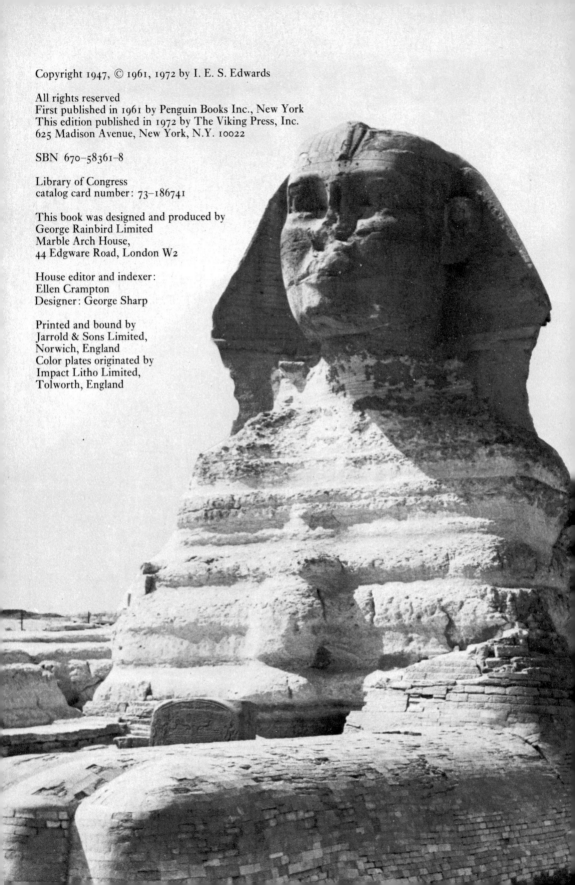

First published in 1961 by Penguin Books Inc., New York
This edition published in 1972 by The Viking Press, Inc.
625 Madison Avenue, New York, N.Y. 10022

SBN 670–58361–8

Library of Congress
catalog card number: 73–186741

This book was designed and produced by
George Rainbird Limited
Marble Arch House,
44 Edgware Road, London W2

House editor and indexer:
Ellen Crampton
Designer: George Sharp

Printed and bound by
Jarrold & Sons Limited,
Norwich, England
Color plates originated by
Impact Litho Limited,
Tolworth, England

Contents

Color Plates

Drawings and Plans

List of Drawings and Plans – continued

Preface

The following chapters are, in the first place, an attempt to describe some of the principal features of a number of pyramids, nearly all of which were built over a period of about a thousand years. Only those pyramids which illustrate most clearly the evolution and subsequent decline of that class of tomb are discussed in any detail, the remainder being merely mentioned in passing. The last chapter gives some account of the methods employed in construction and of the motives which prompted the Egyptian kings to adopt the pyramid form.

Although I have visited most of the pyramids described and have made use of notes which I recorded on their sites, a considerable part of the factual matter is, of necessity, taken from the published reports of various archaeologists who have surveyed or excavated these monuments in the course of the past century. My debt to these archaeologists and to the publishers of their reports will be apparent to every reader. Many of the interpretations given are also based on the works of previous writers; in some cases, however, I have ventured to offer explanations of my own.

Since 1947, when the first edition of this book appeared, discoveries of great importance for tracing the early history of the pyramids have been made, chiefly by the excavations of J.-P. Lauer, Ahmed Fakhry, and the late Zakaria Goneim, all working for the Antiquities Department of the Egyptian government, and by the late W. B. Emery, on behalf of the Antiquities Department and the Egypt Exploration Society. Almost every year something comes to light which enables the history of some architectural feature to be more clearly understood. In order to take into account the additional knowledge made available by these discoveries, the text was first revised and expanded in 1961. The present edition includes information which has been obtained since that date. Some of the photographic illustrations in the earlier editions have been omitted for technical reasons, and a considerable number of new illustrations in both colour and monochrome have been added. For assistance in seeking out and procuring these illustrations and for steering the book through the press I am particularly indebted to Mrs Ellen Crampton and her colleagues on the staff of the present publishers. I must also record my thanks to the museums and photographers mentioned in the lists of illustrations, who have provided the photographs.

No less striking than the discoveries made in the field has been the number of books and articles, on subjects dealing directly or indirectly with pyramids, which have appeared since 1947. A glance at the publications listed in the bibliography will show how many fall into this category. Nevertheless, much work still remains to be done before all the sources of information known at present are fully explored. The study of the fragmentary papyri from the pyramid complex of Neferir-karē at Abu Sir, recently published, is but one example of material at hand which can hardly fail to yield results of the highest value both for reconstructing the equipment of an ancient mortuary temple and for understanding the organization of the resident priests who were responsible for the maintenance of the temple and for the performance of the daily services.

The plans and drawings that appeared in all previous editions have been reproduced again here. They were prepared by the late John Cruikshank Rose, to whom I shall always be grateful both for the care which he devoted to them and for the readiness with which he gave me his assistance.

I. E. S. Edwards

London
December 1971

Introduction

ONE of the first questions which occur to the mind of anyone looking at an ancient monument is its date. In the case of Egyptian monuments it is often difficult, and sometimes impossible, to answer the question in terms of years before the beginning of the Christian era, because our knowledge of Egyptian chronology, especially in the early periods, is still very incomplete. We know the main sequence of events and frequently their relationship to one another, but, except in rare instances, an exact chronology will not be possible until the discovery of material of a different and more precisely datable character than anything found hitherto.

Partly for the sake of convenience and partly because a century of study has demonstrated that it is fundamentally sound, the method of grouping the kings of Egypt into thirty-one dynasties, which is first known to us from Manetho's *History of Egypt*, has been universally adopted by modern historians as a substitute for closer dating. Since the end of a dynasty did not always entail any very marked political or artistic changes, it has also been found convenient to group the dynasties into periods roughly corresponding with the most important of these changes. There are nine main periods, to which the following names and approximate dates may be given:

I–II Dynasties	Early Dynastic Period, 3100–2686 BC
III–VI Dynasties	Old Kingdom, 2686–2181 BC
VII–X Dynasties	First Intermediate Period, 2181–2133 BC
XI–XII Dynasties	Middle Kingdom, 2133–1786 BC
XIII–XVII Dynasties	Second Intermediate Period, 1786–1567 BC
XVIII–XX Dynasties	New Kingdom, 1567–1080 BC
XXI–XXV Dynasties	Late New Kingdom, 1080–664 BC
XXVI Dynasty	Saite Period, 664–525 BC
XXVII–XXXI Dynasties	Late Period, 525–332 BC

The Pyramid Age, *par excellence*, covers the second of these groups – the period beginning with the IIIrd Dynasty and ending with the VIth Dynasty. During this time the kings, with few exceptions, and many of their queens were buried in tombs having superstructures in pyramidal form. Pyramids were also built for several kings and queens of the subsequent dynasties, but they were in the nature of archaisms, lacking not only much of the architectural splendour of their predecessors, but also some of their religious significance. The total number at present known in Egypt is about eighty; many of them, it is true, are reduced to little more than sand and rubble, but they are still recognizable to the archaeologist as having once been pyramids.

Those pyramids which belong to the Pyramid Age were, in almost every instance, built on the fringe of the desert west of the Nile in the neighbourhood of Memphis, between Meidum in the south and Abu Roash in the north. If later tradition is to be believed, Memphis was built on ground which had been reclaimed by Menes, the first dynastic ruler of Egypt, by dyking the Nile so that it flowed through a channel to the east of its original course. Whether or not this tradition is true in detail, there can be little doubt that it was Menes who founded Memphis, for the archaeological remains in its immediate vicinity dating from the time of the Ist Dynasty are plentiful, whereas nothing has yet been found there which can be ascribed to an earlier period. The discovery of a considerable number of pre-dynastic settlements near the Mukattam hills, on the opposite bank of the river, only emphasizes the complete absence of any corresponding settlements at Memphis itself.

Hitherto, it has not been possible to determine with certainty whether Memphis was designed by Menes to be the capital of Egypt or whether it was originally built simply as a fortress-city and became the seat of government at some later date, perhaps at the beginning of the IIIrd Dynasty. The circumstances surrounding the accession of Menes to the throne would undoubtedly favour the choice of just such a place for his capital. Before his reign, Egypt was composed of two separate kingdoms; the one extending possibly from Aswan, in the south, to the neighbourhood of Memphis, and the other covering the remainder of the country northwards, which included the whole of the Delta area. The capital of the southern (Upper Egyptian) kingdom was situated at Nekhen (Hierakonpolis) and the capital of the northern (Lower Egyptian) kingdom at Pe (Buto). Menes, at first king of Upper Egypt only, overcame the northern kingdom and united the two former kingdoms under one crown, establishing himself as ruler over the whole land. Memphis would thus have been the natural place for him to build a strongly fortified city because, being situated almost at the frontier between the two former kingdoms, it would have provided a powerful deterrent against any attempts at retaliation by the vanquished northerners if at any time they had suspected weakness in the south. It would also have been the most convenient centre for administering the newly united country.

By unifying the two kingdoms, Menes performed a military feat which may have been attempted by others before his time, but never with more than temporary success. Menes, however, both achieved the military victory necessary for uniting the two kingdoms and ensured that its effects would be lasting by following it up with an astute political policy on which the greatness of Egypt in the subsequent dynasties was founded. Nevertheless, the historical fact that Egypt had once consisted of two separate kingdoms was never entirely forgotten by its people, for down to the latest times the Pharaohs still included among their titles that of 'King of Upper and Lower Egypt'.

We have scarcely any detailed knowledge of the methods of political administration employed by Menes and his early successors, but it seems clear that they introduced a high degree of centralization. Excavations by W. B. Emery at Saqqara, the necropolis of Memphis, have brought to light a group of large, but severely plundered, tombs dating from the Ist Dynasty, some of which may have belonged to kings and to members of the royal family, while others were certainly built for courtiers and high officials. Many objects found in these tombs, and also in other tombs of the same period elsewhere in Egypt, were inscribed with the names and titles of contemporary officials, from which it is possible to deduce that the king was surrounded by a large body of counsellors and executives; a complete lack of biographical detail, however, precludes any reconstruction of their personal history.

Even before the reign of Menes, Egypt was divided into districts, which we generally call *nomes* after their Greek name. Their number had probably

Sketch-map of Egypt

Lower Egypt

Upper Egypt

Mediterranean Sea

River Nile

[Alexandria]

XVII
VI   XII
Sais
VII   XVI
Buto
V
Busiris   Tanis
XX
XI XV   XIX   XIV
III   XVIII
IV   Bubastis
Athribis
Letopolis   II   X
Abu Roash   XIII
Giza △   Heliopolis
Abu Sir   [Cairo]
Saqqara   I
Dahshur △   Memphis

Lake Moeris   XXI   Mazghuna
Lisht △
Meidum △   XXII
Seila △
Hawara △
Illahun △
Herakleopolis Magna ●
XX

XIX   XVIII   Eastern Desert

XVII

△ Zawiyet el-Mayitin
XVI   ● Beni Hasan

Bahria Oasis   Gulf of
Suez
El-Eshmunien ●   ● El-Bersheh
XV   ● El-Amarna
Cusae ●   XIV

XII   Red Sea
Asyut ●
XIII   ● Badari
XI
X
IX
Beit Khallaf ●
VIII   VII   Dendereh
Abydos ●   VI
V
Deir el-Bahri △   ● Coptos
Nagada (Ombos)   ● Karnak
Deir el-Medina ●   ● Thebes (Luxor)
Armant ●
IV
Gebelein ●
III
El-Kula △
Kharga Oasis   Hierakonpolis ● ● El-Kab
Edfu ●

II

○ Fertile land
Roman numerals indicate Nomes

Miles

0   50   100

I ● Aswan

varied from time to time, as the more powerful had absorbed the weaker or the larger had decayed internally and had disintegrated; the traditional number was forty-two, twenty-two in Upper Egypt and twenty in Lower Egypt. The number in existence at the time when Menes achieved his conquest may have been smaller; thirty-eight or thirty-nine are mentioned in texts dating from the Old Kingdom. Menes allowed the *nomes* to continue as separate units, but placed at the head of each a governor, who was responsible for directing its social and religious affairs. At first these governors, or 'nomarchs' as they are generally called, held office for only a limited period, but by degrees the office became the hereditary right of certain families. Thus there grew up a provincial ruling class which gradually threatened the authority of the king until, at the end of the VIth Dynasty, it played an important part in the collapse of the monarchy.

We know little about the political constitution of the *nomes* or their relations with the capital – though doubtless each *nome* was required to contribute to the royal exchequer, but it seems clear that they were permitted a very high degree of religious independence. Every *nome* possessed its own local deity or deities, usually represented in animal form or in human form with an animal head: Wepwawet, the wolf-god of the Asyut *nome*, Bastet, the cat-goddess of Bubastis, and Harsaphes, the ram-headed god of Herakleopolis, are examples. Some local gods, however, were always represented entirely anthropomorphically, Ptah of Memphis, Min of Coptos, and Osiris being three of the best known.

Within a single *nome* many different deities might be worshipped, their relative importance naturally varying according to the number of their adherents and the wealth of their temples. In the Memphite *nome*, for example, there were, besides the principal god Ptah, also Sakhmet, a lioness-headed goddess, Nefertem, an anthropomorphic god with a lotus-flower head-dress, and Sokar, a falcon-headed god who dwelt in the desert west of Memphis. Each of these deities originally possessed an independent sanctuary, but, in the course of time, Ptah, Sakhmet, and Nefertem came to be considered as a single family and were worshipped in one sanctuary. There were similar triads elsewhere – Osiris, Isis, and Horus forming the most famous.

In permitting complete religious independence to the different *nomes*, the early kings can hardly be accused of having allowed their conduct of affairs to be dictated by reasons of political expediency; in an age when polytheism was the universally accepted philosophy, no alteration in the established religious order would have seemed to them either necessary or desirable. With the possible exception of a few gods connected with the elements, who appear to have gained wider recognition at a very early date, most of the deities were regarded as having authority mainly within fixed geographical limits. It is certainly useless to speculate on the effect which a less liberal policy would have had on the subsequent development of Egyptian religion. But it is of importance to realize that the different elements which determined the character of that religion, as it is known to us, were chiefly local in origin. Herein lies the reason for many of the divergent, and sometimes even contradictory, beliefs held by the Egyptians in dynastic times.

The development of an official religion began in the Pyramid Age. It was derived from the cult of a temple with a powerful priesthood, situated a little to the north of Memphis at the city which the Greeks later called Heliopolis, known to the ancient Egyptians as On and so named in the Book of Genesis, where Potipherah is described as a priest of On. In very ancient times the cult of this temple was represented by a fetish in the form of a pillar, but by the beginning of the IVth Dynasty it had become the centre of the sun religion. The most sacred object within the temple was the *benben*, probably a conically shaped stone which was thought to symbolize the primeval mound which emerged from the primordial waters at the creation of the universe. According to legend it was on this mound that the Sun-god first revealed himself in the form of a phoenix.

Early in their history the priests of Heliopolis evolved a cosmogony which affirmed that Rē-Atum, the Sun-god, had generated himself out of Nun, the primordial ocean. Rē-Atum's offspring were Shu, the god of the air, and Tefnut, goddess of moisture, who in turn had given birth to Geb, the Earth-god, and Nut, the Sky-goddess. From Geb and Nut had sprung Osiris, Isis, Seth, and Nephthys. These nine deities were known as the Great Ennead of Heliopolis. There was also a Little Ennead, composed of a group of lesser gods under the leadership of Horus.

Rē-Atum was not, however, the only form in which the Sun-god was worshipped at Heliopolis: Horakhti – meaning Horus of the horizon – and Khepri, in the form of a scarab, were also venerated there. Some attempt was made by the Heliopolitan priesthood to differentiate between these forms, Khepri being regarded as the morning sun and Rē-Atum as the evening sun, but the distinction was never very strictly observed. The Egyptians of the Pyramid Age clearly found little difficulty in regarding their Sun-god not as a single indivisible being but rather as a composite deity whose various attributes were derived from local solar deities, originally separate and subsequently united, without proper co-ordination, with Rē of Heliopolis. It is not surprising, therefore, that the sun cult contains many inconsistencies as it is presented in the earliest body of religious texts in our possession, namely the texts carved on the walls of the chambers and corridors of pyramids in the late Vth and the VIth Dynasties.

In order to illustrate the divergent beliefs which might exist simultaneously, it is only necessary to cite the various explanations offered to account for the daily passage of the sun across the earth. According to the view most commonly accepted, Rē, accompanied by his retinue, traversed the sky each day in a boat. The moon and the stars were likewise believed to journey across the sky in ships. No method of transport would seem more natural to the ancient Egyptian than a ship, for both he and his ancestors from time immemorial had used the Nile to travel from place to place, and it was only logical that the heavenly bodies should be conveyed on their celestial journey by similar means.

According to another school of thought, the sun was carried through the firmament on wings, like a bird. This belief was particularly associated with the Sun-god in the form of Horakhti, who, since the earliest times, had been regarded as a falcon. Inasmuch as no visible object could support itself for long in the air unless it had wings, it must have seemed only reasonable that the sun should be subject to the same fundamental laws as other bodies. The falcon was chosen because it excelled all other birds known to the Egyptians in its ability to fly at a very great height.

Possibly the most picturesque of all the different ideas concerning the passage of the sun across the sky was that which ascribed to the Sun-god the form of a scarab-beetle; this conception was especially connected with him in his name of Khepri. The ancient Egyptian was familiar with the spectacle of the scarab-beetle pushing a ball of dung along the ground until it found a suitable crevice in which to deposit it. From this ball, he believed, the young scarab, by a process of self-generation, subsequently emerged. In view of an imagined resemblance between the sun, regarded as the source of all life, and the ball of dung from which the young scarab was thought to emerge, it is not surprising that the force which propelled the sun across the sky, namely the Sun-god, should have been pictured as an enormous beetle, which pushed the sun as its earthly counterpart pushed the ball of dung. In this connection it is immaterial that modern entomologists have shown that the ball of dung rolled along by the beetle is simply a reserve food-supply, while the one which contains the egg is not spherical but pear-shaped, and is kept in a hole by the mother-insect until ready to hatch.

The nocturnal course of the sun also gave rise to different theories. There was the natural explanation that it spent the hours of darkness passing by ship through the Underworld, called the Det (commonly known as the Duat), before reappearing above ground each day at sunrise. A more fanciful solution, however, postulated that the sky was formed by the body of the goddess Nut, spanning the earth like an enormous arch, with her head on a level with the western horizon, her groin on the eastern horizon, and her arms and legs extended beneath the horizons. The sun was consumed by this goddess every evening at sunset and traversed her body during the night, to be reborn at sunrise. It was an explanation which never lost its appeal to the Egyptians and which, until the latest times, continued side by side with that of the sun's nocturnal passage through the Det.

The solar cult of Heliopolis, while exercising a predominant influence on the religion of the pyramid-builders, was compelled to recognize, and in time to incorporate within its theology, a cult which was certainly not solar in origin, namely that of the god Osiris. This cult, in the form in which we know it, suffers from almost as many inconsistencies as that of the sun, and from a similar necessity to embody beliefs derived from originally unrelated local gods into the cult of the principal god with whom they had become assimilated.

In remote antiquity, before the union of Upper and Lower Egypt under Menes, Osiris had been probably first the king and then the local god of the ninth Lower Egyptian *nome* with its capital at Busiris. Subsequently his influence spread until he became the chief god of a group of *nomes* in the eastern Delta. At some time during this development he was identified with a local god named Andjeti and assumed his insignia – the shepherd's crook and the flail. Horus, later regarded as the son of Osiris, was at this time a completely independent god, ruling a group of *nomes* in the western Delta. Isis, who figures in pyramid times as the wife of Osiris, seems also to have been a Delta goddess, but nothing is known with certainty about her origin.

After the cult of Osiris had become linked with that of Horus, its influence began to extend southwards until, by pyramid times, Osiris had become identified with Sokar, the god of the Memphite necropolis, Wepwawet, the wolf-god of Asyut, Khentiamentiu, the jackal-god of Abydos, and possibly others. The most important of these associations was undoubtedly that with Khentiamentiu, for, with the advance of time, Osiris came to be connected

Traces of the original paint are still visible on this limestone statue of King Zoser, which shows him in the costume worn by monarchs during the *sed* festival. It was found in the serdab on the north side of the Step Pyramid and removed to the Cairo Museum.

primarily with Abydos, while Busiris, his original home, gradually lost its significance.

Egyptian religious texts, though containing innumerable references to the legend on which the cult of Osiris was based, nowhere give a full and connected account of it. The reason for this omission is not far to seek, for the legend must have been so well known in ancient times that a detailed record was unnecessary. The earliest complete version known at present is that of Plutarch in his work *De Iside et Osiride*, which, though differing in detail, agrees in all important respects with the allusions in the Egyptian texts and must therefore represent substantially the standard account of all time. The following are the main features of the narrative as preserved in Plutarch and the Egyptian texts:

Osiris, the eldest son of the Earth-god Geb and the Sky-goddess Nut, ruled as a just and benevolent king over the whole earth, instructing mankind in the various arts and crafts and converting them from barbarism to a state of civilization. In time, however, his brother Seth, prompted by jealousy, murdered him. Plutarch states that the murder was committed by a cunningly conceived trick: Seth, having prepared a banquet ostensibly in honour of his brother's return to Egypt from a foreign land, invited seventy-two of his friends to attend as guests. In the course of the meal a chest of clever workmanship was carried into the room and offered by Seth as a present to anyone who, when lying down inside it, fitted it exactly. By a prearranged plan, a number of the other guests first tried the chest, but were not of the right size. Osiris then entered it and, owing to his unusual dimensions, exactly fitted it. While he was still inside the chest, however, some of the accomplices closed it and carried it to the Nile. After ferrying it downstream to the Tanite mouth, they cast it adrift in the sea, which at length washed it ashore at Byblos.

Isis, when she discovered that Osiris had been murdered, set out on a long and eventful search for his corpse, which she ultimately found and brought back to Egypt from Byblos. For a time she remained at Khemmis, in the marshes of the Delta, keeping watch over the coffin of Osiris and awaiting the birth of her child Horus, who appears to have been conceived after his father's death. Seth, however, when out hunting, discovered the coffin and removed the body, which he cut up into fourteen or sixteen pieces, scattering them over different parts of Egypt. Isis again went in search of the body, and buried each piece in the place where she found it – the head at Abydos, the neck at Heliopolis, the left thigh at Bigeh, and other parts elsewhere. The only part missing was the virile member, which had been thrown by Seth into the river and devoured by the fish of Oxyrhynchus.

Another version of the story states that, after Isis had found the body, Rē ordered Anubis to embalm it; Isis then fluttered her wings over it and restored it to life. It is an important variant, because the process of embalmment, as we know it from the Egyptian mummies, was certainly connected closely with the Osirian legend. After being restored to life, Osiris became king of the region of the dead and thus assumed the role in which he figures throughout historical times.

The remainder of this legend, which is recorded on an excellently preserved papyrus from the New Kingdom, concerns the long and furious struggle between Seth and Horus, who resolved to slay his uncle and thus avenge his father's death. In the course of the struggle Seth plucked out one of his

Zoser's serdab protected the statue shown on the previous page, which has now been replaced by a cast. In addition to providing a substitute for his body if it were destroyed, the statue was a second home outside the pyramid for his spirit, which could enter and leave at will, despite the absence of doors. Two small holes were cut either to allow the statue to see out or to enable incense to reach it.

nephew's eyes, but Horus triumphed in the end and succeeded to the throne of Osiris. His missing eye was restored by the god Thoth and his title to his father's throne was endorsed by the verdict of a tribunal of the gods of Heliopolis. As a result of this episode, Horus became for all time a model of filial devotion, while the eye which he lost in the struggle was henceforth regarded as a symbol for every form of sacrifice.

The sun cult and the cult of Osiris were certainly not connected either in origin or in their main theological conception. Rē was primarily a god of the living, with whom certain privileged persons might be associated after death, while Osiris was essentially the god of the blessed dead and of the region of the dead. Both gods, however, shared one most important feature in common: they provided a divine example of survival after death. Osiris, though murdered by Seth, had been restored to life by the magic of Isis, and Rē, whose daily disappearance beneath the western horizon was considered as his death, was reborn each morning at sunrise. In the experiences of these gods, the ancient Egyptian found reason to hope for his own survival. But a continuance of life after physical death did not follow as a normal and natural consequence: it was something which could only be assured by observing the proper ritual and by supplying the dead with all the material assistance which had been required by the gods for their own survival. Herein lay the need for providing the dead with a tomb, whether pyramid or otherwise, and with a burial which would conform in all the essential elements with an accepted pattern.

In spite of their meticulous attention to detail in practical matters, the Egyptians of the Pyramid Age never evolved a clear and precise conception of the after-life. That conservatism so noticeable in Egyptian art is even more emphasized in matters of religion; elements which had once been admitted into the canon continued side by side with later innovations, even though they were logically superfluous and sometimes irreconcilable. The impression made on the modern mind is that of a people searching in the dark for a key to truth and, having found not one but many keys resembling the pattern of the lock, retaining all lest perchance the appropriate one should be discarded.

Even in very early times, before the Osirian and solar cults had gained any considerable following, the Egyptians believed that man was composed of body and spirit. They also believed that the spirit could remain alive after physical death if the body were preserved and provided with the necessary sustenance. Where the after-life of the spirit took place is not known, but it may have been in a kind of Underworld to which access was gained, it was thought, through the pit of the tomb.

This simple conception of an after-life closely associated with the tomb and dependent on the preservation of the body was never entirely supplanted by other ideas, with the result that, in later times, we find Egyptian tombs provided with every imaginable article for the use of the dead. The tomb of Tutankhamun with its magnificent equipment, which included even chariots and regal accoutrements, is but a single instance of the persistence of this creed in a highly developed form more than two thousand years after its earliest appearance.

A more advanced conception of a blissful after-life gained as a reward for virtue may have been entertained by adherents to the Osirian cult from remote antiquity, but the absence of any contemporary evidence of its beliefs and tenets renders any attempt to reconstruct the creed in its primitive form very hazardous. Even in early times, however, the Osirian Hereafter was probably regarded as a kind of idealized version of this world, situated below the western horizon and presided over by Osiris. This region, called by the Egyptians the Fields of Reeds and subsequently known to the Greeks as the Elysian Fields, was represented in later times as a group of isles reached by a magic boat, where those who had been accepted by the god could dwell in perpetual spring. As was only fitting to the kingdom of the god of fertility, the ground yielded fabulous harvests, with corn growing to a height of nine cubits. The cultivation of these crops provided the fortunate dwellers of the Elysian Fields with their main occupation.

Abydos assumed a position of unique importance in the Osirian creed, and early supplanted Busiris as the chief centre of the cult. Temples equal in magnificence to any in Egypt were built there and dedicated to the god. It was at Abydos, according to one tradition, that Isis had found and buried the head of Osiris; another tradition alleged that she had buried there the whole of the body with the exception of the virile member. Every year it was the scene of a solemn festival, including a Passion Play in which the principal events in the life and death of Osiris were re-enacted. The thousands of potsherds still lying on the ground testify to the number of offerings presented to the god by pilgrims.

It was inconceivable to the ancient Egyptians, who regarded the after-life as a kind of mirror of this world, that an event of such importance in his earthly life as the annual festival at Abydos should not have its counterpart in the life to come. From the end of the Old Kingdom, therefore, many tombs were equipped with boats to enable their owners to make the journey to Abydos. By the Middle Kingdom, and possibly very much earlier, those who could afford the cost of a second tomb might even build a cenotaph at Abydos; their spirits could thus dwell at will near Osiris and participate in his annual festival while still maintaining through their real tombs the link with their native towns. For instance, Sesostris III, one of the greatest kings of the Middle Kingdom, caused a rock cenotaph to be hewn for himself at Abydos, while his body was buried in his pyramid at Dahshur. Those who could not afford a cenotaph would often set up, near the supposed shrine of Osiris, a stone slab carved with figures in relief and bearing an inscription, generally of a formal character, in order to ensure that their names would remain perpetually in the presence of the god.

In all matters concerning their religion, the Egyptians placed considerable reliance on the magic power of the written word. They believed that, by using the correct formulas, they could impose their will upon the gods. The spells carved on the walls of the chambers and corridors of the late Vth and the VIth Dynasty pyramids are the best examples of this form of magic in the Pyramid Age. A remarkable instance, however, is also provided by the Osirian practice of placing the name of Osiris as a title before the name of the dead, with the object of transforming him into the god himself. The explanation of this universal deification may be that it was an extension of a privilege originally intended for the king alone. During his earthly life he was considered as the embodiment of Horus, the son of Osiris; it was only natural, therefore, that he should be regarded as Osiris when he had died and his son, the next embodiment of Horus, had succeeded him on the throne. In time, the privilege of becoming an Osiris was extended, first to other members of the royal family, then to a few chosen people not of royal blood, and finally it became a right claimed by all. We cannot actually trace these successive stages in the democratization of the Osirian cult, but comparison with the course followed by other religious and funerary practices enables its development to be conjectured with a measure of probability.

In the solar cult also the after-life was originally considered as a royal prerogative. This after-life, however, was not to be spent either in the west or in the Underworld, but in a celestial region in the east. To reach it, the dead king must cross a lake, called the 'Lily Lake', which extended from the northern horizon to that of the south. An austere figure named 'He-who-looks-behind-himself' – a name resulting from the belief that he performed his duties facing backwards – ferried him across the lake, but only after he had been convinced that the king was entitled to enter the 'Fields where the gods were begotten, over which the gods rejoice on their New Year's Days', as the eastern side was called. In order to convince the ferryman, the king could resort to a number of different stratagems: he could try to persuade him that he was bringing the Sun-god something which he needed; he could pretend that the Sun-god required him to perform some function, or he might have recourse to magic and take with him a jar containing a substance which would render the ferryman impotent to resist his demands. If other means failed, the king could entreat the Sun-god himself to instruct the ferryman to grant him a passage.

Having crossed the lake, the king arrived at the gates of the Other World. Heralds were standing in readiness to announce the news of his arrival and the gods immediately gathered to greet him. One of the pyramid texts describes the scene in the following words: 'This king Pepi found the gods standing, wrapped in their garments, their white sandals on their feet. They cast off their white sandals to the earth; they threw off their garments. "Our heart was not glad until thy coming," they say' (Spell 518).

Once he had been admitted into this Other World, how was the king to employ his time? The Egyptian texts are very inconsistent on this point. In one of the earliest pyramid texts it is asserted that he becomes the Sun-god's secretary and his duties are thus described: 'King Unas sits before him [Rē]; King Unas opens his chests [of papers]; King Unas breaks open his edicts; King Unas seals his documents; King Unas dispatches his messengers who weary not; King Unas does what he [Rē] says to King Unas' (Spell 309). Yet other texts present a picture of the king ruling in all the splendour which had accompanied his earthly sovereignty: courtiers surround his throne while his subjects prostrate themselves before him and kiss the ground at his feet. He even sits in judgement and issues edicts as he used to do on earth.

Every day the king would accompany the Sun-god on his voyage across the skies. Sometimes he is described as a rower in the barque, for example: 'King Pepi receives to himself his oar; he takes his seat; he sits in the bow of the ship of the Two Enneads; he rows Rē to the West' (Spell 469). Elsewhere he is promoted to the position of captain of the barque. At night the voyage would be performed in the reverse direction, through the Underworld, thereby giving light to ordinary deceased mortals who were thought to dwell there.

With the advance of time, the dead king became even more closely associated with the Sun-god until, by the VIth Dynasty, he had become completely identified with him. One of the texts in the Pyramid of Teti expresses the relationship in the following terms: 'O Rē . . . thou art Teti and Teti is thou . . . make Teti sound and Teti will make thee sound' (Spell 405). An even more striking instance occurs in the pyramid texts of Merenrē, where the king is addressed thus: 'Thou embarkest therein [the Sun's barque] like Rē; thou sittest down on the throne of Rē that thou mayest command the gods; for thou art Rē who came forth from Nut, who brings forth Rē every day' (Spell 606).

Closely connected with the problem of the location of the after-life and its occupations was the question of the form which the king would assume when entering upon it. The physical body was probably at all times thought to dwell in or near the tomb, while the immaterial element was believed to become at death a separate entity termed the *ba*. In early hieroglyphic writings the *ba* was represented by a stork with a tuft of feathers on the front of its neck; later the sign was changed to a bearded human-headed bird preceded by a lamp. Possibly the later sign was a relic of an ancient belief that the stars were simply innumerable *bas* lit up by their lamps. Although the physical and spiritual elements were thus separated, they were still interdependent; for the well-being of the *ba* could only be ensured, it was believed, if the body were preserved intact and able to receive it. Herein lay a further reason for the elaborate care taken to protect the body from disturbance and decay.

Another entity which played an important part in the fortunes of the king was his *ka*. In Egyptian symbolism the *ka* was represented sometimes as a bearded human figure with a crown composed of two upraised arms bent at the elbow, and sometimes as the two arms in the same position but without the human figure. It came into existence at the time of the king's birth and remained with him after death. Two famous groups of reliefs in the temples of Deir el-Bahri and Luxor, which date from the XVIIIth Dynasty, show the god Khnum creating at the same time both the royal child and his *ka* by moulding them on a potter's wheel.

The precise nature of the *ka* is far from clear. Many different explanations have been suggested: Gaston Maspero, one of the greatest of French Egyptologists, regarded it as a twin or double of its owner, made of the same substance and coeval with him; Adolf Erman thought it was the embodiment of the life force – that mysterious element which distinguishes the living from the dead; J. H. Breasted believed it was a protecting genius comparable with the Christian conception of a guardian angel; H. Kees detected in it the personification of those abstract qualities, such as might, prosperity, reverence, splendour, which were essential for a continuance of this life. Sir Alan Gardiner considered that it embraced the entire 'self' of a person regarded as an entity to some extent separable from that person. Modern concepts, he suggested, to which that of the *ka* occasionally corresponded were 'personality', 'soul', 'individuality', and 'temperament': the word might even mean a man's 'fortune' or 'position'. All these explanations can be justified in different contexts and it seems necessary to postulate that the ancient Egyptians did not always entertain one single and immutable conception of the *ka*, but allowed their ideas to be modified, even in fundamental respects, according to their different doctrines of the human make-up.

Whatever may have been the true function of the *ka* in relation to its owner during his earthly life, it is certain that the expectation of close

association with it in the Next World provided him with one of his most
cherished hopes of the after-life. The dead king and his *ka* are often mentioned in the pyramid texts as being together, sometimes in the kingdom of
the Sun-god where the *ka* acts as his guide, even introducing him to the god
or providing him with the food necessary for his subsistence, and sometimes
in the tomb, where the *ka* shares its benefits with the owner. Indeed, one of
the Egyptian names for a tomb was the 'house of the *ka*', and the priests responsible for its maintenance were called the 'servants of the *ka*'. It is hardly
surprising therefore that the Egyptian texts occasionally refer to the dead
as those 'who have gone to their *kas*', so important an element in a blissful
after-life was the union considered.

Mastabas and early burial customs

B.Y far the greater part of the rich collections of Egyptian antiquities now in the museums of Egypt, Europe, and America has been obtained from tombs – a fact which is easily explained because tombs dating from pre-dynastic times and from nearly every period during the three thousand years of Egypt's dynastic history have been found in considerable numbers, whereas few of the houses in which the people lived or of the buildings in which they worked have survived. Even capitals of the importance and size of Memphis and Thebes have disappeared, leaving hardly any trace. Nothing remains of the palaces of those kings whose pyramids have been from ancient times among the most famous monuments in the world; it is not even known whether they were built in Memphis itself or somewhere nearer to the actual sites of the pyramids. So complete a disappearance can only be due to the nature of the materials and to the methods employed in construction. Houses and palaces were almost certainly composed mainly of mud-brick, wood, and gesso; they were built, moreover, above ground. Tombs, on the other hand, lay partly below the ground, and those elements which stood above ground were, after the early dynasties, generally either hewn out of rock or built of stone. Although the total number which has survived to the present day is large, it is but a fraction of those which once existed; successive generations inhabiting the country have drawn liberally on the edifices of their predecessors when building for their own requirements.

In a land where stone of excellent quality could be obtained in abundance, it may seem strange that the rulers and governing classes should have been content to spend their lives in buildings of inferior quality to their tombs. The ancient Egyptian, however, took a different view; his house or palace was built to last for only a limited number of years and could be renewed or replaced whenever necessary, but his tomb, which he called his 'castle of eternity', was designed to last *for ever*. Its construction was normally finished during his lifetime. In the event of death befalling him before the completion of his tomb, it sometimes happened that the original plan was modified in detail and the building brought to an abrupt finish, either in order that he might occupy it with the minimum delay or possibly so that his relatives might save themselves the expense necessary for further work on it. Equally, if he lived to see his tomb well advanced towards completion, he might enlarge it and provide himself with a bigger and more imposing resting-place than that which he had originally contemplated.

Ancient Egyptians were accustomed to travel on the Nile by boat. They also believed that the Sun-god Rē used this method of transportation on his daily journey across the sky. This is a model of a full-size boat found buried near Cheops.

The motive which prompted the ancient Egyptian to devote such labour to the construction of his tomb was his belief that the attainment of the after-life which he desired was dependent on the fulfilment of two primary conditions: his body must be preserved from disturbance or destruction, and the material needs of both himself and his *ka* must be supplied. This motive remained constant throughout the whole course of Egyptian history. Changes in the form of the tomb occurred not infrequently as a result of experience gained or of new religious developments, but the fundamental purpose of the tomb continued unaffected.

In pre-dynastic times the dead were buried in rectangular or oval pits dug in the sand. The body, laid on its side in a contracted posture, was wrapped in a reed mat, around which were placed a few personal belongings, such as necklaces, bangles, hunting implements, and pots containing food and drink. Sometimes these graves were lined with wooden boards lashed together by thongs at the corners, forming a kind of coffin around the body. No examples of their superstructures have been preserved, but it is unlikely that they consisted of anything more substantial than a heap of sand supported at the sides by a wooden frame. With the passage of time, the sand was always liable to be blown away, with the result that the body and its appurtenances would become exposed and, unless immediately reburied, must suffer destruction. Experience doubtless taught the successors of these early Egyptians that few bodies, when once exposed, were likely to be reburied.

From the beginning of the dynastic era, the kings and nobles overcame the risk of their graves being destroyed by the elements by building over the burial-pit a superstructure composed of sun-baked mud-brick. This form of tomb has become known in modern times as a 'mastaba' – an Arabic word meaning a 'bench'. It was so named because, when engulfed in drift-sand to nearly its full height, it resembled the low bench built outside the Egyptian house of the present day where the owner sits and drinks coffee with his friends.

Mastaba dated to the reign of King Aha

1. burial chamber
2. outer face of the super-structure
3. and **4**. two walls separated by a mud-packed pavement

Some of the most interesting mastabas of the Ist Dynasty, and certainly the most informative for tracing the early stages in the architectural development of the pyramid, were excavated at the northern end of the necropolis at Saqqara by W. B. Emery between the years 1935 and 1956. The oldest mastaba in this group, which is also the simplest in design, is dated to the reign of Aha, the second king of Upper and Lower Egypt. Below ground-level, it consisted of a shallow rectangular pit, which was roofed with timber and divided by cross-walls into five separate compartments. The middle compartment probably contained the body, enclosed in a wooden coffin, while some of the most intimate possessions were placed in the adjoining chambers. So far, it was only an enlarged version of the pre-dynastic tomb. Above these chambers and covering a considerably greater area was a brick superstructure, the interior of which was divided into twenty-seven cells, intended for the storage of wine-jars, food-vessels, hunting implements, and other necessities of life. The outer faces of the walls of the superstructure, which inclined inwards from the base to the top, were built in the form of alternate panelled projections and recesses. Some of the later mastabas in the group were surrounded by a low terrace, to the upper surface of which were attached by means of wooden pegs life-size heads of cattle modelled in clay and provided with real horns. The shape of the roof can only be conjectured, for no large mastaba of this period has yet been found with its roof intact, but the evidence afforded by contemporary subsidiary tombs suggests that it was convex. Two walls, also built of brick and separated by a mud-packed pavement, enclosed the building. A coating of white lime-stucco, decorated with coloured geometric patterns, was laid over both the superstructure and the enclosure walls.

Dug in the ground about forty yards outside the north wall was a boat-shaped cavity lined with mud-brick which had contained a wooden boat intended for the use of the deceased owner in his after-life. Between the boat and the mastaba stood two groups of dummy buildings, made of rubble cased with mud and overlaid with lime-stucco, but when found they were so badly damaged that it was impossible to decide whether they had been models of religious or secular buildings.

Mastabas of this kind were almost certainly close copies of noblemen's houses and royal palaces, thus demonstrating that the tomb was regarded as the place where the dead were believed to dwell. Without doubt, the arrangement of the cells in the superstructure was adapted to fit the particular requirements of the tomb, but they must have represented the various rooms in the residence. Corridors, which would have weakened the building, were unnecessary, because it was thought that the spirit of the deceased could pass unhindered through material barriers. By an extension of this concept it was also supposed that the spirit could enter the dummy buildings outside the tomb even though they were completely solid. Attendants who had been members of the owner's household were sometimes buried in small mastabas arranged in rows outside the enclosure wall of the main tomb, evidently in the belief that they could continue in his service in the after-life. They were certainly buried at the same time as their masters, but not alive as might be supposed. In all probability their death was the result of a lethal dose of poison accepted voluntarily as a duty required by their terms of employment.

Whether or not some of the elaborate mastabas at Saqqara were built for the kings of the Ist Dynasty is a problem which has not yet been solved. That many of these kings, and at least two of their successors in the IInd Dynasty, possessed 'tombs', albeit of a different pattern, at Abydos is however not open to doubt. If, as is not unlikely, a king built residences for himself in different parts of the country, he could well have constructed more than one 'tomb' for the use of his spirit in the after-life. The choice of Abydos for a cenotaph may have been prompted either by its sacred associations (p. 21) or by the fact that it was the ancestral home of the early kings, while Saqqara, it may be argued, was the natural burial-place because of its proximity to Memphis, the capital and consequently the site of the chief royal residence. A further possibility is that the 'tomb' at Abydos was intended for the king in his capacity of ruler of Upper Egypt and the mastaba at Saqqara was the counterpart symbolizing his rulership over Lower Egypt. This explanation would account for the difference in design of the two buildings, which would otherwise be difficult to understand, and would be compatible with the general conception of providing the dead king with an alternative residence.

Many years ago Professor G. A. Reisner advanced the theory that the almost totally destroyed superstructures of the royal 'tombs' at Abydos from the reign of Djer, the third king of the Ist Dynasty, onwards were brick-built monuments which rose in two or three deep steps to the summit, but his hypothetical reconstructions have never gained general recognition among Egyptologists. Indeed, H. Ricke, in a more recent study, has come to the conclusion that the superstructures were low, flat-topped mounds of sand supported at the sides by walls of mud-brick. J.-P. Lauer is in general agreement with Ricke, but considers that Ricke's estimate of the height (about 4 feet) should be approximately doubled and suggests that the top was curved.

One of the many difficult problems which confront an archaeologist excavating badly damaged buildings composed of brick and partly filled with sand and rubble is to trace the design of the interior. Architectural elements of considerable size may not be distinguishable from filling material unless there is some reason for suspecting their existence at an early stage in the process of dismantling the ruined structure. Thus, in the excavation of the Saqqara group of mastabas, it was not possible to recognize at first a feature of considerable importance embodied in the core of the super-structures of at least some of the earliest tombs. This feature was a rectangular

Heads of cattle modelled in clay and provided with real horns were placed on the terrace of this Ist Dynasty brick mastaba.

mound of sand and rubble, overlaid with a casing of bricks, which had been erected on ground-level directly above the central pit and beneath the innermost storage cells of the superstructure. It is not hard to imagine that this mound represented the pile of sand which in pre-dynastic times had been placed over the simple pit-graves. Some magical significance had no doubt been ascribed to it, even though in origin its purpose was purely utilitarian, and consequently it was retained when a new pattern of tomb was introduced. A mound of sand and rubble covered with a layer of bricks must, however, have provided an insecure basis for that part of the super-structure which stood above it, and it is not surprising that, before the end of the Ist Dynasty, a firmer platform was devised by surrounding the mound on all four sides with a perpendicular wall, against the outer sides of which were erected sloping embankments of sand and rubble cased with bricks laid in a stepped fashion. With this support, the mound was well protected against any tendency to spread outwards when subjected to pressure from above by the weight of the roof and intervening filling of the mastaba. As an additional precaution against this risk a terrace composed of brick and sand with stepped outer faces was built as a kind of girdle which gave further reinforcement to the central mound without depriving it of its essential nature as a separate architectural element.

By the IInd and IIIrd Dynasties the superstructures of mastabas of officials and private persons, while retaining the outward form of a house, had become a solid mass of rubble covered by an outer skin of brick. The recesses in the walls were often reduced to two – one near each end of the eastern wall, the southern recess being developed into an offering-room, built sometimes entirely within the body of the superstructure and sometimes purely outside it. In the western wall of this offering-room there was a niche which served as a false door, through which the spirit could leave and re-enter the tomb at will. The substructure, on the other hand, had in-creased in size and importance to such a degree that it was often composed of a kind of central hall, out of which led a number of side-chambers, intended, in the main, to store those objects which had formerly been placed in the superstructure. Among these underground apartments, hewn out of solid rock, a closet was sometimes included. The hall was entered through a door opening southwards at the bottom of a deep vertical shaft which had been driven down from the ground-level. A flight of steps or a ramp, starting from the northern end of the mastaba, met this shaft at a point several feet above its base. It was by this ramp or staircase that the body and some of the most personal belongings were taken to the tomb. After everything had been placed inside the tomb, a portcullis consisting of a heavy slab of stone, which had previously been supported by props, was allowed to slide down two perpendicular grooves flanking the doorway. The shaft and stairway were then filled up with gravel or rubble and covered with an outer layer of brick.

To account for the transference of the storerooms from the superstructure to the substructure, it is fair to deduce that measures to provide greater protection for the body and its belongings had become imperative. The introduction of the mastaba had coincided with a marked elaboration in the equipment of the tomb, and, as a consequence, the risk of robbery must have been substantially increased. While this equipment was mainly stored in a brick structure above the ground or in shallow pits beneath the centre of the

Overleaf: A stepped mound in a 1st Dynasty mastaba at Saqqara.

1st Dynasty mastaba with central mound, ground plan and cross-section

structure, tomb-breakers would have experienced little difficulty in forcing a way to their quarry. Deeper burial, however, would certainly present the robber with a serious hindrance, but it would also complicate the task of the tomb-builder.

In 1901 Alessandro Barsanti discovered at Saqqara beneath the mortuary temple of King Unas, at a depth of about 21 feet below ground-level, a vast subterranean tomb approximately 130 yards in length and embodying more than seventy chambers hewn in the rock on each side of a central corridor. Within this tomb were clay jar-stoppers with seal impressions of Hetep-sekhemui and Rēneb, the first two kings of the IInd Dynasty, whose order of

1st Dynasty mastaba with stepped central mound, ground plan and cross-section

sequence is uncertain. In every probability this tomb may be ascribed to whichever of these two kings was the later. A second tomb of comparable design lying about 140 yards to the east of the first was excavated in 1937–8 by Selim Bey Hassan and this tomb has been attributed, also on the basis of seal impressions, to the third king of the Dynasty, Ninetjer. The owner of a IVth Dynasty tomb at Saqqara, named Shery, recorded in his inscriptions that he was the overseer of the priests in charge of the tombs of Sened and Peribsen, the fifth and sixth kings of the IInd Dynasty and, since Shery is unlikely to have been buried far from his place of work, it may be deduced that the tombs of these two kings are also at Saqqara and await discovery. The fact that Peribsen possessed a 'tomb' at Abydos, which was found by Émile Amélineau in 1897–8 and re-excavated three years later by Sir Flinders Petrie, cannot be regarded as a hindrance to the acceptance of this theory if, as many authorities suppose, the practice of building tombs in more than one place had already been established by the kings of the Ist Dynasty. Khasekhemui, the last of the line of nine or possibly ten kings who comprised the IInd Dynasty, also built a 'tomb' at Abydos, but hitherto no evidence is available to show that he had a second tomb at Saqqara. The design of this 'tomb' is reminiscent of the two earlier tombs found at Saqqara, but it is smaller in size, its length being only 75 yards. Situated roughly half-way along its main axis is a chamber measuring 17 feet by 10 feet and built entirely of dressed limestone. Peribsen's 'tomb' consisted of a rectangular chamber 24 feet in length by $9\frac{1}{2}$ feet in breadth, surrounded by a corridor on the outer sides of which lay a series of small cells. Apart from Khasekhemui's chamber both these 'tombs' were built of mud-brick. Nothing remains of the superstructures either at Saqqara or at Abydos, but doubtless they also were made of mud-brick.

Many mastabas of the IVth Dynasty were still built of brick, but it was the introduction into general use of stone, previously reserved for royal monuments, which marked the most significant development of this period. Even in the brick mastabas, the offering-room and subterranean chambers were often faced with stone. The stone employed for the purpose was a fine quality limestone quarried at Tura in the Mukattam hills. This limestone was also used to face the superstructures of the stone mastabas, while a stone of inferior quality taken from neighbouring quarries was used to build their inner cores.

In their substructures, the IVth Dynasty mastabas, whether made of brick or of stone, present many new features. Both types often had a single room with a deep recess in one of its walls for a coffin made of wood or stone. In the south-east corner of this room the stone mastabas sometimes had a pit, the purpose of which is not certainly known, but it was probably intended to hold the viscera which had been removed from the body of the deceased in order to help in its preservation. After the burial, the entrance to this room was blocked by a heavy limestone portcullis. The vertical shaft leading to the top of the superstructure was then filled with rubble and its mouth covered with a slab of dressed stone. The ramp adjoining the shaft, which was regularly found in the IInd and IIIrd Dynasties, was generally omitted from the stone mastabas, though it was frequently retained in those made of brick.

The superstructures of IVth Dynasty mastabas sometimes embodied two notable innovations which did not, however, become general until the Vth

Dynasty. The first was a statue of the owner of the tomb, occasionally accompanied by statues of other members of his family, and the second was the decoration of the stone walls of the offering-rooms with scenes carved in relief and painted. The statues were placed in a chamber built within the body of the mastaba and known in modern times as the 'serdab' – an Arabic word meaning a 'cellar'. It was so called because, having no doors, windows, or apertures of any kind, apart from a hole or narrow slit in one wall approximately on a level with the face of the statue, scarcely any light was admitted into the interior.

Decorated offering-rooms were only the beginning of a process of development whereby, in the Vth and VIth Dynasties, the inside of the super-structures was gradually filled with chambers and columned halls, all of which had their walls covered with reliefs. One famous mastaba of the VIth Dynasty contained more than thirty chambers so decorated. Among the scenes most commonly carved on the walls were those which showed servants bearing offerings of food and drink to their deceased master, harvest scenes, manufacturing processes, the owner of the tomb inspecting his estates or hunting, and a wide variety of other episodes closely associated with his occupations during life.

The important developments in the mastaba from the IVth Dynasty onwards were a direct result of the realization that the measures which had been taken to defeat the elements and the robber had also defeated their own ultimate object, namely the preservation of the body. An inevitable consequence of burying the body in a deep chamber far from the drying influence of the hot sand was that it decomposed unless some method of embalmment were employed. The earliest mummy hitherto discovered is one dating from the Vth Dynasty found by Sir Flinders Petrie at Meidum in the season 1891–2. Even during the Early Dynastic Period, however, attempts were sometimes made to imitate the external form of the living body by wrapping each limb separately and inserting under the wrappings linen pads soaked in resin and moulded to the shape of the individual members. A further development, for which evidence is available from the IVth Dynasty, was the painting in green of the facial features on the outside of the wrappings covering the head, while in some cases, although rarely before the Vth Dynasty, a coat of plaster was applied either to the head alone or to the entire body and modelled to the required shape.

There can be no doubt that the Egyptians were fully aware of the inadequacy of their precautions to preserve the body from molestation and decay. As an additional safeguard for the continuation of life after death they therefore resorted to magic.

In the cult of the dead, the Egyptians believed that, without depriving the deceased person of the virtues of the prototype, a model could be substituted for any article which it was not practicable to supply in actuality. For instance, in some IInd Dynasty mastabas dummy vases were used instead of vessels filled with provisions and were thought to be equally beneficial to the owner of the tomb. Similarly, a statue or even a figure carved in relief was considered to be an effective substitute for the human body in the event of its destruction. One of the best-known mastabas of the IIIrd Dynasty was provided with figures of the deceased owner, a high official named Hesy-Rē, carved in relief on wooden panels which fitted into the recesses on the east side of the superstructure. The figures were certainly intended to enable

Engaged columns representing single stems of plants with flowers or leaves are an important feature of Zoser's temple enclosure at Saqqara. His mortuary temple may be a stone replica of the royal palace at Memphis. Imhotep, the principal royal architect and a priest during Zoser's reign, was responsible for the construction of this pyramid complex.

Hesy-Rē to leave and re-enter his tomb. Outside panels of this kind were, however, very vulnerable and the serdab was devised so as to give the figure better protection without any corresponding loss of efficacy. Even greater security was obtained by the introduction of stone figures to take the place of those made of wood. As a variant to the complete figure in the serdab, but not necessarily instead of it, a stone representation of the head of the dead person was sometimes, in the IVth and Vth Dynasties, placed in the burial-chamber. These so-called 'reserve' heads were undoubtedly portraits of their owners, perhaps given by the king to privileged members of the court, male and female, as a mark of special favour. The ears, in the surviving examples, are generally broken off and in some instances an incision has been scored in a line running from the top to the back of the skull, but the reason for these deliberate mutilations is unknown. Presumably the owner's intention was that the reserve head should serve as substitute for the actual head if the latter were destroyed or damaged.

When once the principle of substitution by means of a representation had been recognized, it was but a step to extend its scope to cover not only individual objects, such as food-vessels or statues, but also composite scenes illustrating episodes in the life of the deceased which he wanted to enjoy again in the after-life. Scenes depicting him hunting, fowling, or inspecting his estates were therefore believed to provide him with the means to continue these pursuits after his death. Likewise, scenes of harvesting, slaughtering of animals, brewing, and baking were thought to guarantee a constant supply of the commodities thus produced.

In order to eliminate any risk of the spirit of the deceased failing to recognize his statue, it was usually inscribed with his name and titles in hieroglyphs. Similarly, in the scenes carved in relief, short explanatory inscriptions were inserted as a kind of commentary, often giving the names of the persons represented and sometimes describing the actions which they performed. These persons were generally relatives of the deceased or his servants, who were thus assured of an after-life in the service of their master.

In spite of all the different devices for securing subsistence which were included in the equipment of the tomb, a regular supply of fresh provisions was always thought essential for the well-being of the deceased. They were laid on a low flat altar, which stood in front of the false door built into the west wall of the offering-room constructed on the east side of the super-structure. This position probably resulted from the practice of building mastabas on the high desert west of the Nile, so that the deceased, when looking out of the false door, would be facing the valley whence the offerings were usually brought.

Possibly the first offerings were presented by a son who, in providing for his deceased father's needs, symbolized Horus, the son of Osiris. Subsequent offerings would generally be brought by mortuary priests (like Shery mentioned above in connection with the royal tombs of the IInd Dynasty) who were engaged by written contract and paid for their services. Payment took the form of land bequeathed by the deceased to the priests. As an instance, one of the sons of Chephren, the builder of the second pyramid at Giza, bequeathed at least twelve towns as a mortuary endowment of this kind. Such land, having become the property of the priests, would be passed on by them to their heirs, who would also inherit the accompanying obligations with respect to the tomb. Experience must, however, have shown that

The Step Pyramid of Zoser was the first edifice in ancient Egypt to be constructed entirely of stone rather than of mud brick. An inscription left by a visitor to the pyramid during the New Kingdom venerates Zoser as 'he who opened the stone'.

even the most binding contracts would not be observed for longer than a limited period, and, at an early date, the so-called 'funerary stela' was introduced into the tomb to serve as a substitute for the actual offerings. This stela contained a magic formula declaring that the deceased had received the daily offerings in abundance; above the formula there was generally a scene, carved in relief, showing him seated at a table heaped with offerings presented to him by members of his family. While not intended to dispense with the regular supply of fresh provisions, the stela, by means of the magic power of its written word, provided the deceased with a valuable method of re-insurance against starvation and neglect.

However primitive and materialistic the Egyptian conception of the after-life may seem, it must be conceded that it was responsible for the production of some of the greatest artistic masterpieces in antiquity. Without the impetus provided by a practical motive, it is doubtful whether a fraction of the statues, reliefs, or inscriptions which are now so universally admired would ever have been produced.

The reserve heads of a woman (*left*) and of Seneferu-senb have been deliberately mutilated.

Step Pyramids

UNTIL the end of the Early Dynastic Period both kings and nobles, to judge from the evidence now available, were buried in tombs built of brick. In the IIIrd Dynasty, however, the kings began to use stone – a material which had previously been used only for isolated parts of buildings. The construction of the first tomb of this kind has always been ascribed to Imhotep, the architect of Zoser, who is credited by Manetho with having been the inventor of the art of building in hewn stone. Some indirect confirmation of his connection with Zoser's tomb is provided by the occurrence of his name on the pedestal of a statue which was found outside the tomb when it was excavated. His achievements became legendary among later generations of Egyptians, who regarded him not only as an architect but as a magician, an astronomer, and the father of medicine. In Saite times he was deified, being considered the son of Ptah, while the Greeks identified him with their own god of medicine, Asklepios.

The site which Imhotep selected was a stretch of high ground at Saqqara overlooking the city of Memphis. It covered an area measuring approximately 597 yards from north to south and 304 yards from east to west. A short distance to the north lay the large cemetery of Ist and IInd Dynasty mastabas which included those mentioned in the preceding chapter. Zoser was buried not in a mastaba, but beneath a monumental step pyramid. It was the central and dominating feature of a large complex of stone buildings and courtyards intended for various ceremonies connected with the after-life of the king. Around the perimeter of the complex was a massive stone enclosure wall. Tura limestone was used throughout for the outer facings of the buildings and local stone for their inner cores.

Although most of the subterranean parts of the Step Pyramid had been thoroughly explored during the nineteenth century it was not until the last thirty-five years that anything was known about the surrounding buildings. Time and deliberate destruction had reduced everything except the pyramid itself to ruined heaps of masonry over which lay a thick layer of sand. Scientific excavation, followed by painstaking restoration by C. M. Firth, J. E. Quibell, and J.-P. Lauer, working for the Service des Antiquités of the Egyptian Government, have now enabled a fairly complete picture to be formed of the whole complex as it appeared at the time of Zoser's burial.

In its final form the Step Pyramid was a massive structure rising in six unequal stages to a height of 204 feet. Its base measurements were approximately 411 feet from east to west and 358 feet from north to south. Before attaining these dimensions, however, it had undergone a number of changes of plan, some of which can be clearly detected, while the remainder are admittedly hypothetical and cannot be demonstrated without dismantling a considerable part of the building. Those alterations which can be proved lie in the places where the monument has been most severely damaged and where, in consequence, surfaces which were once covered by later layers of stone have now become exposed. It is an instance, by no means unique, of archaeological knowledge being gained at the expense of artistic loss.

It is clear that the nucleus of the monument is a solid box-like structure consisting of a core of local stone faced with an outer layer of dressed Tura limestone. This nucleus, 26 feet in height, appears to have been a mastaba of unique shape with a square ground-plan, each side being oriented approximately to face one of the four cardinal points and measuring about 207 feet. When completed, it was extended by about 14 feet on all four sides and a second facing of dressed limestone was added. The height of this extension, however, was about 2 feet less than that of the original mastaba, and so a

The Step Pyramid enclosure

step mastaba was formed. A further enlargement added about 28 feet to the east side only, making the tomb oblong with the longer axis running from east to west.

Before the facing of this accretion had been dressed, an entirely different design was adopted. The mastaba, which was extended by $9\frac{1}{2}$ feet on each side, became the lowest stage of a four-stepped pyramid. On its northern side a beginning was made with the construction of a mortuary temple, but before either building had been finished it was decided to extend the pyramid further towards the north and west. If this enlargement had been completed the height of the pyramid would have been increased and the number of steps would have been augmented to six, but this plan also was abandoned at the level of the fourth step. The sixth and last extension of the pyramid added a little to each side; the six steps were completed and the whole building was cased with a final layer of dressed Tura limestone.

The substructure of the Step Pyramid consists of a deep shaft giving access to a maze of corridors and rooms forming a hypogeum without parallel among the other pyramids of the Old Kingdom. Owing to the fact that the construction of some of these subterranean apartments was never finished, it is not always easy to detect which were part of Zoser's design and which were additions by later explorers or robbers. The main plan of Zoser's hypogeum and the successive stages of its construction can, however, be determined with certainty. First, a shaft, approximately 23 feet square, was sunk to a depth of about 28 feet into the limestone substratum. A tunnel, with its ceiling 23 feet below the surface of the ground, was then driven northwards from the shaft for a distance of about 66 feet. At that point, having passed the northern limits of both the mastaba and the four-stepped pyramid, the tunnel was continued for a further 70 feet in the form of an open trench, its floor sloping gradually upwards until it reached ground-level. Work on the shaft was then resumed until it had reached a total depth of 92 feet. Concurrently with the deepening of the shaft, the floor of the tunnel was lowered so that it became a ramp with a progressively steeper gradient. The floor was not, however, lowered to the full depth of the shaft, but only to a point about 40 feet above its base.

In design, the vertical shaft and ramp of the substructure of the Step Pyramid resembled the corresponding elements of the contemporary private mastabas. In the latter, however, a door at the bottom of the shaft gave access to a central hall surrounded by a number of rooms, one of which contained the body, whereas in the Step Pyramid the tomb-chamber itself became the central feature. This chamber, approximately 9 feet 9 inches in length and 5 feet 6 inches both in width and in height, was built entirely of pink granite from Aswan and was situated at the bottom of the shaft. At its northern end a hole was bored in one of the slabs spanning the roof, in order to admit the body at the time of burial. After the body had been placed in the chamber, the hole was filled with a granite plug, measuring about 6 feet in length and weighing approximately 3 tons. Above this tomb-chamber there was a room entered by a door from the ramp; it was here that the granite plug was stored until it was lowered into position. Nothing remains of this room, but it was probably built of limestone blocks. Its roof, which may have been corbelled, must have been very strong, because it bore the weight of the rubble with which the remainder of the shaft was subsequently filled.

At a distance of about 70 feet from the tomb-chamber and roughly parallel with its sides, four long galleries were hollowed out of the native rock. Flights of steps leading down from doors in the east and west walls of the ramp gave access to passages which connected the galleries one with another. Some of these passages and galleries were never finished, but it is likely that the original intention was to cover many of their walls with panels of small blue-glazed tiles, so arranged as to resemble the reed mats which hung on the walls of Zoser's palace. Tiled panels of this kind were found in the east gallery, which was only discovered in 1928, and in two rooms near the south-east corner of the tomb-chamber. The panelling on the west wall of the east gallery was interrupted in three places by limestone reliefs of the king performing religious ceremonies. Around the outer edge of the recesses containing these reliefs there were inscriptions giving the king's name and his titles. Similar inscriptions also flanked a doorway separating the two rooms decorated with blue tiles. Both this doorway and some of the tiles were taken to the Berlin Museum in 1843 by the German Egyptologist, Richard Lepsius.

It is probable that, when Zoser's monument was first planned, the substructure was intended to consist only of the two chambers at the bottom of the shaft, the four surrounding galleries, and the connecting passages, but, after the superstructure had been enlarged for the first time, eleven vertical shafts were sunk into the ground on its east side to a depth of about 108 feet. At the bottom of each shaft a corridor was directed westwards under the superstructure. Two fine alabaster coffins, one of which contained the re- mains of a child, were found at the far end of the fifth corridor from the north, while limestone pedestals for similar coffins remained in some of the other corridors. It is clear, therefore, that these shafts and corridors were tombs, almost certainly those of members of the royal family. Possibly each

The Step Pyramid, cross-section looking south (above), substructure and ground plan (below)

1. square mastaba with core of local stone faced with Tura limestone

2. extension of 14 feet

3. extension of 28 feet to the east side

4. extension of 9 feet 6 inches on each side and mortuary temple begun on north side

5. extension towards the north and west

5'. facing of dressed Tura limestone

6. shaft and burial chamber

7. 11 vertical shafts with corridors leading westward from them

8. rooms containing panels of blue-glazed tiles

9. tunnel and trench leading to ground-level

10. new access route to underground chambers

11. steps giving access to passageways connecting galleries

12. east gallery

13. mortuary temple

14. serdab

tomb was originally intended to have its independent superstructure, but ultimately they were all buried under the third extension of the monument, and the only means of access to them was by a long stairway leading to the northernmost tomb.

Until the fifth extension of the superstructure, the subterranean chambers and corridors were reached by descending the open trench and ramp from the north side. The open trench, however, was blocked with rubble when the superstructure was extended northwards, and it became necessary to dig a new tunnel in its place. Beginning with a flight of steps situated some distance to the north of the final superstructure, the tunnel followed a line to the west of the former trench and curved eastwards to join the original ramp near its upper end. Its course seems unnecessarily circuitous, and it is difficult to understand the motives which prompted such an expenditure of labour.

With the exception of the mortuary temple and the serdab, the buildings surrounding the Step Pyramid are without any known precedent or parallel. The mortuary temple in its ground-plan is reminiscent of a brick temple found at Saqqara by W. B. Emery in 1954 within the enclosure wall of a mastaba dated to the reign of Qaa, the last king of the Ist Dynasty. Both temples moreover were built to the north of their respective tombs. This orientation is notable, almost every similar edifice in the true pyramids being situated, like the offering-room of the normal mastaba, east of the tomb. Zoser's mortuary temple, a large rectangular building attached to the lowest step of the pyramid, was entered through a doorway in its eastern wall. No doors were fitted into this entrance, but an imitation of an open door was carved in the stone wall adjoining the northern jamb. Many other buildings in the complex were fitted with similar imitation doors, often carved to fit the exact measurements of the doorway. Beyond the entrance a long corridor with numerous turns led to two open courts, from one of which the staircase descended towards the substructure of the pyramid. At the southern end of each court there were three gangways opening into a wide gallery. Short walls, flanked on the north side by fluted engaged columns, formed the divisions between the gangways. Engaged columns with various decorations constituted, like the imitation doors, one of the most characteristic features in the architecture of this complex. Their design, which will be discussed at a later stage in the description of the complex, was invariably suggested either by the single stem of some plant or by a number of stems bound together. Two rooms on the west side of the open courts, each with a stone basin in its floor, and a sanctuary with two recesses sunk into the face of the pyramid, complete the few elements of this temple which are sufficiently preserved to be recognizable.

It is impossible to divine with any certainty the archetype by which Imhotep was guided when designing this mortuary temple, but it is tempting to regard it as a stone representation of the royal palace at Memphis. This explanation would be in keeping with the generally accepted opinion that most of the other buildings in the complex were copies of constructions in the palace compound. Whatever may be the true explanation, it is noticeable that most of the principal architectural features (e.g. courts, ablution rooms, and the recesses in the sanctuary) occur in pairs, suggesting that the temple was designed for the celebration of some ritual which had to be repeated. Such a ritual would have been performed for the king, once as ruler of Upper Egypt and a second time as ruler of Lower Egypt.

The serdab, which has suffered relatively little damage, is situated a short distance to the east of the entrance to the mortuary temple. It is built entirely of dressed Tura limestone, its front wall inclining inwards at an angle of 16° from the perpendicular to correspond with the angle of the lowest step of the pyramid, which provides its back-wall. Placed inside is a cast of a limestone statue of the king seated on a chair, the original having been transferred to the Cairo Museum at the time of its discovery. He is dressed in a long robe, which leaves only his hands, his feet, and the top of his shoulders exposed. On his head is a long wig covered by a linen head-dress. The eyes, probably made of rock-crystal set in copper sockets, and part of the artificial beard attached to his chin – a symbol of royalty – have now disappeared. Two holes were cut in the front wall of the serdab opposite the face, either to allow the smoke of incense to reach the statue or to enable the statue to look out.

Outside the serdab lies a small enclosure with two entrances, a narrow one at the south-east corner and the main one on the north. Sculptured representations of wooden doors were carved on the walls at each side of the main entrance, giving the impression of doors swung open so that the serdab could be seen from the open court outside the enclosure.

Two large rectangular buildings with curved roofs dominated the whole area lying east both of the serdab court and of the pyramid. Each was composed of a solid core of masonry overlaid with dressed Tura limestone. The southern face of each building was decorated with four engaged columns, which, together with a broad pilaster at each side, supported a cornice following the curve of the roof. In the more northern of the two buildings vertical flutings were carved on both the engaged columns and the pilasters. In the southern the engaged columns were similarly fluted, but the pilasters were ribbed. The capitals of the engaged columns resembled two large pendent leaves, a design found only in this complex. Near the top of the engaged columns were two square holes and, in the southern building, a pair of bosses into which brackets supporting insignia may have been fitted. An alternative explanation that the holes were intended for wooden imitations of the horns or the tusks of an animal seems less probable.

Situated asymmetrically near the middle of the southern face of each building was an entrance giving access to a narrow passage which led, by way of two right-angled turns, to a small cruciform sanctuary. Three niches, intended either for offerings or for statuettes, were sunk into the walls of the sanctuary. In the northern building there were also two niches in the wall at the end of the passage. The stone ceilings of the passages were carved to resemble the log rafters with which similar corridors were roofed in buildings composed of wood and mud-brick. West of the entrance, concealed from view behind the stone facing, there was a second passage leading to a small chamber which may once have contained a statue.

In front of the two buildings were open courts, the southern being considerably the larger. Surrounding the courts was an enclosure wall, in the east side of which, near the corner of each building, there was a broad recess. In the northern court this recess was decorated with three engaged columns, each representing a single papyrus stem and flower. The recess in the southern court contained only one engaged column, which appears to have represented a lily.

The precise purpose which these buildings were intended to serve in Zoser's after-life has never been satisfactorily explained. At one time they were believed to be the tombs of two of his daughters, Intkaes and Hetephernebti, whose names were carved on some stelae found nearby, but recent excavation has failed to reveal anything of a funerary character in their composition and a different explanation must be sought. The decoration of

Engaged papyrus column

Capital composed of
pendent leaves

the recesses in the courts seems to provide a clue, for it is known that the lily and the papyrus were the emblems of Upper and Lower Egypt respectively. Possibly, therefore, the southern building represented the pre-dynastic national sanctuary of Upper Egypt, which was situated at Hierakonpolis, while the northern building represented the corresponding sanctuary of Lower Egypt at Buto. The presence of an altar, shaped like a horse's hoof, in the court of the southern building would certainly imply that the buildings fulfilled a religious rather than a secular function.

South of the enclosure wall of the southern building lay another oblong court, the east and west sides of which were occupied by a series of dummy chapels composed of solid masonry. In front of each chapel was a small court provided with an imitation open door. A projection from the middle of its south wall screened a niche sunk into the base of the chapel façade. Architecturally, the façades of ten out of the thirteen chapels on the west side bore a striking resemblance to the façades of the northern and southern buildings. They consisted of three engaged columns, decorated with vertical flutings and supporting a curved cornice, the ends of which joined two broad pilasters. The capitals of these engaged columns, like those of the northern and southern buildings, were composed of two pendent leaves. A single round hole, cut between the leaves, probably supported a bracket holding an emblem. The façades of the remaining chapels of the west side and all those on the east seem to have been plain, except for a torus moulding at the top and sides.

This court and its surrounding buildings were designed to provide Zoser with the setting necessary for repeating in his after-life his jubilee ceremony, known in Egyptian as the *heb-sed*. Every king of Egypt was entitled to celebrate the *heb-sed* after occupying the throne for a certain number of years, the period varying from time to time. The origin of the festival is very obscure, but it seems to have been a relic from the remote past when kings reigned for only a limited period before being ceremonially put to death. Underlying this primitive custom was doubtless the belief that it was essential for the welfare of the kingdom that the physical vigour of its king should be unimpaired. The *heb-sed*, by enabling the king to regain his vigour through the exercise of magic, obviated the necessity of replacing him by a younger man.

One of the most important elements in the *heb-sed* was a re-enactment of the coronation. In this ceremony a procession led by a priest would enter those of the chapels surrounding the *heb-sed* court in which were gathered the gods of the *nomes* of Upper Egypt. Having obtained from each god consent to the renewal of his kingship, the king would be conducted to the more southern of two thrones, placed on a dais beneath a canopy, in order to be crowned with the white crown of Upper Egypt. A similar ceremony would be repeated in the chapels of the gods of the Lower Egyptian *nomes* before the king ascended the northern throne to receive the red crown of Lower Egypt. The unification of the two kingdoms would be symbolized at a later stage by lacing lotus (or lily) and papyrus flowers around a stake driven into the ground.

The significance of another ceremony in the *heb-sed* is not so apparent. The king, carrying a flail, would run a fixed course, accompanied by 'the priest of the souls of Nekhen'.* One of the reliefs discovered in the Step Pyramid seems to show Zoser performing this rite. It may have been

* The 'souls of Nekhen' were the prehistoric kings of Upper Egypt.

derived from a primitive belief that the fertility of the fields depended in some way on the physical agility of the king.

In addition to the chapels already described, the *heb-sed* court of the Step Pyramid still preserves at its southern end the coronation dais. The façades of the second and third chapels on the west side near the dais contained recesses approached by flights of steps. Possibly they were intended for statues of the king, the more southern statue as King of Upper Egypt and the more northern as King of Lower Egypt. The proximity of these recesses to the dais suggests that the buildings to which they belonged represented the pavilions where the king remained while the priests performed the ceremonies preceding the double coronation.

A passage leading from the south-west corner of the *heb-sed* court connected it with a smaller court in which stood a building of medium size. Its outer walls, built with a slight batter, were undecorated, apart from having a torus moulding on the southern face. Internally, it consisted of an imposing entrance-hall, three inner courts and a group of side-chambers. Projecting from the middle of the west side of the entrance hall were three tongue-walls, two of which terminated in engaged columns decorated with vertical flutings. The two alcoves formed by these tongue-walls may have contained statues, but whether they were images of the king or of gods cannot be deduced while the function of the building remains obscure. Its relation to the *heb-sed* court would seem to imply that its use was in some way associated with the *heb-sed*. Possibly it was the pavilion in which the king resided for the duration of the ceremonies and to which he retired between the various episodes in order to change his vestments. In support of this explanation both A. Hermann and H. Ricke have pointed out that the ground-plan shows many affinities with that of a small house of the time of Zoser which has been excavated at Saqqara.

Engaged fluted column

More difficult to understand is the purpose of a maze of corridors and chambers which led out of the *heb-sed* court at the south-east corner. In the absence of any distinctive architectural features, it has been conjectured that they too had some connection with the *heb-sed*.

A corridor linked the *heb-sed* court with the eastern end of a colonnade, close to a gateway in the enclosure wall – the only entrance into the complex. This colonnade consisted of a long, narrow passage running westwards between a series of alcoves formed by tongue-walls which projected from each side. These tongue-walls, of which there were forty, terminated in engaged columns with a ribbed decoration, the ribs varying in number from seventeen to nineteen. Within the alcoves there may have been statues of the king, those on the south side representing him as King of Upper Egypt and those on the north side as King of Lower Egypt. Since, however, the alcoves so nearly correspond in number with the forty-two *nomes*, it has been suggested that each contained a double statue of the king and a *nome*-god, but, although groups of this kind are known in the IVth Dynasty, excavation has revealed no trace of such sculpture in this colonnade. The whole building was covered with a flat stone roof, carved on the underside to imitate rounded logs of wood. Slits cut at an oblique angle in the side walls near the roof admitted beams of light which may have been directed on the sculpture in the alcoves.

Attached to the western end of the colonnade was a small transverse vestibule. Its roof, which resembled in pattern that of the colonnade, was

Engaged ribbed column

Overleaf: This
reconstruction shows a
panel of blue-glazed tiles
as it appeared in the
south mastaba of Zoser.
The tiles were meant to
imitate woven reed
mural hangings.

supported by eight ribbed columns joined in pairs by cross walls. In its west wall was a reproduction in stone of an open door giving access to a large open court which occupied the whole area from the south face of the Step Pyramid to the enclosure wall. The side walls of the court were made of dressed limestone, decorated with recessed panelling. At its northern end, near the pyramid, was an altar approached by a ramp. There were also two constructions, each in the form of a pair of hooves, south of the altar. Possibly they marked the limits of some ceremonial procession, but no evidence of its nature has hitherto come to light.

In the south-west corner of the southern court adjoining the enclosure was a rectangular building composed almost entirely of solid masonry. Its outer walls of dressed limestone were decorated at the top with a frieze of cobras. Inside, it contained only two elongated chambers set at right angles to each other. Unless this building was connected in some way with the ceremonies of the southern court, it must have served as the offering-room for a large mastaba, the superstructure of which, with its longer axis running exceptionally from east to west, was mainly concealed within the body of the enclosure wall. Its position on the north side of the mastaba would correspond with the orientation of the mortuary temple in its relation to the Step Pyramid.

The substructure of this south mastaba shares many features in common with the Step Pyramid. A tomb-chamber, made of blocks of pink granite, was built at the bottom of the vertical shaft. Its only entrance was a hole (which was subsequently stopped with a granite plug) in the flat roof. Immediately above the tomb-chamber was a second room, intended for storing the plug before the burial, its roof supporting the rubble-filling of the shaft. The side-ramp, however, instead of entering this room like its counterpart in the Step Pyramid, skirted it on the south side and gave access directly to the galleries, all of which were situated east of the tomb-chamber. In one gallery there were three separate reliefs of the king engaged in the performance of religious ceremonies. In a parallel gallery, a short distance to the west, the backs of three doors were carved in the limestone facing of the wall. Their position, approximately behind the reliefs, suggests that the panels containing the reliefs were regarded as false doors through which the king was in the act of emerging. The walls of several of these galleries were covered with the blue-glazed tiles imitating mural hangings made of reeds.

Since Zoser was almost certainly buried under the Step Pyramid, it is difficult to account for the construction within the same complex of a second tomb having every appearance of being intended for him. We know that the kings of Egypt did sometimes build more than one tomb – Seneferu, the first king of the IVth Dynasty, for instance, had two pyramids – and the reliefs on the false doors of the south mastaba are strong evidence that Zoser intended the tomb for his own use. The granite tomb-chamber, however, measured only 5 feet 3 inches square, which could not have contained the body of a person of normal stature unless in a contracted position – a manner of burial which is unlikely to have been used for a royal person of the IIIrd Dynasty. It has, therefore, been suggested that the tomb was either a dummy, intended for use in the symbolic sacrifice of the king during the *heb-sed*, or the actual burial-place of his entrails, which were removed from the body to aid its preservation. More recent discoveries in the neighbouring pyramid enclosure of Sekhemkhet, which will be mentioned later in this chapter, do not, however, support either of these explanations.

Two parallel structures of solid masonry covered nearly the whole of the west side of the complex. The outer wall of the first structure, where it faced the south court, was decorated with recessed panelling, which gave it a uniform appearance with the walls on the south and east sides of the court. The second structure, which was higher than the first, had a curved roof resembling the roof of the south mastaba. It may therefore have been the superstructure of a row of tombs belonging to Zoser's attendants, but, owing to the friable nature of the underlying rock, complete excavation has hitherto been impossible. Beyond these two structures was the thick enclosure wall.

The area between the mortuary temple and the northern enclosure wall may never have been finished, its only recognizable features being a large terrace with courts and a platform, measuring approximately 50 feet square, cut out of the native rock. This platform, which was faced with dressed limestone, was nearly in line with the north-south axis of the pyramid, and it is very possible that it served as an altar. The body of the enclosure wall on this side was built in the form of cells with dividing walls of stone. Since no trace of any object which might have been placed in these cells was discovered during excavation, it is unlikely that they were ever used for the purpose of storing funerary equipment. Beneath them, however, were subterranean chambers containing bread, fruit, and other means of subsistence for life in the Next World.

The enclosure wall of the Step Pyramid complex measured approximately 33 feet in height and had a peripheral length of more than a mile. It was composed of a thick inner core of masonry faced, partly inside and entirely outside, with dressed Tura limestone. On the outside, at intervals of $13\frac{1}{2}$ feet, there were rectangular bastions, all of uniform size apart from fourteen which were larger. On each of these larger bastions, which were spaced irregularly around the wall, an imitation was carved of closed double doors, giving the bastions the appearance of towered gateways. The only actual doorway, which has now been rebuilt, was situated near the southern corner of the east side, where two towers flanked a narrow passage leading to the entrance colonnade. Imitations of double doors, but in an open position, were also carved on the walls inside the towers. The whole outer face of the wall was panelled, and its upper half was decorated with small rectangular insets arranged vertically in rows of eight. These insets undoubtedly represented apertures of a similar pattern found in walls of mud-brick into which were fitted pieces of wood, perhaps for bonding purposes or for keeping the wall dry, but it is difficult to understand why the insets in this enclosure wall should have been confined to the upper half.

Walls composed of alternating projections and recesses are found in Egyptian tombs dating from the earliest dynastic times. The brick mastabas of the Ist Dynasty which lie a short distance to the north of the Step Pyramid are only one group of the many examples known. In those mastabas, however, the enclosure walls were not crenellated, but plain. The bastions and the fourteen gateways in Zoser's wall may have had their counterpart in the enclosure wall of his palace. It is, however, not impossible that the whole wall was a stone copy of the famous 'White Walls' built around Memphis by Menes. The 'White Walls', it must be supposed, were made of mud-brick overlaid with white gesso.

To review the Step Pyramid as a whole: it is certainly not an exaggeration to describe it as one of the most remarkable architectural works produced by the ancient Egyptians. That later generations regarded it with exceptional esteem is clear, not only from the veneration which they accorded to Imhotep, but also from hieratic graffiti on the passage walls of the northern and southern buildings, which record the admiration felt by some Egyptians who visited the monument more than a thousand years after it was built. No other known pyramid was surrounded with such an array of imposing buildings to supply the needs of the king in his after-life. In their place the kings who ruled two dynasties later were content with pictorial representations carved in relief. As an example, the pyramid complex of Sahurē, the second king of the Vth Dynasty, contains only reliefs of the *heb-sed*; it has no court with buildings specially designed for use in the ceremony.

Doubts have sometimes been entertained whether so high a degree of architectural perfection could have been achieved without having been preceded by a long process of development. There is, however, no evidence that stone had been employed in any earlier building, except for the construction of isolated parts. Moreover, the Step Pyramid displays many features which suggest that its builders lacked experience in the use of stone. Small blocks which could be easily handled were used instead of the massive slabs found in later buildings, showing that the technique of quarrying and manipulating heavy pieces of stone had not then been mastered. Again, engaged columns were probably not the outcome of artistic preference, but of doubt regarding the strength of the free-standing pillar. In decoration too the patterns chosen were copied from the wood, reed, or brick elements of earlier buildings; independent forms suited to stone had not yet been evolved.

Although the prototypes of the papyrus and the lily columns, which decorated the recesses in the eastern façades of the courts of the northern and the southern buildings, are evident at a glance, it is not easy to recognize what the sculptor was endeavouring to reproduce in the case of the ribbed and the fluted columns. H. Ricke has expressed the opinion that the ribbed columns, which are found only in the entrance colonnade, are not in reality columns but merely representations of buffers or fenders made of palm-ribs and laid as a cover over the exposed ends of brick walls in order to protect them from damage. J.-P. Lauer, however, maintains that these columns are imitations of wooden pillars representing bundles of reeds or palm-ribs which had been used as supports in more primitive constructions. This explanation, he believes, would account for the traces of red paint which remain on the columns, because red was the colour used to represent wood, whereas green would have been employed to represent the stems of plants.

Before attempting to summarize the principal theories of their origins, it is necessary to note that the fluted columns, in their occurrence in this complex, show certain differences. Those attached to the façades of the northern and southern buildings and the chapels in the *heb-sed* court were slender (tapering from about 1 foot 9 inches at the foot to $11\frac{1}{2}$ inches at the top), lacked bases, and had the so-called 'pendent leaf' capitals. The columns in the mortuary temple and the pavilion behind the *heb-sed* court, on the other hand, were thicker (about 2 feet 6 inches at the foot and 1 foot 8 inches at the top), were provided with circular disc-bases, and had rectangular block-capitals. All these columns were painted red from the top to a narrow band (lacking in the columns of the *heb-sed* court) 2 feet above the base, which

Stem of the *Heracleum giganteum*

was white, and black from the band downwards. Both Lauer and Ricke are in agreement in regarding the black colour as representing a protective covering of leather placed on the lower portions of similar columns made of softer materials. They are also essentially in agreement in interpreting the white band as a representation of a strip of metal, probably copper, which was intended to reinforce the lower part of the column. They regard the columns as reproductions in stone of the trunks of trees, perhaps conifers, the flutes being merely stylized representations of the incisions made in the wood by the curved cutting-edge of the tool used for dressing the surface. Ricke, who argues that the term 'column' is architecturally incorrect, has explained the so-called 'pendent leaf' capitals as being composed of a block representing the exposed end of a purlin supporting the framework of the roof and two cleats which were intended to strengthen the joint of the purlin with the framework and with the column. The corrugated surface of the cleats, he believes, may be explained, like the flutes of the columns, as reproductions of the grooves made in the wooden prototype by the metal tool. The outward curve of the tips of the 'leaves', he suggests, was a device for deflecting rainwater away from the joint.

Although Lauer and Ricke differ widely in their interpretation of several details, including the nature of the objects placed in the holes beneath the pendent leaf capitals, they concur in their views on two fundamental matters: both agree that the ribs on the columns of the entrance colonnade represent stems, probably palm-ribs, and that the fluted columns imitate trunks of trees. P. E. Newberry, who was a botanist as well as being an Egyptologist, however, maintained that these two columns shared a common prototype in an umbelliferous plant, the *Heracleum giganteum*, the hollow stems of which, when green, are ribbed but, when dry, are fluted. In support of this identification he claimed that the pendent leaf capitals were imitations of the petioles of the leaves which hang down over the stem. This explanation is attractive for many reasons: it places the ribbed and the fluted columns in the same category as the papyrus and the lily columns, each being a representation of a single stem of a plant; the *Heracleum giganteum*, when fully grown, possesses sufficient strength to have been used in primitive structures for the framework over which reed-matting was placed; neither the papyrus nor the lily, by reason of the weakness of their stems, could have been used, at least singly, as supports, but if the Egyptians were already employing the *Heracleum giganteum* for structural skeletons it would have been simple, when reproductions in wood or stone took the place of the actual plant, to introduce variations, and the papyrus and the lily, because of their symbolic significance, would have been the most obvious plants to choose; lastly, the resemblance of the petioles to the pendent leaves of the capital seems too close to have been accidental.

Newberry's interpretation of the columns would probably have received more general acceptance than has yet been accorded to it if he could have shown that the *Heracleum giganteum* grew in Egypt, but, although this plant is widely distributed in its occurrence, there is no evidence that it has ever flourished in the Nile Valley. (Newberry was aware of this difficulty and had previously suggested another umbelliferous plant, the *silphium*, which was almost certainly a North African species of *Ferula*, either *Ferula communis* or *Ferula tingitana*, both of which have tall, rigid stems fluted externally.) Several other plants, however, which were once common in Egypt have long

The Pyramid of Meidum in its final form was a geometrically true pyramid. Originally planned as a step pyramid, it underwent successive alterations until, finally, the steps were filled in and overlaid with a smooth casing. Layers of masonry applied around a core formed the step pyramid; these were methodically stripped off by plunderers, leaving the strangely shaped monument we see today.

become extinct there, and it is conceivable that the *Heracleum giganteum* belongs to this class. On architectural grounds it may be argued that the pendent leaf capital is found only in the engaged columns of the northern and southern buildings and the *heb-sed* court, but the petioles, unlike the flowers of the papyrus and the lily, were without symbolical meaning and their omission from the engaged columns of the pavilion and the mortuary temple could be understood as an artistic variation. A stronger case can be presented against the theory that the ribbed columns also owed their origin to the *Heracleum giganteum* because their capitals appear to have no clear parallel in the plant itself unless it be that the stem was slit vertically at the top and the strips, still attached at the base, were folded downwards over the outside in order to double the thickness and thus provide greater strength. It must, however, be conceded that the absence of any indication of a tie at the base of the capital is difficult to reconcile with this explanation.

Size, architectural design, and decorative elements were not the only respects in which Zoser's pyramid excelled the tombs of his predecessors. It was also equipped on a scale never attempted before. In spite of being subjected to plundering over a period of at least four thousand years, it has yielded in the course of excavation thousands of beautifully shaped vases and dishes made of alabaster, schist, porphyry, breccia, quartz crystal, serpentine, and many other stones. Considerable quantities still await removal from the tombs of the royal family, where they may be seen lying in heaps reaching from the floor to the ceiling. No food or other commodity was placed in most of these vessels; their very presence, possibly in conjunction with the recitation of a magic formula by the priest, was enough to ensure a constant supply of their appropriate contents for the king.

Before its destruction, the enclosure must have contained a considerable number of statues. Only the seated figure of Zoser in the serdab has been preserved substantially intact, but fragments of other statues have also been found. At the northern end of the *heb-sed* court there is a limestone pedestal on the top of which are carved eight human feet; it must, therefore, have supported a group of four statues, possibly those of the king, queen, and two princesses. In the same court there were found three large monolithic figures, only one of which had been finished. At first sight these figures resemble caryatides, but it is highly unlikely that they were designed to stand as independent columns; they were probably intended to be built into niches. Fragments of other statues, including at least one of the king, were discovered outside the enclosure wall and in a recess in the south wall of the entrance colonnade. All these statues, and possibly several more which have now disappeared without trace, were made not to commemorate the persons whom they represented, but to provide their spirits with a substitute for their bodies during the various ceremonies performed within the pyramid enclosure. Since only two royal statues dating from an earlier period – both representing a predecessor of Zoser, Khasekhem – have hitherto been discovered, it is highly probable that Zoser's reign marked a big advance in the production of sculpture in the round. The figure in the serdab, if it may be regarded as typical, suggests that the collection of statues once contained in the enclosure was of a quality comparable with the finest masterpieces of the succeeding dynasties.

Before the recent excavations nothing remained visible of Zoser's monumental works except the pyramid itself, stripped almost entirely of its

Chephren, builder of the second Giza pyramid, is here portrayed wearing the royal beard and headdress. The high-backed throne supports a Horus-falcon with outstretched, protecting wings.

outer casing; inside also the pyramid had suffered grievously. All the rubble-filling of the central shaft and part of the blocking built into the side-ramp after the burial were systematically removed by ancient plunderers, so that today it is possible to stand on the granite roof of the tomb-chamber and, with the aid of a powerful electric torch, to see the underside of the lowest layer of stones which covered the mouth of the shaft when the first mastaba was built. Beneath these stones the plunderers, when removing the rubble-filling, had constructed a stout wooden platform, only a few fragments of which now remain. That the stones, lacking the support of either the filling or the platform, have not collapsed into the shaft is little short of miraculous.

Apart from the stone vessels, nothing has been preserved of Zoser's tomb furniture. In the tomb-chamber, however, some human remains were found; although there is no proof that they belonged to Zoser, the method of their burial would have been consistent with the practice of his time. The eleven tombs of the royal family were similarly plundered, leaving only the two alabaster coffins already described. One of these coffins – that containing the skeleton of a child – was lined with six layers of wood, each less than a quarter of an inch in thickness. They were laid with their grains running alternately in vertical and horizontal directions, and were held together by small wooden pegs. Some gold rivets, found in the innermost layer, suggest that this wooden lining was originally overlaid with gold.

It is impossible to estimate with any accuracy when the plundering of the Step Pyramid was begun. The graffiti in the northern and southern buildings suggest that the surrounding structures were substantially intact during the New Kingdom, but it does not follow that the tomb itself had not been robbed of its most valuable furniture by that time. The three reliefs of Zoser in the eastern gallery may provide evidence that access could be gained to the subterranean chambers and corridors during the Saite Period. Each relief has been divided by ink lines into squares, indicating that a scale reproduction of it was planned. Since the Saites are known to have modelled some of their sculpture on the works of the Old Kingdom, it is not unlikely that they were the artists who drew these grids over the reliefs. Other intruders were guided by baser motives, and a steady process of denudation probably continued without hindrance until the present century.

The Service des Antiquités, under the direction of J.-P. Lauer, has done a considerable amount of restoration work within the enclosure. The entrance colonnade, the south-east corner of the enclosure wall including the portal, and isolated parts of several other buildings have been reassembled.

Although none of Zoser's successors in the IIIrd Dynasty has left a monument comparable in magnificence with his pyramid enclosure, there is clear evidence that they followed the example which he had set in building tombs of a step pyramid form. One of these kings chose a site close to the south-west corner of Zoser's complex and laid out an enclosure roughly equal in length to the enclosure of the Step Pyramid, but only about two-thirds of its width. The excavation of this site was first undertaken by Zakaria Goneim on behalf of the Service des Antiquités of the Egyptian Government in 1951–5 and through his labours a very considerable amount of information was obtained, although he was unable to complete the task before it became necessary to suspend the Service's activities in the field. Work was resumed in 1963 under J.-P. Lauer, but only on a limited scale.

Inscribed clay stoppers of jars discovered in this pyramid showed that it

The Pyramid of Sekhemkhet,
cross-section looking west
(top), substructure and ground
plan (bottom)

1. trench and tunnel
leading to substructure

2. arch carved in south wall

3. vertical shaft rising through
core of pyramid

4. 132 subterranean magazines

5. burial chamber

was built by Sekhemkhet, a king who is otherwise known only from three
representations carved in relief on a rock at Wady Maghara in Sinai and
mistakenly attributed by Egyptologists in the past to Semerkhet, the penultimate king of the Ist Dynasty. How soon after his accession Sekhemkhet
began to build his pyramid is unknown, but, if he has been correctly identified
with a king whose personal name is given as Zoser-Ti or Zoser-Teti in the
king-lists, his reign lasted for no longer than six years and it is not surprising
that a very considerable amount of the projected work was never carried out.
Planned on a base measuring about 395 feet square, the superstructure
would probably have risen by seven steps to a height of about 230 feet. Since
the monument was used as a quarry in later times it is impossible to estimate
the height to which it had been built when work was abandoned; all that has
survived to the present day is a few layers of the inner core nowhere higher
than about 23 feet above ground-level. In order to reach the required depth

for the substructure an open trench with sloping floor was cut in the rock, its shallow end being situated far beyond the northern face of the pyramid. When the trench had been hewn to a depth of about 40 feet below the surface of the rock it was continued as a tunnel for a further 29 feet before this plan was abandoned, probably because the rock at that level was found to be unsound. The trench was then filled with rubble to about half its depth and a second tunnel was cut immediately above the first. Although the floor of the new tunnel continues the gradient of the trench its flat ceiling is horizontal as far as a point 38 feet, measured on the incline, from the entrance where an arch, rounded on the under side, 3 feet in thickness and 13 feet in height, is carved in the rock which forms the south wall of this section of the corridor. Beyond the arch the ceiling, roughly curved, slopes at about the same angle as the floor, but its continuity is interrupted by a vertical shaft, about 9 feet square in section, which rises through the rock and the core of the pyramid. Shafts comparable in design and position were constructed in mastabas of this period at Beit Khallaf, their purpose being to enable heavy stone portcullises to be lowered to the corridor and block it after the body had been placed in the tomb. A doorway in the west wall of the corridor immediately beneath the shaft gives access, by way of an L-shaped passage, to a series of 132 subterranean magazines arranged in staggered fashion on each side of a level corridor running first from east to west and continued at both ends with arms extending southwards. From the doorway leading to these magazines the sloping corridor continues downwards until it becomes flat at a point only a few yards short of the burial-chamber, a roughly hewn compartment measuring about 30 feet from north to south, 17 feet in width and 16 feet 6 inches in height. Recesses extending from floor to ceiling, each 6 feet 6 inches in depth, were cut approximately in the middle of the east and west walls, but their purpose is not evident. A doorway in the south wall of the burial-chamber leads to a blind gallery, one of four similar galleries, the northernmost of which would probably have been accessible by a connecting passage from the sloping corridor if work had not been terminated when the passage had been tunnelled to within $8\frac{1}{2}$ inches of the corridor. It may be conjectured on the analogy of Zoser's pyramid that the walls of some at least of these galleries would ultimately have been decorated with blue-glazed tiles and possibly also with carved representations of the king performing religious ceremonies.

In spite of the unfinished condition of this pyramid hopes were raised in the course of its excavation that it would prove to contain the body of the king. It is true that the vertical shaft had been used in later times for the burial of animal-bones, but these bones, and also a group of sixty-two papyri written in demotic (a cursive script developed indirectly from hieroglyphics and employed from the XXVth Dynasty onwards), were buried in the sand-filling near the top of the shaft, while beneath it, in the corridor, the excavator found a collection of gold jewellery which he dated without hesitation to the IIIrd Dynasty. Moreover, not only was the corridor sealed in three places, at its entrance, below the shaft, and at the doorway of the burial-chamber, by thick blocking walls of stone, which were still intact, but also there was no trace of any tunnel by which robbers could have circumvented these obstacles. Most significant of all, however, seemed to be the fact that a closed sarcophagus, on which a wreath had been placed, was discovered in the burial-chamber. This sarcophagus, carved from a single

The Layer Pyramid of Zawiyet el-Aryan, a step pyramid of the IIIrd Dynasty, may have been built by an obscure king named Khaba.

rectangular block of alabaster, was exceptional in one respect: instead of having the whole top as a lid, it had, at one end, a sliding panel which could be raised and lowered by a rope passed through a U-shaped boring at the top of the panel. Rib-shaped tenons on the sides and the base of the panel fitted into grooves cut in the sides and base of the aperture in the sarcophagus. Some plaster which could be seen in the grooves suggested that the panel had not been moved since it was ceremonially closed at the time of the funeral. All these indications, however, proved deceptive: the sarcophagus when opened was found to be empty. Unless it is to be assumed that the body and its costly appurtenances were stolen with the connivance of those in charge of the burial, it seems necessary to suppose that the tomb, or at least the sarcophagus, was never occupied.

Too little work has yet been done on the clearance of the enclosure to show how far the construction of the various buildings had progressed when operations were brought to an end, presumably because of the king's death. Exploratory pits sunk at intervals along the perimeter revealed that the foundations of the outer walls had been laid; in all probability, several of the upper courses had also been built but had been wilfully dismantled by later generations to provide material for their own monuments. As first planned the enclosure was about 215 yards shorter from north to south than in its final form. A considerable part of the original north wall still remains standing; it is composed of a thick core of local stone faced with fine limestone. Like the enclosure wall of Zoser's pyramid, it is panelled and rectangular bastions project outwards from its northern side. It is in fact almost an exact copy of Zoser's wall, both the panels and the bastions being of the same measurements as the corresponding features in the Step Pyramid enclosure, and doubtless imitations of closed double doors would have been carved on the irregularly spaced larger bastions if they had been completed. Greater economy in the use of Tura limestone as well as in its preparation is, however, to be detected in the construction of Sekhemkhet's wall: the outer skin is only one course in thickness (about 1 foot) and each block is about twice as high (approximately 20 inches) as the facing blocks in Zoser's wall. When it was decided to enlarge the enclosure, this wall, which had been built to the level of the sixth course, was left to serve as the southern retaining wall of a terrace, which appears to reach as far as the new northern boundary of the complex, and the eastern and western walls were also extended northwards but, for reasons which are not yet apparent, these extensions are not in direct alignment with the earlier walls, each being stepped inwards by about 6 feet. Perhaps future excavations will provide an explanation of this strange feature and will also bring to light at least the foundations of other constructions within the enclosure, only one of which has yet been explored, though some walls on the north side of the pyramid, probably belonging to the mortuary temple, have been located.

Like Zoser, Sekhemkhet built a mastaba on the south side of his pyramid, but its superstructure was not concealed in the core of the enclosure wall. It was constructed of stone blocks and it stood on the terrace about halfway between the pyramid and the original enclosure wall, its main axis running from east to west. Before its almost complete demolition the superstructure measured about 35 yards in length and 18 yards in breadth. The substructure, which has been excavated by J.-P. Lauer, consists of a vertical shaft under the western end of the superstructure, a sloping corridor and a

The Layer Pyramid of Zawiyet
el-Aryan, cross-section looking
west, ground plan

1. vertical shaft 62 feet 6 inches
deep
2. burial chamber
3. transverse corridor with 32
compartments cut in the inner
wall
4. *cul-de-sac*

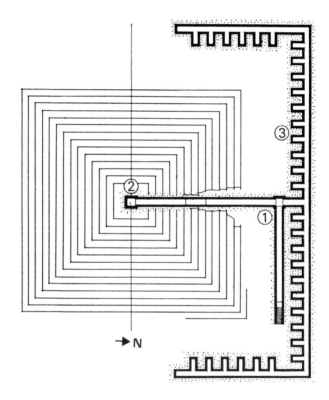

level passage leading to the tomb-chamber. The shaft, which has been sunk
through the terrace and the underlying rock to a depth of about 95 feet,
penetrates the roof of the level passage near its junction with the sloping
corridor. It was filled with sand and rubble when the tomb was closed. In
spite of this obstruction the ancient robbers were able to bore a tunnel through
the blocking of the sloping passage, skirt the base of the shaft and reach the
tomb-chamber. Fortunately they did not remove the entire contents of the
chamber, though they must have taken everything of value to them except
a few fragments of gold foil embossed with a reed-mat design which Lauer
found near the entrance to the chamber. Apart from these fragments he

also found some stone vessels, pottery, animal bones and the skeleton of a child in a decayed wooden coffin with panelled sides. The style of the coffin proves that the burial dates from the IIIrd Dynasty, but nothing has yet come to light to establish the identity of the child. While this discovery casts considerable doubt on the theories hitherto advanced concerning the purpose of Zoser's south mastaba, it presents a new problem to which no solution can now be offered. The entrance to the sloping passage has not yet been located.

Not the least valuable result of the excavation of the Pyramid of Sekhem-khet was the light which it shed on the date of another step pyramid, the so-called Layer Pyramid at Zawiyet el-Aryan. G. A. Reisner, who examined this pyramid some years after it had been excavated by Alessandro Barsanti, at first ascribed it to the IIIrd Dynasty; subsequently he revised his opinion in favour of the IInd Dynasty. Its superstructure, of which only the lowest courses of the inner core have been preserved, covers an area of 276 feet square. In every probability the architect planned a monument with six or seven steps, but it seems that the building was never completed. A flight of steps to the north of the superstructure, about 13 yards from the north-east corner, descends to a rock-cut tunnel which runs to a point outside, and approximately in line with, the middle of the north face where it joins the base of a vertical shaft, 62 feet 6 inches in depth. At the same level in the shaft two other tunnels have their entrances, one in the south wall leading by way of a horizontal corridor and a second flight of steps to the tomb-chamber measuring approximately 12 feet (north – south) by 8 feet 9 inches and 9 feet 10 inches in height, and the other in the north wall giving access by a con-necting passage to a long transverse corridor running from east to west with short arms at each end directed southwards. Thirty-two compartments, all oriented towards the pyramid and about 15 feet in length, were cut in the inner wall of this corridor. At a higher level in the shaft another corridor, a cul-de-sac, was tunnelled southwards.

Although the design of the substructure of this pyramid differs in detail from the Pyramid of Sekhemkhet, it is essentially similar and the surviving remnants of the two superstructures are almost identical. Perhaps the resemblance would have been even closer if the work on the substructure of the Layer Pyramid had been completed, for the original intention of the architect may well have been to add side-galleries near the tomb-chamber. The absence of the sarcophagus and funerary equipment suggests not only that the pyramid was never occupied, but also that work had not reached an advanced stage when discontinued. It is possible that its builder was Khaba, an obscure king whose name was inscribed on some stone vessels which Reisner found in a group of IIIrd Dynasty brick mastabas situated on a plateau to the north of the pyramid. The discovery, it must be conceded, did not necessarily show that Khaba ruled in the IIIrd Dynasty because objects bearing the names of kings of an earlier date were often placed in tombs built in the times of their successors. Nevertheless, it is now clear that the chronological position of this pyramid lies close to, and possibly immediately after, the Pyramid of Sekhemkhet, the evidence of which was not available to Reisner when, influenced by its general similarity to the rock-cut stairway mastabas of the IInd Dynasty, he made the tentative suggestion that it was built in the IInd Dynasty.

Nothing is known with certainty about the history of four small step pyramids situated at Seila, Zawiyet el-Mayitin, Nagada, and El-Kula. A Belgian expedition under Jean Capart in 1946 conducted an exhaustive investigation of the environs of the pyramid at El-Kula, but without finding an entrance to its substructure. The superstructure was surveyed in 1949 by another expedition, also organized by the Fondation Égyptologique Reine Élisabeth, with the result that the interesting discovery was made that the corners, and not the four sides, were oriented towards the cardinal points. When complete, the monument, which covers an area of about 61 feet square,

The Pyramid of El-Kula, cross-section looking south-east

rose in three steps, the uppermost of which has now almost entirely disappeared. Only the core, consisting of coarse limestone quarried near by, has been preserved and the suggestion has been made that it was originally covered with a layer of mud overlaid with white plaster; fine-grained limestone was not available in that locality. The Pyramid of Nagada, a four-stepped monument almost identical both in size and in general construction with the Pyramid of El-Kula, may provide a solution to the problem of the location of the substructures of the other three pyramids in this group. When Sir Flinders Petrie conducted his excavations at Nagada in 1896 he found that the substructure was a simple pit roughly hewn in the rock immediately beneath the centre of the pyramid and not connected by a tunnel with any entrance outside the pyramid; it would, therefore, have been inaccessible from the time when the lowest course of the superstructure had been laid. Unfortunately, the pit proved to be empty so that he obtained no evidence of the date of the burial. Some allowance must be made for the inexperience of the builders, as compared with those who worked in the Memphite necropolis, in erecting large stone monuments, but even so these four pyramids present the appearance of being early creations. Only by further excavations, and probably by dismantling considerable portions of their superstructures, is it likely that it will be possible to determine their date more precisely and perhaps also to discover the reason for their construction at places far distant from the capital.

The transition to the true pyramid

A T the beginning of the IVth Dynasty an important development occurred in the design of the royal tomb: the step pyramid was superseded by the true pyramid, a monument with a square base and sides sloping inwards to a point at the summit. By a lucky chance it is possible to trace this development in the badly damaged pyramid at Meidum which lies about thirty miles south of Memphis. In its present condition the monument resembles a high rect-angular tower rather than a pyramid. This shape is not entirely fortuitous, but is partly due to the method of its construction, the main features of which became known through Sir Flinders Petrie's excavations in 1891. Subsequent investigations, conducted at different times by G. A. Wain-wright, Ludwig Borchardt, and Alan Rowe, have added many important details to Petrie's discoveries.

Like Zoser's pyramid, the Pyramid of Meidum attained its final form after undergoing a number of transformations. The initial building may have been a mastaba or possibly a small step pyramid, the superstructure of which would now be concealed within the surviving core; its shape cannot, therefore, be determined with certainty. Some blocks recovered in the course of excavation bore drawings scratched by quarrymen which showed pyramids with two, three, and four steps, possibly representing successive alterations in the original design. The first ascertainable form of the superstrucure is that of a seven-stepped pyramid. This form was achieved by increasing the height of the earlier construction and making the tower-like building so produced furnish both the nucleus and the top step of the pyramid. Six thick coatings of masonry, diminishing in height from the centre outwards, were then built against the four sides of this nucleus, their upper portions supplying the six remaining steps. Each of the coatings, which inclined inwards at an angle of about $75°$, consisted of a core of local stone cased from top to bottom with Tura limestone. They were not bonded together, but depended on their angle of incline for cohesion. Only the casing which covered the steps was dressed, the remainder being left rough.

When the seven-stepped pyramid had been completed, a considerable enlargement of the superstructure was undertaken. The top step was raised by about 45 feet and each successive step was built up to a level somewhat higher than the one above it in the previous design; a new step was added to the base. Again the material used was local stone cased with Tura limestone, which was dressed where it was exposed.

The superstructure now visible is composed of parts of the third and fourth steps of the seven-stepped pyramid, the whole of the fifth and sixth steps of the eight-stepped pyramid and a small part of the seventh step. If the coatings which were built around the nucleus had been bonded together, the ruined superstructure would doubtless have assumed a very different appearance from that which it presents today. In the course of its destruc-tion, systematic stripping of the sides, coating by coating, would have been impossible, and the pyramid would probably have been reduced to a shape-less heap of stones.

This pyramid was not, however, destined to remain as a step pyramid, although it is evident that both the seven- and the eight-stepped designs were, in their turn, intended to be final. For reasons which cannot readily be explained, the steps were filled in with a packing of local stone, and the whole structure was overlaid with a smooth facing of Tura limestone. By this means, the monument was transformed into a geometrically true pyramid. Substantial portions of the lower half of the ultimate form still remain intact, but are now almost completely covered by accumulations of sand.

The entrance to the pyramid at each stage of its development was in the northern face. From a point in the outermost casing, situated a little above the lowest step of the penultimate design, a corridor leads downwards at an angle of about 28°, first through the core of the superstructure and then into the substratum of rock. At a distance of about 190 feet from the entrance, the gradient ceases and the corridor continues on an even plane for a further 31 feet. Near the bottom of the gradient there is a pit in the floor, but its purpose is not apparent. Beyond the pit there may have been a wooden door, the frame of which would have fitted into grooves cut in the walls, roof, and floor of the corridor. Two recesses, each about 8 feet 6 inches in width and 4 feet in depth, open out of the sides of the level section of the corridor, the first on the east and the second on the west. The purpose of these recesses too is obscure, but it is tempting to think that they were intended for storing, during the construction of the pyramid, stone plug-blocks which would have been too large to be lowered down the corridor after the burial. The area of both recesses would have been sufficient for manoeuvring blocks of considerable size, and the space left vacant when they had been moved into position could have been filled with masonry. Some limestone blocks found in the recesses may actually have been used for this purpose. Such a method of sealing the passages to the tomb-chamber may well have led to the invention of the side portcullises found in the next pyramid to be described.

At the end of the corridor a vertical shaft leads upwards, emerging in the floor of the tomb-chamber at its north-east corner. Built partly in the rock substratum and partly in the core of the superstructure, it measures 19 feet 6 inches from north to south and 8 feet 6 inches from east to west. It is entirely

The Pyramid of Meidum, cross-section looking west

1. first ascertainable form of the superstructure, a seven-stepped pyramid

2. enlargement to an eight-stepped pyramid

3. extension to a geometrically true pyramid

4. entrance to the pyramid

5. burial chamber

composed of limestone, its roof consisting of overlapping layers in the form of a corbel vault. The floor also is paved with slabs of limestone, some of which have now disappeared. In the south wall there is a hole made by robbers in search of hidden treasure. Both in the shaft and in the chamber there are wooden baulks which may have been used for some purpose by the builders or, alternatively, may have been required for moving heavy funerary equipment, perhaps a stone sarcophagus. No trace of such a sarcophagus was, however, found in 1882 by Sir Gaston Maspero, the first archaeologist to enter the pyramid in modern times, or nine years later by Petrie, although he discovered some fragments of a wooden coffin which might have been placed inside an outer sarcophagus of stone.

The buildings belonging to this pyramid were arranged according to what subsequently became the standard design for an Old Kingdom pyramid complex, the essential elements of which were always the pyramid itself and at least one subsidiary pyramid standing on high ground within an enclosure, a mortuary temple, a sloping causeway, and a building on the western fringe of the cultivation. The valley building was connected with the river by a canal dug in order to enable the funeral procession of boats to reach the complex without a long journey overland.

A wide mud-plaster pavement, bounded by a stone wall, surrounded this pyramid. Between the south face and the wall lay the subsidiary pyramid, now reduced to a few stones covering the substructure. No evidence was found to suggest that it had been transformed into a true pyramid. Within the enclosure on the north side was a large mastaba – an unusual feature in such a position – which has completely disappeared. Built against the middle of the east face of the pyramid, and still almost intact, is the mortuary temple composed entirely of Tura limestone. It is a very simple building, covering an area of little more than 34 feet square and rising to a maximum height of 9 feet. A door in the southern corner of its front wall opens into a passage set at right angles to the door; beyond lies a single chamber running parallel with the passage and an open court which backs directly on to the pyramid. No carvings of any kind decorate the walls of the passage or the chamber, neither of which has any opening for light except the door. In the middle of the court, opposite the door leading from the chamber, there is a low lime-stone altar intended for the daily offerings of food and drink for the dead king. Two tall monolithic slabs of limestone with rounded tops, mounted on low rectangular bases of similar material, stand one on each side of the altar. Although no inscriptions have been carved on these slabs, it is clear from their shape that they were designed as funerary stelae which might have been expected to bear the various names and titles of the king. The absence of such an inscription, together with the fact that the stones forming the lowest courses of the temple walls have been left undressed, would strongly suggest that the building was never finished.

An open space measuring about 80 feet in width separated the mortuary temple from the eastern enclosure wall. At a point in the wall nearly opposite the temple entrance, a narrow opening gave access to the causeway which connected the pyramid area with the building situated slightly south of due east on the edge of the valley. A shallow depression in the sand is the only indication of this causeway now visible. When intact, it measured 235 yards in length. Its floor of mud-plaster was laid on a bed, 10 feet in width, hewn out of the rock substratum. Bounding each side was a stone wall 7 feet in

Mortuary temple of the Pyramid of Meidum

1. passage set at right angles to the door
2. single chamber parallel with the passage
3. open court with low limestone altar and two uninscribed stelae
4. eastern enclosure wall
5. stone wall bounding side of causeway

height, which decreases in thickness from 5 feet at the base to 4 feet at the top. A coping-stone with the upper surface rounded, which came to light in the course of Flinders Petrie's excavations, showed that the walls did not support a roof. The only break in these walls was near the upper end, where two doors allowed the causeway to be entered from the sides. Two deep recesses at the junction of the causeway and the enclosure wall may once have contained statues of the king, the southern as King of Upper Egypt and the northern as King of Lower Egypt; on the other hand, they may have been used for the performance of some ritual during the funeral ceremony. At the lower end of the causeway, close to where it joined the valley building, there was a double door, the pivots of which fitted into two sockets cut in the rock beneath the mud-plaster floor. It is difficult to account for the presence of a door in such a position, but it may be surmised that it was intended to debar those not entitled by their office to proceed further than the valley building.

Complete excavation of the valley building has so far proved impracticable owing to the sodden condition of the ground, caused by a rise in the level of the Nile bed since the days when this pyramid complex was built. Its walls are reduced nearly to ground-level and the simplicity and modest dimensions of the mortuary temple would certainly suggest that the valley building also was unpretentious.

No contemporary inscriptions giving the name of the builder of this pyramid have been found at Meidum. In the passage and chamber of the mortuary temple, however, there are a number of graffiti, scribbled on the walls by visitors during the XVIIIth Dynasty, which show that the pyramid was at that time considered to be the work of Seneferu, the first king of the IVth Dynasty. As an example, one of these graffiti may be translated as follows: 'On the twelfth day of the fourth month of summer in the forty-first year of the reign of Tuthmosis III, the Scribe Aa-Kheper-Rē-senb, son of Amenmesu [the Scribe and Ritualist of the deceased King Tuthmosis I], came to see the beautiful temple of King Seneferu. He found it as though heaven were within it and the sun rising in it. Then he said: "May heaven rain with fresh myrrh, may it drip with incense upon the roof of the temple of King Seneferu." ' Other graffiti in the temple dating as early even as the VIth Dynasty mention the name of Seneferu, but do not state explicitly that the temple belonged to him.

The information given in the graffiti alone would be considered sufficient to enable the pyramid of Meidum to be attributed to Seneferu if no other pyramid with a comparable claim were known. Twenty-eight miles north of Meidum, at Dahshur, there are, however, two pyramids, the southern of which was certainly built by Seneferu, and the evidence at present available suggests that he also built the northern pyramid. Before the question of ownership can be discussed more fully, it is necessary to describe the chief architectural features of these two pyramids. Although the southern pyramid was no doubt planned as a geometrically true pyramid, it was not completed as such; at a point somewhat above half its height the angle of its incline decreases abruptly from $54° 31'$ to $43° 21'$. It has, therefore, been variously named the 'Bent', 'False', 'Rhomboidal', and 'Blunted' Pyramid. More than a century ago Sir J. Gardner Wilkinson suggested that it was finished in haste and that its height had accordingly been reduced. To some extent this suggestion was confirmed by J. S. Perring, who examined the composition of the superstructure in 1839 and observed that the stones in the upper part were laid with less care than those below.

Built on a square ground-plan, each side of the Bent Pyramid measures approximately 620 feet at the base; its vertical height, when complete, would have been about 336 feet. It is oriented roughly on the four cardinal points, but Sir Flinders Petrie, when making his survey in 1887, found that the error from true north and south in its orientation was greater than that of either the Great Pyramid or the Pyramid of Chephren at Giza. Externally, it is the best preserved of all the surviving pyramids; no other has retained so much of its outer casing of Tura limestone. A contributory cause of its preservation may have been the technique employed in building the casing: the stones are not laid in flat courses, but, like those of the step pyramids, incline downwards towards the interior of the monument, thus giving it greater cohesion. This method of laying rectangular blocks also had the advantage of reducing the amount of trimming necessary to bring their exterior surface into alignment with the slope of the pyramid.

Internally, the Bent Pyramid is unique among the pyramids of the Old Kingdom in having two separate entrances. An aperture approximately in the middle of the northern face and at a height of about 39 feet above ground-level gives access to a narrow low-roofed corridor, which descends at a gradient of 25° 24′, first through the core of the pyramid and then into the subterranean rock. At a distance of about 241 feet 6 inches from the entrance, the corridor becomes level for a further 2 feet 8 inches, where a corbelled roof suddenly rises to a height of 41 feet 6 inches and a kind of lofty, narrow vestibule, 16 feet 2 inches in length, is formed. Immediately beyond lies the lower of two chambers, measuring 20 feet 6 inches from north to south and 16 feet 6 inches from east to west, with a height of about 57 feet. The most remarkable feature of this chamber is its corbelled roof, which is made by stepping a few inches inwards each of the fifteen upper courses of all four limestone walls, leaving at the top a span only 5 feet 3 inches long and 1 foot wide. In the south wall of the chamber, opposite the entrance, there is a passage 10 feet in length leading to a deep pit, which, until it was excavated in 1946–7 by Abdessalam Hussein, was filled with cut blocks of stone and paved. Above the pit a blind shaft rises perpendicularly to a height of 42 feet 6 inches; a second passage, vertically above the first, runs from the roof of the chamber to a point higher up in the shaft. Two blocks of stone were placed in recesses in the shaft, one on the north side immediately below the opening from the upper passage and the other on the south side near the top of the shaft, apparently for the purpose of closing the shaft, but neither of these trap-doors had been lowered into position. Like the pit, the floor of the chamber was built up with blocks of stone to a height of 20 feet 6 inches above the floor of the vestibule.

A second corridor with its entrance about 15 yards south of the middle of the west face of the pyramid leads to the upper chamber. It is the only known instance during the Old Kingdom of such a corridor running from any direction except the north. Sloping first at a gradient of 30° 09′ and then at a gradient of 24° 17′ it descends through the core of the superstructure for a distance of 211 feet until it reaches ground-level, where it continues horizontally for a further 66 feet to join the chamber. This chamber is not built immediately above the one connected with the northern entrance, but lies to the south-east. It has a corbelled roof, and its floor, like that of the lower chamber, was built up to a height of about 14 feet by layers of small blocks of stone. When this blocking was removed in 1946–7 it was found

The Bent Pyramid, cross-sections
looking east (top) and south (bottom)

1. and **4.** two separate entrances
2. lower chamber with corbelled roof
3. upper chamber with cedarwood
framework beneath the floor

that a kind of framework of thick cedar-wood poles had been constructed against the walls and across the part of the chamber which had previously lain beneath the floor. What motive could have prompted the builders to place the framework in this position is uncertain, but the stoutness of the poles and their arrangement suggest that it was intended to counter lateral pressure on the walls and thus provide support until the floor had been built up. Structural weaknesses must have become apparent while the pyramid was being built, because, as Perring observed, plaster had been used by the builders to fill up cracks which had developed in the walls of the lower chamber, and similar repair work had also been carried out in the upper chamber.

Until as recently as 1951 access to the upper chamber could not be gained by way of the corridor, which had remained partly blocked with stones, and its entrance was sealed with the outer casing of the pyramid. The only means of approach was through a roughly hewn passage running from a hole in the south side of the roof of the lower chamber to a point in the horizontal section of the upper corridor. To Perring belongs the credit of being the first to describe a pair of portcullises which he saw in the upper corridor, one on

1. and **4.** two separate entrances
2. lower chamber with corbelled roof
3. upper chamber with cedarwood
framework beneath the floor

each side of the mouth of the passage leading from the lower chamber.[1] They were considerably wider than the corridor and were not constructed in the normal way to drop perpendicularly, but to slide sideways across the corridor from recesses in the side-walls. A wooden prop was probably used to keep the portcullis from sliding into position prematurely. Only the outermost of the two portcullises, however, had been closed; the one nearer to the chamber still remained in its recess. Since the closed portcullis was plastered not only on the outer side but also in the inner side, Perring concluded that it must have been closed at a time when the passage leading to the lower chamber and also the two sloping corridors were open; otherwise the workmen who laid the plaster would have been trapped within the pyramid. Perring's observations have since been confirmed and it is evident that the passage was not the work of later robbers, as the roughness of its fashioning would at first suggest. It would not be the only example of such a passage being hurriedly hewn through the masonry of a pyramid; the Great Pyramid offers a striking parallel, which will be considered in the next chapter.

Apart from some 'cordage and ancient baskets' of uncertain date which Perring discovered in one of the corridors, the only objects which have been recovered from the Bent Pyramid are the dismembered remains of a bird, identified as an owl, and parts of the skeletons of five bats, all wrapped together and placed inside a wooden box laid in a cavity in the floor of the upper corridor. No trace of a sarcophagus was found either in the upper or in the lower chamber. The name of Seneferu, written in red ochre, was however identified on a block lying beneath the floor of the upper chamber and also on a stone at the north-east corner of the outer casing.

At a distance of about 60 yards to the south of the pyramid and within its stone enclosure wall a second and much smaller pyramid was built. Each of its sides measures 181 feet at the base. When complete it rose to a height of 106 feet 9 inches, but the top 38 feet and most of the outer casing are now missing. Internally it consists of a corridor which descends steeply from an entrance above ground-level in the centre of the northern face, a short horizontal passage with a portcullis and an ascending passage opening westwards into a corbel-roofed chamber measuring about 7 feet 8 inches square. In front of the entrance stood a small one-roomed chapel with a pit in the centre of the floor. Two round-topped limestone stelae, about 16 feet in height, were erected between the eastern side of the pyramid and the enclosure wall, roughly in line with the east-west axis of the pyramid. Only the pedestal of one of these monoliths has survived, but the other, though broken, is almost entirely preserved. Carved on its outer face in low relief of striking delicacy is a seated figure of the king wearing the Double Crown and a short linen garment of a kind usually associated with the *heb-sed* festival, and holding a flail in his right hand. The figure occupies the bottom left-hand corner of a rectangular frame surmounted by the falcon of Horus, the remainder of the space within the frame being filled with the names and titles of the king. Between the stelae, and somewhat further to the east, traces of what may have been a brick altar were found, but its date could not be ascertained.

Subsidiary pyramids of this kind, varying in number, are regularly found within the main pyramid enclosures. It has generally been supposed that they were built for the queens. Some may have been used for that purpose, but others could not possibly have been tombs. In this instance it seems likely

A substantial portion of the outer casing remains intact near the top of Chephren's pyramid at Giza.

that it was intended to fulfil the same function as the south mastaba in the Step Pyramid enclosure.

The original plan of the Bent Pyramid does not seem to have included a mortuary temple worthy of the name, but only an open offering-place with an altar and two limestone stelae. Fragments of the stelae recovered during excavation show that they were nearly twice as high as those outside the subsidiary pyramid, similar in shape and decorated with the king's names and titles. The altar, formed like the hieroglyphic sign for an offering, consisted of three limestone blocks with an alabaster offering-table inserted in a cavity cut to receive it in the top surface of the blocks. At an early date the offering-place was enclosed within protecting walls of brick and, perhaps even earlier, an antechamber was built further towards the east with its entrance in the south-east corner. The altar was also roofed over with flat slabs of stone resting on two stone walls. Some reconstruction work was undertaken at a later date, possibly during the Middle Kingdom, and the general plan was modified in detail, but these changes had little effect on the fundamentally simple character of the initial offering-place.

In almost every respect the causeway with its unroofed corridor resembled the causeway of the Meidum pyramid, except insofar as it was considerably longer and it joined not the eastern enclosure wall but the northern wall near the eastern end. The pavement, about 10 feet in width, consisted of mud-plaster laid on a bed of limestone chips. Stone blocks were used for the walls, which were built with a batter on both faces; they measured 6 feet 6 inches in thickness at the base and rose to a height of 6 feet 2 inches. Two deep recesses were constructed at the upper end of the causeway where it joined the enclosure wall, the eastern recess being provided with a doorway in the north wall through which priests who lived near the pyramid could reach the mortuary temple without having to go first to the lower end of the causeway and then return between its walls, a distance of 772 yards.

The excavation of what has been regarded as the valley building in the season 1951-2 by the Service des Antiquités, under the direction of Ahmed Fakhry, produced results which far surpassed expectations. In contrast with the extreme simplicity of the mortuary temple, this building was monumental in size and, although it suffered systematic destruction at a time which cannot yet be determined, enough has been preserved of the decoration to show that it would have borne comparison with anything now known of its kind dating from the Old Kingdom. Rectangular in its plan and surrounded by an enclosure wall, the entire building was composed of local stone and faced with Tura limestone; the floor was paved with mud-plaster. In front of the entrance, which was in the middle of the southern façade, lay a narrow court, the long outer wall of which was a continuation of one of the walls of the causeway. At each end of this wall, on the outer side, stood a limestone stela decorated with the names and titles of the king; in shape and size they resembled the stelae outside the subsidiary pyramid. The building itself was divided into three main parts: an entrance hall flanked on each side by two chambers, an open court, and six shrines at the back of a pillared portico. Its floor dimensions were approximately 51 yards from north to south by 28 yards 1 foot from east to west. Scenes were carved in bold relief on the walls of the entrance hall, on the rectangular monolithic pillars and on the side walls of the portico and at least the two westernmost shrines. Statues of the king, larger than life-size, were attached to niches in the back walls

The Giant Sphinx at Giza incorporates a portrait head of King Chephren with the body of a lion, which the ancient Egyptians regarded as the guardian of sacred places. A knoll of rock left by quarrymen who worked on the Great Pyramid was used as its core; when complete it was probably overlaid with plaster and painted. The Sphinx has been cleared of sand drifts many times. Only the head and shoulders were visible early in the nineteenth century.

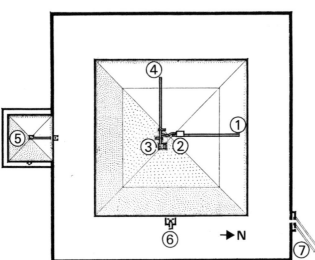

The Bent Pyramid, ground plan

1. and **4**. two separate entrances

2. lower chamber with corbelled roof

3. upper chamber with cedarwood framework beneath the floor

5. smaller pyramid built in same enclosure

6. open offering-place with altar and two limestone stelae

7. point where causeway joins enclosure wall

of some, and possibly all, of the shrines; they were thus in the nature of figures carved in very high relief and not free-standing sculptures like the seated statue of Zoser in the serdab of the Step Pyramid. Some idea of the destruction wrought in later times to these sculptures may be gained from the bare fact that more than 1,400 decorated fragments were recovered in the course of excavation and very few pieces of sufficient size to enable their scenes to be interpreted in detail. The best preserved were the reliefs forming a kind of dado in the entrance hall and on the side walls of the portico which showed female offering-bearers personifying the royal estates and bringing produce from the estates to the pyramid. Among the many other scenes in the building, of which only fragments have been preserved, were episodes in the *heb-sed* and representations of the king performing various ritual ceremonies in the presence of the gods.

Valley building of the Bent Pyramid

The Bent Pyramid –
portcullis in open
position

1. portcullis block
2. corridor
3. wooden prop

Mortuary temple of the
Bent Pyramid

1. antechamber to
Mortuary Temple
2. and 3. open offering-
place with altar and two
limestone stelae, later
roofed over

* The subsidiary pyramid
belonging to the Bent Pyramid
was not a tomb in the sense
intended here.

† Owing to the considerable
accumulations of sand and rubble
which today encumber the
lower part of the sloping
corridor, the first two chambers
can be entered only with
difficulty. The third, probably
the burial-chamber, is
completely inaccessible without
the aid of tackle, which cannot
be introduced until the corridor
has been cleared. Perring,
however, reached this chamber,
and the following description is
based on his account.

Until further investigations have been conducted towards the east some doubt must be felt concerning the precise identification of this building. In later pyramids, as at Meidum, the valley buildings are located on the eastern fringe of the desert where it joins the cultivation. This building, however, lies in a depression at some distance from the cultivation and consequently was not directly accessible by canal from the river. H. Ricke has expressed the opinion that another building may have stood at the edge of the valley on a site now occupied by the tomb of a sheikh. The present building, he believes, represents the temple in which the funerary rites of Seneferu as King of Lower Egypt were performed, while the corresponding ceremonies on his behalf as King of Upper Egypt were celebrated in the mortuary temple. An important difference between the two ceremonies was that the rites of Lower Egypt alone required four chapels for the viscera and two chapels for royal crowns, relics of very ancient royal mortuary customs practised respectively at Buto and Saïs. Ricke considers that the four easternmost shrines in this building were intended for the rites of Buto (one for each of the deities known as the Four Sons of Horus, under whose protection the viscera were regularly placed) and the two westernmost shrines for the rites of Saïs. In support of his theory he claims that the two groups of shrines differed in their decoration and also in the size of the niches in their back walls; only the shrines of the viscera, the walls of which he believes were plain, contained statues, while the two shrines of the crowns bore reliefs but no statues. This interpretation is the result of an extensive study into the history of early Egyptian burial customs by its author and his collaborator, Siegfried Schott; whether it is right or not in detail it offers a satisfactory reason for the building and accounts for its principal architectural features.

A short distance to the north of the Bent Pyramid stands the earliest tomb known to have been completed as a true pyramid.* Externally, its most noticeable feature is its very flat angle of inclination. Instead of rising at the normal angle of about 52°, the sides of this pyramid incline at an angle of only 43° 36′, approximating very closely in this respect to the upper portion of the Bent Pyramid. An aperture in the northern face, several feet above ground-level, gives access to the sloping corridor which descends at an angle of about 27° through the masonry core of the superstructure. At the end of the corridor there are three chambers,† one beyond another, the second lying directly under the apex of the pyramid. The first two chambers are almost identical in size and shape, each measuring about 31 feet from north to south and nearly 12 feet from east to west. Both these chambers, which are founded on the rock substratum, have high corbel-vaulted roofs. The third chamber, the floor of which has been removed to a depth of 14 feet, is reached by a short passage opening out of the south wall of the middle chamber at a height of about 25 feet above the floor. It is the largest of the three, measuring 13 feet 6 inches from north to south and 31 feet from east to west; its corbel roof rises to a height of 50 feet.

To whom did this pyramid belong? Until the adjoining buildings have been excavated it is unlikely that this question can be answered with certainty, but the evidence at present available points to Seneferu, whose so-called Horus-name, Neb-maet, was written in red ochre on a casing-block found at the north-east corner of the pyramid. Ink inscriptions of this kind are, however, sometimes misleading; as an example, Unas, the last king of the

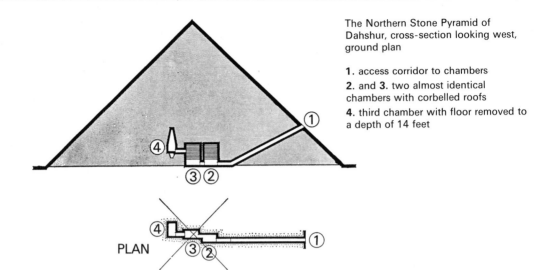

The Northern Stone Pyramid of
Dahshur, cross-section looking west,
ground plan

1. access corridor to chambers
2. and **3**. two almost identical
chambers with corbelled roofs
4. third chamber with floor removed to
a depth of 14 feet

PLAN

Vth Dynasty, used blocks in building his pyramid which bore the name of
his predecessor Isesi, probably from a dismantled temple of that king.
More indicative seems to be the fact that mastabas in the immediate
neighbourhood belonged to Seneferu's courtiers and there would appear to
be no reason for locating them in that position if the king who built the
pyramid had not been their sovereign. Some authorities attach considerable
significance to an inscription, said to have been found on the edge of the
cultivation near the pyramid. This inscription, which has been known since
1905 when it was published by Ludwig Borchardt, is dated in the twenty-
first year of the reign of Pepi I of the VIth Dynasty and its purpose was to
record a decree issued by that king exempting from certain duties and taxes
the priests of the 'Two Pyramids of Seneferu'. Although there is no reason
to doubt the information given to Borchardt with regard to its place of
discovery, it must be recognized that its value for the purpose of identifying
the owner of the pyramid depends mainly on the proximity of this position
to the pyramid and also on the unverifiable supposition that it had not been
moved to that place from somewhere else either in ancient or in later times.

If the evidence concerning the ownership of the Pyramid of Meidum and
the two stone pyramids at Dahshur be marshalled it will be apparent that
two assertions can be made without reservation: first, that inscriptions
dating from the Old Kingdom show that Seneferu possessed two pyramids,
and secondly, that one of his pyramids was the Bent Pyramid, a fact which is
clearly demonstrated by the stelae and other contemporary inscriptions
found in the adjoining buildings. It is, moreover, highly probable that the
Bent Pyramid was sometimes called the Southern Pyramid of Seneferu; a
false door from the Vth Dynasty mastaba of Duarē at Dahshur bears an
inscription in which a son of the owner is described as the Overseer of the
Southern Pyramid of Seneferu, while the same designation of the pyramid
to which he was attached occurs on a figure of a priest of the Middle Kingdom
which was actually discovered in the valley building of the Bent Pyramid.

King Seneferu probably
gave this inlaid box-lid
as a gift to his wife,
Queen Hetepheres. It was
used as a container for
the linen curtains which
hung round her bed-
canopy (*see page 95 top*).

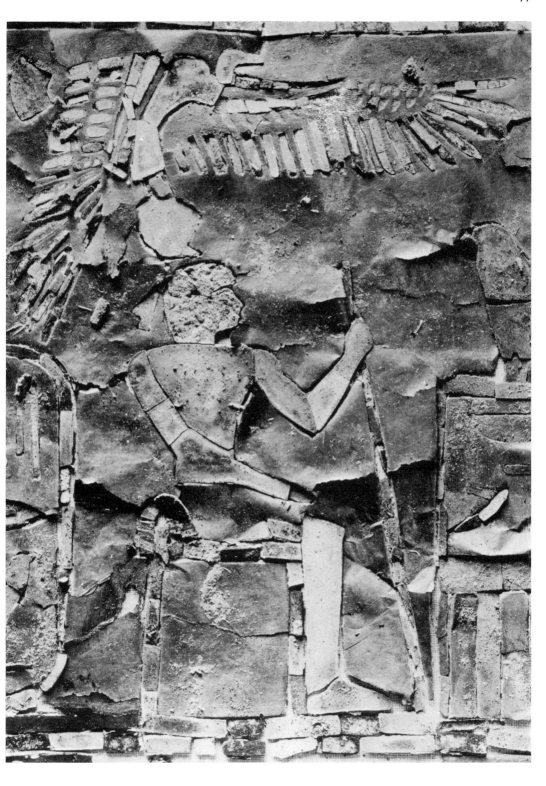

Since Meidum lies south of Dahshur it seems logical to infer that the Bent Pyramid would only have been called the Southern Pyramid of Seneferu if the Northern Stone Pyramid had also been built by the same king. It is, however, possible that the Two Pyramids of Seneferu and the Southern Pyramid of Seneferu were both intended to have only a local application with reference to Dahshur and, if so, the Pyramid of Meidum may also have belonged to Seneferu. On the whole it seems less improbable to suppose that Seneferu possessed three pyramids than that the Egyptians of the XVIIIth Dynasty were mistaken when they attributed the mortuary temple of Meidum to him in their graffiti.

One helpful feature in examining this problem is the fact that constructional methods in the building of pyramids were changed in an important respect at the beginning of the IVth Dynasty and this change is clearly illustrated in these three monuments. It has already been stated that the technique of laying the stones in inclined courses, employed in all the known step pyramids, was also used in the construction of the Bent Pyramid. In the Northern Stone Pyramid at Dahshur, however, the stones are laid in level courses, and since that method was regularly used in subsequent pyramids, the order of sequence of these two monuments seems plain. The Pyramid of Meidum, rather surprisingly, shares technical affinities with both the pyramids at Dahshur: the stones of the inner step pyramid are laid in inclined courses while those of the outer true pyramid are flat. If technique were the only criterion it would be difficult to determine the relative chronological positions of the inner pyramid and the Bent Pyramid, but the step-design of the former appears to allow little room for doubt that it antedates the latter monument. The outer pyramid, on the ground of constructional technique, can only be posterior to the Bent Pyramid; its relationship to the northern stone pyramid may be indicated by some casing-blocks which are dated in the twenty-first and twenty-third years of the reign of an unnamed king, while similar blocks dated in the twenty-first and twenty-second years of Seneferu have been found at the Northern Stone Pyramid. If the unnamed king was in fact Seneferu it must follow that work on the construction of the outer Pyramid of Meidum and the Northern Stone Pyramid at Dahshur must at some stage have been carried on concurrently. The exact position which the dated blocks, now fallen to the ground, once occupied in the Pyramid of Meidum cannot be accurately determined, but since the lower part of the casing is still intact they seem to have belonged to the upper portion. In the Northern Stone Pyramid of Dahshur, on the other hand, one of the dated blocks is situated in the lowest courses of the casing. It therefore seems likely that when these blocks were laid work was further advanced at Meidum than at Dahshur.

While the adjoining buildings of the Northern Stone Pyramid at Dahshur and the valley building at Meidum remain unexcavated no complete comparison of the three monuments is possible. It is however significant that the mortuary temple of the Pyramid of Meidum, which must belong to the same period as the outer pyramid, is architecturally more developed than its counterpart in the Bent Pyramid complex. In all probability the original mortuary temple of the step Pyramid of Meidum was built on the north side of the pyramid and was dismantled when the outer covering was superimposed.

A possibility which has not yet been mentioned is that only the outer

Relics of Seneferu include these fragments: the head of a statue from the valley building of the Bent Pyramid (*top left*), part of an engaged statue of the king (*top right*), and a portion of a relief showing Seneferu inhaling the divine breath of Sakhmet, the lioness-headed goddess (*bottom*).

The pyramids of Dahshur (*left*) include the Bent Pyramid and the Northern Stone Pyramid. Both are at present attributed to Seneferu.

Pyramid of Meidum was the work of Seneferu while the inner pyramid belonged to his predecessor, an obscure king named Huni who was formerly thought to have been the owner of the Bent Pyramid. In favour of this hypothesis it may be argued that the engineering feat of building three pyramids, embodying approximately nine million tons of stone without taking into account the stone used in the temples, causeways, and enclosure walls, would have required greater technical and physical resources than are likely to have been available to Seneferu alone. It may also be claimed that the inscriptional evidence should be taken at its face value and not be interpreted as referring only to the two pyramids at Dahshur. Two pyramids could be understood to symbolize Seneferu's sovereignty over Upper and Lower Egypt, but a third pyramid would seem to have no justification, practical or symbolical. Huni, to whom the Turin king-list ascribes a reign of twenty-four years, must surely have built a pyramid, but it does not follow that his pyramid was indeed the step Pyramid of Meidum; other possible locations, particularly a large enclosure to the west of the pyramids of Zoser and Sekhemkhet, must be explored and be found lacking before the absence of an alternative tomb can be considered as a valid reason for associating him with the Pyramid of Meidum. It is moreover necessary to remember that no single mention of his name has yet been found at Meidum. Admittedly Seneferu acquired the reputation of having been a beneficent king, but it may well be questioned whether his sense of piety towards his predecessor would have led him to transform the design of his tomb; later kings, whose predecessors' monuments were incomplete at the time of their death, were generally content to make only summary additions in brick and plaster, and in at least one instance, in the Vth Dynasty, a valley building and a causeway built by one king were actually usurped by his successor.

It is hard to believe that further excavations, particularly at the Northern Stone Pyramid of Dahshur and at the Pyramid of Meidum, will fail to reveal the true solution to this problem. They may even suggest a reason for the architectural transformation of the Pyramid of Meidum. The excavation of the Bent Pyramid enclosure has already produced results which have not only reduced appreciably the extent of what was previously unknown, but have also shown that evidence of a kind suitable for affording proof of ownership may be recovered from the buildings within the enclosures of these monuments.

The Pyramid of Meidum, sketch of section showing details of construction

1 Vyse and Perring, *The Pyramids of Gizeh*, Vol. III, p. 69.

The Giza Group

SENEFERU'S son and successor to the throne was Khufu, better known as Cheops, the Greek form of his name. Inspired possibly by the magnitude of his father's constructions, he chose a plateau, situated on the edge of the desert about five miles west of Giza, and erected at its north-west corner a pyramid of even vaster dimensions. Two later kings of the IVth Dynasty, Chephren and Mycerinus, followed his example by building their pyramids on the same plateau, a short distance to the south. Together, these three pyramids constitute possibly the most celebrated group of monuments in the world.

The Pyramid of Cheops, or the Great Pyramid, marks the apogee of pyramid-building in respect of both size and quality. No exact computation of the amount of hewn stone contained in it is possible, because the centre of its core consists of a nucleus of rock, the size of which cannot be precisely determined. It has, however, been estimated that, when complete, the core of local stone and the outer facing of Tura limestone were composed of about 2,300,000 separate blocks, each averaging some 2½ tons in weight and reaching a maximum of 15 tons.

Many attempts have been made by writers on the Great Pyramid to illustrate its size by comparison with other famous buildings. It has, for instance, been calculated that the Houses of Parliament and St Paul's Cathedral could be grouped inside the area of its base and still leave considerable space unoccupied.[1] According to another estimate there would be room for the cathedrals of Florence and Milan, and St Peter's Basilica, as well as for Westminster Abbey and St Paul's Cathedral.[2] It has also been reckoned that, if it were sawn into cubes measuring a foot in each dimension and these cubes were placed in a row, they would extend over a distance equal to two-thirds of the earth's periphery at the Equator. One computation of this kind has been attributed to Napoleon during his campaign in Egypt. When some of his Generals returned from climbing to the top of the pyramid, Napoleon, who had declined to make the ascent himself, greeted them with the announcement that, according to his calculations, the three pyramids on the Giza plateau contained enough stone to build a wall, measuring 10 feet in height and 1 foot in width, around the whole of France. The mathematician Monge, who was among the savants accompanying Napoleon on this campaign, is alleged to have confirmed this calculation.[3]

No monument in Egypt has been surveyed and measured so often and with so much care as the Great Pyramid. Even before the theories regarding the supposed esoteric significance of its angles and dimensions had been invented, Edmé-François Jomard, another of Napoleon's staff of savants, Colonel Howard Vyse and J. S. Perring (1837–8) and other pioneers of Egyptian archaeology had measured the monument with as high a degree of accuracy as is required by most modern excavators. The first exhaustive survey of the monument was, however, conducted by Sir Flinders Petrie, who spent the greater part of two seasons (1880–2) at the task. His published results remained the standard work on the subject until 1925, when they were partly superseded by a fresh survey undertaken with the help of more modern instruments by J. H. Cole of the Survey Department of the Egyptian Government.[4] From this survey it was ascertained that the following were the original measurements of the four sides at the base: north, 755·43 feet; south, 756·08 feet; east, 755·88 feet; west, 755·77 feet. While, therefore, no two sides were absolutely identical in length, the difference between the longest and the shortest was only 7·9 inches. Each side was oriented almost exactly in line with true north and south or east and west, the following being the estimated errors: north side, 2' 28" south of west; south side, 1' 57" south of west; east side, 5' 30" west of north; west side, 2' 30" west of north. As the accuracy of this orientation implies, the four corners were almost perfect right angles, their exact measurements being: north-east, 90° 3' 2"; north-west, 89° 59' 58"; south-east, 89° 56' 27"; south-west, 90° 0' 33". When complete, it rose to a height of 481·4 feet, the top 31 feet of which are now missing. Its four sides incline at an angle of about 51° 52' to the ground. The area covered by its base is 13·1 acres.

Although the Great Pyramid, when viewed from a distance, gives the impression of being preserved substantially intact, closer observation reveals that it has suffered severely at the hands of despoilers. About a dozen courses and the capstone, possibly made of granite, have been removed from the apex. The whole of the outer facing of Tura limestone, with the exception of a few pieces at the base, has been stripped off the sides. In the north face, a little below the original entrance, there is a large aperture roughly cut in the core. According to Moslem tradition, this aperture was made during the latter part of the ninth century at the command of the Caliph Ma'mun, son of Harun al-Rashid of Arabian Nights fame, in the mistaken belief that the pyramid contained hidden treasure. Until that time the pyramid, though doubtless robbed of its former contents, had probably remained structurally intact. Subsequently it became a copious and convenient quarry, providing the stone required for bridges over irrigation canals, houses, walls, and other buildings in the neighbourhood of Giza and Cairo.

The chambers and corridors of the Great Pyramid, if their arrangement is to be understood, must be considered in conjunction with its structural development. In contrast with the Pyramid of Meidum, the transformations which the Great Pyramid underwent in the course of construction were mainly, if not entirely, internal; its ultimate external shape and dimensions were probably those intended from the beginning. The entrance is in the north face at a height of about 55 feet, measured vertically, above ground-level. It is not situated exactly midway across the face, but at a point about 24 feet east of the centre. From the entrance a corridor, measuring about 3 feet 5 inches in width and 3 feet 11 inches in height, descends at a gradient of 26° 31' 23" first through the core of the pyramid and then through the rock. At a distance of about 345 feet from the original entrance, the corridor becomes level and continues horizontally for a further 29 feet before terminating in a chamber. On the west side of the level section of the corridor, near the entrance to the chamber, there is a recess, the cutting of which was never completed. The chamber also is unfinished, its trenched floor and rough walls resembling a quarry. A square pit sunk in the floor may represent the first stage in an unfulfilled project for deepening the chamber. According to Vyse and Perring, who measured the chamber in 1838, its dimensions are:

Overleaf: The relative sizes of the three pyramid complexes at Giza, belonging to Cheops (*left*), Chephren (*centre*) and Mycerinus (*right*), can be judged from this aerial photograph.

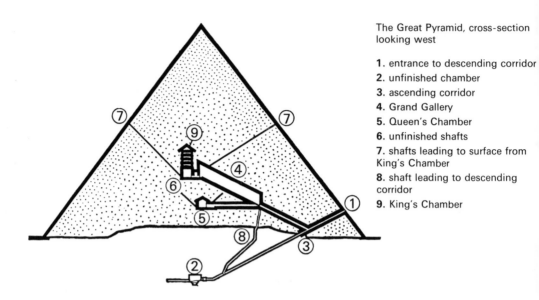

The Great Pyramid, cross-section looking west

1. entrance to descending corridor
2. unfinished chamber
3. ascending corridor
4. Grand Gallery
5. Queen's Chamber
6. unfinished shafts
7. shafts leading to surface from King's Chamber
8. shaft leading to descending corridor
9. King's Chamber

height 11 feet 6 inches; east–west, 46 feet; north–south, 27 feet 1 inch.

In the south wall of the chamber, opposite the entrance, there is an opening to a blind passage, roughly hewn in the rock and obviously unfinished. The presence of this passage suggests that, if the original plan had been executed, there would have been a second chamber beyond the first and connected with it by a corridor. Such an arrangement would have as a parallel the Northern Stone Pyramid at Dahshur, the main difference being that in the latter the second chamber lies directly beneath the apex and the first to the north of it, whereas in the Great Pyramid both chambers would have been situated south of a point perpendicularly under the apex.

It is of some interest to compare the half-finished rock-chamber with the brief but graphic description of the subterranean part of the Great Pyramid given to Herodotus when he visited Egypt in the middle of the fifth century BC. Beneath the pyramid, he was told, were vaults constructed on a kind of island, which was surrounded by water brought from the Nile by a canal. On this island the body of Cheops was said to lie. No trace, however, of either the canal or the island has yet been found, and it is most unlikely that they ever existed. Although the pyramid had almost certainly been opened and its contents plundered long before the time of Herodotus, it may easily have been closed again during the Saite Period, when a number of ancient monuments were restored. The story which Herodotus relates – the veracity of which he does not claim to have confirmed from his own observations – may well have been embroidered by generations of pyramid guides extending over the greater part of two centuries.

At the time when the decision was made to alter the original project and to substitute a burial-chamber in the body of the pyramid for the one under construction in the rock, the superstructure had already been built to a height of several feet. A hole was therefore cut in the masonry roof of the earlier descending corridor at a point about 60 feet from the entrance and a new ascending corridor was hewn upwards through the core. The mouth of this corridor was filled, after the burial, with a slab of limestone, so that it became indistinguishable from the remainder of the roof at the upper end of the descending corridor. The block could not, however, have been securely fastened, because it collapsed when Ma'mun's men were boring their tunnel near by. According to Moslem historians it was the noise made by the fall of this block to the floor of the descending corridor which enabled the tunnellers to locate the pyramid corridors, their previous operations having been directed too far to the west.

The ascending corridor, which is approximately 129 feet in length, corresponds in width and height with the descending corridor; its gradient of 26° 2′ 30″ also tallies to within a fraction of a degree. At its lower end, immediately above the gap left by the missing limestone slab, are three large plug-blocks made of granite and placed one behind another. These plugs, which completely fill the original corridor, were by-passed by Ma'mun's men, who simply cut a passage through the softer limestone of the west wall as far as a point beyond the uppermost plug. Borchardt, while making a detailed study of the walls of this corridor, observed that the stones at the lower end were laid approximately parallel with the ground, whereas nearly all those at the upper end were parallel with the gradient of the corridor. From this fact he deduced that the point at which the angle changed marked the height to which the pyramid had already been built when it was decided to transfer the tomb-chamber to the superstructure. Borchardt also noticed that the joints of the stones at the lower end were irregular, whereas the stones at the upper end fitted closely – a feature which certainly supports his contention that the lower part of the corridor was cut through rough core-masonry already laid, while the upper part was built *pari passu* with the construction of the pyramid. The only stones in the upper part which are not laid parallel with the gradient are the so-called 'girdle-stones', a name used to describe either single stones or two stones, one above the other, through which the corridor has been hewn. These 'girdle-stones', placed at regular intervals of 17 feet 2 inches, may offer a clue to the structural composition of the Great Pyramid which will be discussed in a later chapter.

When the ascending corridor was being constructed, the builders probably intended the burial-chamber to occupy a position in the centre of the superstructure and at no great height above ground-level. Such a chamber was actually built at the end of a passage leading from the top of the ascending corridor. Called by the Arabs the 'Queen's Chamber' – a misnomer which it has retained – this chamber lies exactly midway between the north and south sides of the pyramid. Its measurements are 18 feet 10 inches from east to west and 17 feet 2 inches from north to south. It has a pointed roof, which rises to a height of 20 feet 5 inches. In the east wall there is a niche with corbelled sides; its original depth was only 3 feet 5 inches, but the back has now been cut away by treasure-seekers. Its height is 15 feet 4 inches and the width at the base 5 feet 2 inches. Presumably it was designed to contain a statue of the king, which may, however, never have been placed in position.

There are many indications that work on the Queen's Chamber was abandoned before it had been completed. The floor, for instance, is exceedingly rough; if the chamber had been finished it would probably have been paved with finer stone. Again, in the north and south walls there are small rectangular apertures from which shafts run horizontally for a distance of about 6 feet 6 inches and then turn upwards at an angle of approximately 30°. These apertures were not cut at the time when the chamber was built – an omission which can only be explained on the hypothesis that the chamber was never finished – but in 1872 by an engineer named Waynman Dixon, who had been led to suspect the existence of the shafts by their presence in the King's Chamber above. Unlike those in the King's Chamber, however, the shafts leading from the Queen's Chamber seem to have had no outlet in the outer surface of the pyramid; the absence of such an outlet provides further evidence of an alteration in the original plan. Possibly the same explanation also accounts for the different levels in the floor of the passage which connected the ascending corridor with the chamber. At first the passage is only 3 feet 9 inches in height, but nearer the chamber a sudden drop in the floor increases its height to 5 feet 8 inches.

The abandonment of the Queen's Chamber led to the construction of two of the most celebrated architectural works which have survived from the Old Kingdom, namely the Grand Gallery and the King's Chamber. The Grand Gallery was built as a continuation of the ascending corridor. It is 153 feet in length and 28 feet in height. Its walls of polished limestone rise vertically to a height of 7 feet 6 inches; above that level each of the seven courses projects inwards about 3 inches beyond the course on which it rests, thus forming a corbel vault of unparalleled dimensions. The space between the uppermost course on each side, measuring 3 feet 5 inches in width, is spanned by roofing slabs, every one of which is laid at a slightly steeper angle than the gradient of the gallery. Sir Flinders Petrie, commenting on this method of laying the slabs, says it was done 'in order that the lower edge of each stone should hitch like a pawl into a ratchet cut in the top of the walls; hence no stone can press on the one below it, so as to cause a cumulative pressure all down the roof; and each stone is separately upheld by the side walls across which it lies'.[5] At the foot of each wall a flat-topped ramp, 2 feet in height and 1 foot 8 inches in width, extends along the whole length of the gallery. A passage measuring, like the roof, 3 feet 5 inches in width runs between the two ramps. At the lower end of this passage there is now a gap, caused by the removal of the stones which formerly linked the floor of the passage with that of the ascending corridor and also covered the mouth of the horizontal passage leading to the Queen's Chamber. In the gap, the lowest stone in the western ramp has been removed, revealing a shaft which descends partly perpendicularly and partly obliquely, first through the core of the pyramid and then through the rock, until it emerges in the west wall of the descending corridor. Its apparent purpose and the significance of some other peculiar features in the Grand Gallery will be considered after the King's Chamber has been described.

A high step at the upper end of the Grand Gallery gives access to a low and narrow passage leading to the King's Chamber. About a third of the distance along its length the passage is heightened and enlarged into a kind of antechamber, the south, east, and west walls of which are composed of red granite. Four wide slots have been cut in both the east and west walls of the antechamber, three extending to the floor and one – the northernmost – stopping at the same level as the roof of the passage. The long slots were intended for three portcullises, no traces of which have survived. According

This diminutive ivory statuette, just five inches high, is the only known figure of Cheops, builder of the Great Pyramid.

to Borchardt these portcullises were designed to be lowered by means of ropes which ran over wooden rollers mounted at the top of each slot. Stretching across the antechamber and fitting into the short slot, there still remain two blocks of granite, one resting on the other; a third block may originally have filled the space between the upper block and the ceiling. Without such a barrier, robbers could, by climbing through the gap, have passed unhindered over the first two portcullises.

The King's Chamber, built entirely of granite, measures 34 feet 4 inches from east to west, 17 feet 2 inches from north to south, and 19 feet 1 inch in height. In the north and south walls, at a height of about 3 feet above the floor, are the rectangular apertures of shafts which differ from those of the Queen's Chamber only in penetrating the core of the pyramid to the outer surface, the northern shaft at an angle of 31° and the southern one at an angle of 45°. The object of these shafts is not known with certainty; they may have been designed for the ventilation of the chamber or for some religious purpose which is still open to conjecture. Near the west wall stands a lidless rectangular granite sarcophagus which once contained the king's body, probably enclosed within an inner coffin of wood. In appearance it is rough, many of the scratches made by the saw when cutting it being still clearly visible. Sir Flinders Petrie discovered that the width of the sarcophagus was about an inch greater than the width of the ascending corridor at its mouth; he therefore concluded that it must have been placed in position while the chamber was being built.

The roof of the King's Chamber has no exact architectural parallel. Above its flat ceiling, which is composed of nine slabs weighing in aggregate about 400 tons, there are five separate compartments, the ceilings of the first four being flat and the fifth having a pointed roof. The purpose of this construction, it appears, was to eliminate any risk of the ceiling of the chamber collapsing under the weight of the superincumbent masonry. Whether such extreme precautions were required by the character of the building may be debatable; they have, however, been justified by subsequent events. Every one of the massive slabs of granite in the ceiling of the chamber and many of those in the relieving compartments have been cracked – presumably by an earthquake – but none has yet collapsed.

Access to the lowest of the relieving compartments is gained by a passage leading from a hole at the top of the east wall of the Grand Gallery. When or by whom this passage was cut is unknown; the first European to mention it was a traveller named Davison who visited the pyramid in 1765. The four upper compartments were not discovered until 1837–8, when Colonel Howard Vyse and J. S. Perring forced a way to them by hollowing out a shaft from below. Some of the walls in these upper compartments are composed of limestone; since they were not intended to be seen their surfaces were not dressed and, in consequence, many of the blocks still retain the red ochre markings painted on them at the quarry. Among these quarry marks are the only instances of the name of Cheops found in the pyramid.

Owing to its upward slope, the blocking of the ascending corridor of the Great Pyramid after the funeral presented unusual difficulties. In other pyramids the corridors either slope downwards or are approximately level, so that they could easily be packed with large plug-blocks which would have been stored outside the pyramid until required. The descending corridor of

Deep inside the Great Pyramid lies the corbel-vaulted Grand Gallery, one of the most remarkable architectural works of the Old Kingdom.

the Great Pyramid could have been blocked in this way, but not the ascending corridor. Not only would the task of raising heavy granite plugs through the hole in the roof of the descending corridor have caused many mechanical difficulties, but plugs so inserted would have served no useful purpose because they could not have been firmly secured. No alternative remained, therefore, but to store the plugs somewhere in the pyramid while it was under construction and to move them down the ascending corridor after the body had been put in the burial-chamber. That such a method was adopted is clear from the fact that the three plugs which still remain in position at the lower end of the ascending corridor are about an inch wider than its mouth and, consequently, could not have been introduced from the descending corridor. Two problems, however, arise from this deduction: where were the plugs stored before being lowered down the ascending corridor, and how did the men who must have pushed the plugs from behind escape from the pyramid after completing their work?

Until Petrie discovered that the horizontal passage leading to the Queen's Chamber was an inch too small in both width and height to hold the plugs, it was generally supposed that they had been stored either in that passage or in the Queen's Chamber. The necessary width and height could have been found in the gap between the top of the ascending corridor and the lower end of the Grand Gallery passage, but the length of the gap would have been insufficient to accommodate the plugs if placed end to end. Moreover, there can be little doubt that this gap was bridged with slabs of stone at the time when the plugs were awaiting removal to their final position. Lack of height would also exclude the passage leading to the King's Chamber, and, in consequence, the chamber itself. Petrie therefore concluded that the plugs were stored in the Grand Gallery passage, where all the requirements of space would have been satisfied. Such an explanation, as Petrie recognized, was open to the objection that the plugs, by blocking the passage, would have obstructed the funeral procession – which must have either climbed over the plugs or proceeded up the side-ramps – but considerations of size seemed to preclude any other solution.

Borchardt, while accepting Petrie's main thesis that the plugs were stored in the Grand Gallery, pointed out that it failed to account for the presence of twenty-eight holes cut at regular intervals in the upper surface of each side-ramp. Two other features which remained unexplained by Petrie, but which appeared to be connected with the holes, were small blocks of stone which had been inserted in the side-walls opposite the holes, each with a slot cut roughly in its surface, and a long continuous groove sunk in the lower part of the third projecting lap from the bottom of each side-wall. This groove, which is nearly an inch in depth, extends along the whole length of both sides of the gallery. Borchardt, after a careful examination of the evidence, suggested that the holes and slots were designed to hold wooden uprights supporting a platform, also made of wood, the sides of which fitted into the long grooves. The purpose of the platform would have been to store the plugs so that the funeral cortège could pass up the passage without obstruction. Its length, which would seem excessive for the storage of only three plugs, may have resulted from an original and possibly discarded plan for filling in the whole of the ascending corridor with plugs. To have succeeded in moving even three plugs into position was a remarkable achievement because they are rather less than half an inch narrower than the

The Great Pyramid, Grand Gallery.

corridor and the gap between the tops of the plugs and the ceiling of the corridor is only about $1\frac{1}{4}$ inches.

From the moment when the first plug was introduced into the upper end of the ascending corridor, the workmen who were charged with the task of transferring the plugs to their final position would have been unable to leave the pyramid by the normal way. They had, however, provided themselves with a means of escape down the shaft which leads from the gap at the upper end of the ascending corridor to the descending corridor. It is idle to speculate whether this shaft was constructed with or without the knowledge of Cheops, but the burial of living persons was certainly not practised by the Egyptians of the Pyramid Age. The shaft would have been completely concealed at the time of the funeral by the slabs of stone bridging the gap and by the lowest stone in the western ramp, which is now missing. The removal of these stones would have presented no difficulty to the workmen when the time came for making their descent. After the last of the workmen had reached the bottom of the shaft, the opening in the west wall of the descending corridor would have been covered with a slab of stone so that it would have been indistinguishable from the remainder of the corridor. At the same time also the mouth of the ascending corridor beyond the first of the plugs would have been covered with the stone which fell to the floor of the descending corridor when the Caliph Ma'mun was forcing a way into the pyramid.

Some speculation regarding the method of closing the entrance to the pyramid has been caused by a statement made by Strabo. In his *Geographica*, written at about the beginning of the Christian era, he states that the Great Pyramid, 'a little way up one side, has a stone that may be taken out, which being raised up there is a sloping passage to the foundations'. Petrie interpreted this statement as meaning that the Great Pyramid had a flap-door composed of a single slab of stone which swung on pivots near the top of each side. In support of his theory he was able to point out that, both in the northern corridor of the Bent Pyramid and in the Pyramid of Meidum, there were sockets cut in the side-walls near the entrance which were apparently intended for holding door-pivots. Owing to the loss of the outer casing, it is impossible to say whether the entrance to the Great Pyramid was provided with similar sockets. It is, however, difficult to believe that the door described by Strabo, if his words have been correctly understood, dated from the time when the pyramid was built. Plugs and portcullises would certainly not have been used to block the corridors of pyramids if subsequent access to the internal chambers was contemplated; a flap-door would have presupposed such access. Possibly the entrance to the Great Pyramid, like the western entrance to the Bent Pyramid, was originally covered with a layer of casing-stones which rendered it indistinguishable from the remainder of the outer surface. When the pyramid was first violated – probably during the period of anarchy which followed the end of the Old Kingdom – the robbers must have forced a way through the blocks covering the entrance. How long it remained open cannot be known, but it may have been sealed and again violated on more than one occasion during the subsequent dynasties, until eventually – possibly under the Saites – a door, corresponding with the one described by Strabo, was fitted. If this highly speculative surmise be correct, it is also necessary to assume either that the existence of the door was forgotten or that the entrance was again blocked with facing stones at some time during the period between Strabo's visit and the ninth century. No other explanation would account for the inability of the Caliph Ma'mun to find the entrance until he had forced a new passage through the core of the pyramid.

Although the buildings which once completed the Great Pyramid complex have either entirely or partly disappeared, the surviving remnants are enough to show that the general layout conformed with the standard pattern. Nothing is now visible of the enclosure wall, but part of the fine limestone pavement which covered the area between the wall and the pyramid has been preserved.

Opposite the middle of the east face of the pyramid stood the mortuary temple, a rectangular building of limestone measuring about 171 feet from north to south and about 132 feet from east to west. It was connected with the upper end of the causeway by a doorway in the east façade. Immediately beyond lay a court paved with black basalt and surrounded by a cloister. The roof of the cloister, to which a stone staircase in the south-west corner gave access, was supported by granite columns, all of which were square in section with the exception of those in the four corners which were oblong. Its walls were decorated with scenes delicately carved in low relief. On the west side was a deep cruciform recess. What lay beyond the recess is not known; J.-P. Lauer, who succeeded in tracing the plan of the temple in 1946, conjectured that it was the sanctuary and that two false doors stood against its west wall. H. Ricke, however, has suggested that the sanctuary, consisting of an altar flanked by two round-topped stelae, was erected in the open space between the centre of the back-wall of the temple and the base of the pyramid. Some statues of the king may have been placed either in the recess or behind it, but no actual evidence to support this possibility was found.

North and south of the temple, outside the eastern enclosure wall of the pyramid, are two boat-shaped pits hewn in the rock; a third pit of the same kind lies on the north side of the causeway near the temple. All these pits, when excavated, proved to be empty. A fourth pit south of the enclosure wall, however, contained a wooden boat, 143 feet in length, which had been partly dismantled before burial. The boat, found by Kamal el-Mallakh in 1954, is to be reassembled outside the pit. On the same side of the pyramid, near the western end, a further pit has been located, but until its stone roofing slabs have been removed it cannot be known whether the boat has been preserved.

The burial of boats suitable for navigation, although not uncommon in the enclosures of the large brick mastabas of the Ist Dynasty, seems to have been limited in the Old Kingdom to the royal pyramid complexes. Some of these boats may have been used at the time of the funeral, but others were probably intended to provide the dead king with a means of transport in his after-life, the precise region in which they were to be employed being still obscure. In the solar cult, a boat would be required for accompanying the Sun-god on his daily journey across the heavens and his nightly journey beneath the earth; it would also be needed for reaching the region beyond the eastern horizon, where the gods were thought to dwell. Until more is known about the religious beliefs of the period preceding the Vth Dynasty, the full significance of the boats is likely to remain conjectural.

At right angles to the upper end of the causeway, on the south side, lies a row of three subsidiary pyramids, each with a small ruined chapel adjoining its eastern face. Beside the first pyramid there is a small boat-pit. Reisner

The linen curtains stored in the box shown on page 77 were hung round this portable bedchamber (*top*) belonging to Queen Hetepheres.

One of the objects interred with Queen Hetepheres, mother of Cheops, was this carrying-chair (*bottom*) made of wood partly overlaid with sheet gold.

believed that this pyramid belonged to Cheops's favourite queen who, in accordance with Egyptian custom, may also have been his full-blood sister. Concerning the second pyramid, Herodotus recounts the following legend: 'The wickedness of Cheops reached to such a pitch that, when he had spent all his treasures and wanted more, he sent his daughter to the stews, with orders to procure him a certain sum – how much I cannot say, for I was not told; she procured it, however, and at the same time, bent on leaving a monument which should perpetuate her own memory, she required each man to make her a present of a stone towards the works which she contemplated. With these stones she built the Pyramid which stands mid-most of the three that are in front of the Great Pyramid, measuring along each side a hundred and fifty feet.'[6] Happily there is no reason for believing that the details of this story bear any relation to historical fact. To judge from the few fragments which have survived, the walls of the chapel of this pyramid, built against the middle of the east face, were decorated with carvings in low relief equal in quality to the reliefs in the king's mortuary temple. The third pyramid was ascribed in later times to Queen Henutsen, who may have been only a half-sister of the king. By the XXIst Dynasty she had been identified with the goddess Isis and had been given the name Isis-Mistress-of-the-Pyramid. At that time also the small chapel adjoining the pyramid was enlarged in order to provide a suitable sanctuary for the goddess.

Mortuary temple of the Great Pyramid

1. upper end of the causeway
2. court surrounded by a cloister
3. cruciform recess
4. space between the temple and the base of the pyramid

The causeway consisted of a corridor, built either directly on the rock-bed or, in those places where the level of the rock-bed was too low, on an embankment of masonry. According to Herodotus, the construction of the causeway and the other buildings at the foot of the pyramid occupied ten years. Today nothing of the corridor remains intact, but some of the embankment is still standing in a small quarry, which it bridged, and again at the point where it crossed the edge of the plateau. Georges Goyon, who conducted an exploratory survey in 1964, estimated that it was about 720 yards in length and 60 feet in width at the base. The lower end of the causeway and whatever may have been preserved of the valley building still lie unexcavated beneath the modern village of Kafr es-Samman. A tunnel was constructed near the middle of the causeway, so that those who wished to cross it could do so without having to make a long detour around either the pyramid or the valley building.

Herodotus, in his description of the causeway, stated that it was built of polished stone on which were carved pictures of animals. The veracity of this statement was doubted by some archaeologists because no traces of carving in relief had been found in any of the IVth Dynasty pyramids or in their adjoining buildings, although they were certainly included in some of the contemporary private mastabas. To account for their absence, it was necessary to suppose that the architects of the period were preoccupied with mastering the technique of using granite and with learning the art of building in megalithic masonry. In the light, however, of the recent discovery that the walls of the mortuary temple were decorated with reliefs, a strong presumption is created in favour of the accuracy of Herodotus's statement regarding the causeway.

South of the causeway, close to the first of the subsidiary pyramids, the Boston-Harvard expedition directed by Reisner found in 1925 the only undisturbed royal tomb of the Old Kingdom hitherto known. It lay at the bottom of a vertical shaft which had been blocked with masonry to its entire depth of 99 feet. Within this chamber were stored the fine alabaster sarcopha-gus and funerary equipment of Queen Hetepheres, wife of Seneferu and mother of Cheops. Although the sarcophagus proved to be empty, the viscera, which had been removed from the body to help in its preservation, were found in an alabaster chest – the so-called Canopic chest. To explain the absence of the body, since the chamber had never been plundered, Reisner suggested that Hetepheres was buried in a tomb at Dahshur near the Northern Stone Pyramid, which he ascribed to Seneferu, but that soon after her burial robbers had broken into the tomb and removed the body with its jewellery and gold ornaments. Before they were able to steal the remainder of the equipment, however, news of the violation of the tomb had reached the king. Hoping to prevent further despoilment, Cheops, who may not have been told of the disappearance of the body, decided to transfer his mother's tomb – possibly in secret – to Giza, where it would receive the same degree of protection as his own pyramid. As an additional precaution, not only was no superstructure built above the new tomb, but a coating of plaster was spread over the stones covering the mouth of the shaft and finally the whole cavity was overlaid with a layer of limestone gravel so that no trace of its presence was visible. The fact that it remained undetected until the twentieth century, when the American excavators literally swept the sand from the rock-bed, is the best testimony to the success of the stratagem.

Among the smaller objects found in this chamber were alabaster vessels, a copper ewer, three gold vessels, gold razors and knives, copper tools, and a gold manicure instrument, pointed at one end for cleaning the nails and curved at the other end for pressing down the quick; a toilet-box contained eight small alabaster vases filled with unguents and kohl. Inside a jewel-case were twenty silver anklets, each inlaid with dragonflies of malachite, lapis lazuli, and carnelian. The larger objects included a canopy-frame made of wood cased with gold, and two armchairs and a bed which were partly cased with gold sheeting. On the foot-board of the bed was a panel of gold inlaid with a blue and black floral design. A carrying-chair, also made of wood, partly cased with gold sheeting, bore an inscription, written in hieroglyphs of gold set in ebony panels and repeated four times, which read: 'The mother of the King of Upper and Lower Egypt, follower of Horus, she who is in charge of the affairs of the harem[?] whose every word is done for her, daughter of the god [begotten] of his body, Hetepheres.'

No description can do justice to the artistic excellence and technical perfection of the equipment of Hetepheres; in comparison with its exquisite simplicity of design, much of the tomb furniture used in the later periods appears tawdry. Only the woodwork had suffered with the passage of time; inevitably it had either become decayed or shrunk to such a degree that it could not be used when the objects were reconstructed by the experts of the Boston–Harvard expedition before being delivered, in accordance with the terms of the excavators' agreement, to the Cairo Museum. Reisner was of the opinion that at least some of the objects had been used by Hetepheres during her lifetime. There is nothing improbable in the suggestion. Belongings of a personal kind were certainly not placed in the tomb until the time of the funeral, although vases and jars containing stores were often made expressly for the tomb and may well have been deposited there in advance. Whether the objects actually formed part of the furnishings of the queen's apartments in the palace is, however, a matter of only secondary importance. The real interest of the discovery lies in the light which it throws on the practical and artistic achievements of the IVth Dynasty and in the concrete evidence which it provides of the kind of equipment which was once to be found in other contemporary royal tombs.

Not the least significant of the various elements designed to add to the impressive effect of the Great Pyramid was its architectural setting. Other pyramids were surrounded by the tombs of officials and relatives of their owners, but little attention seems to have been given to their layout. East and west of the Great Pyramid enclosure wall, however, large cemeteries of mastabas were arranged in parallel rows several feet apart. South of the pyramid only a single row was built, while on the north there were none. The ownership of the tombs was also carefully planned, those in the eastern cemetery being allotted to close relatives of the king and those in the western cemetery – the larger – to officials. Although most of these mastabas have now lost their entire outer casing, it must be supposed that they were all originally faced with Tura limestone; their colour, therefore, would have been uniform with that of the vast pyramid rising in their midst. H. Junker, who excavated a part of the western cemetery, has aptly remarked that the Egyptian conception of the dead ruler continuing in the after-life to be surrounded by his relatives and loyal followers has never found so vivid an expression as in the arrangement of the tombs in this necropolis. It may be claimed, with equal truth, that the difference between the divine majesty of the ruler and his mortal subjects was never more strongly emphasized than in the contrast between the towering pyramid and the simple flat-topped mastabas.

Cheops's obvious wishes for the architectural setting of his tomb appear to have commanded little respect from subsequent generations. Already in the Vth and VIth Dynasties the symmetry of the original design was being destroyed by the construction of smaller mastabas in the spaces between the rows. The owners of these tombs were either officials of the necropolis or mortuary priests who, during their lifetime, had performed the various duties deemed necessary for securing the well-being of the dead king and his associates. In later times, particularly under the Saites, burial in the vicinity of the three Giza pyramids was believed to confer special benefits on the dead, with the result that the whole area became honeycombed with tombs and the regularity of the earliest design must have been obscured beyond recognition.

South of the Great Pyramid complex and near the valley building of the second pyramid lies the giant Sphinx. A knoll of rock, which had been left by the builders of the Great Pyramid when quarrying stone for its inner core, was fashioned in the time of Chephren into a huge recumbent lion with a human head. It was probably overlaid with a coating of plaster and painted. The length of this colossus is about 240 feet, its height 66 feet, and the maximum width of the face 13 feet 8 inches. On the head is the royal head-dress; other emblems of royalty are the cobra on the forehead, and the beard, now largely missing, on the chin. Although the face has been severely mutilated, it still gives the impression of being a portrait of King Chephren and not merely a formalized representation. A figure, possibly of the king, was carved in front of the chest, but scarcely any trace of it now remains. Between the outstretched paws stands a large slab of red granite bearing an inscription which purports to record a dream of Tuthmosis IV of the XVIIIth Dynasty

Mycerinus wearing the white crown of Upper Egypt, a detail from a schist triad showing him between the goddess Hathor and the goddess of the jackal *nome*, displays the strength and vitality characteristic of his energetic dynasty. The complete triad may be seen on page 114.

Overleaf: The pyramids of Giza viewed from the south are, from the foreground, the three subsidiary pyramids of Mycerinus, the Pyramid of Mycerinus, Chephren's pyramid, and the Great Pyramid of Cheops.

before he ascended the throne. According to this inscription the prince, when hunting, decided to rest at midday in the shadow of the Sphinx. During his sleep the Sphinx, which was regarded at that time as an embodiment of the Sun-god Harmachis, promised him the Double Crown of Egypt if he would clear away the sand which had nearly engulfed his body. Unfortunately, the latter part of the inscription is too badly weathered to be legible, but it may be surmised that it related how the god's wish was fulfilled and how the prince was finally rewarded with the Crown of the Two Lands. In addition to clearing away the sand, Tuthmosis IV may have repaired damaged portions of the body by the insertion of small blocks of limestone – an operation which was repeated in Ptolemaic or Roman times, when the sand was once more removed and an altar was erected in front of the figure. The first excavation of the Sphinx in modern times was conducted by Captain Caviglia in 1818 at a cost of £450. Sixty-eight years later it was again freed of sand by Gaston Maspero and lastly, in 1925, the Service des Antiquités undertook once more its clearance and restoration.

Although the Greeks may have adopted the idea of the Sphinx from Egypt, perhaps indirectly by way of Syria, the hybrid which they developed differed widely from its Egyptian counterpart both in form and in attributes. The name also may have been suggested by the Egyptian epithet *shesep-ankh*, 'living image', which the Greeks may have wrongly associated with their own word meaning 'to bind', the Sphinx being composed of human and animal elements *bound* together. In Egyptian mythology the lion often figures as the guardian of sacred places. How or when this conception first arose is not known, but it probably dates back to remote antiquity. Like so many other primitive beliefs, it was incorporated by the priests of Heliopolis into their solar creed, the lion being considered as the guardian of the gates of the Underworld on the eastern and western horizons. In the form of the Sphinx, the lion retained the function of a sentinel, but was given the human features of the Sun-god Atum. An inscription, which dates from a period considerably later than the time of Chephren, puts the following words into the mouth of a sphinx: 'I protect the chapel of thy tomb. I guard thy sepulchral chamber. I ward off the intruding stranger. I hurl the foes to the ground and their weapons with them. I drive away the wicked one from the chapel of thy tomb. I destroy thine adversaries in their lurking-place, blocking it that they come forth no more.' A possible reason for the identification of the Sun-god's features with those of the deceased king may be the Heliopolitan belief that the king, after his death, actually became the Sun-god. The giant Sphinx would therefore represent Chephren as the Sun-god acting as the guardian of the Giza necropolis.

An unusual feature about this alabaster representation of Mycerinus is the locks of hair protruding from beneath his wig. A resemblance to Chephren, Mycerinus's father, can be observed by comparing the features of this statue and the one on page 99 with Chephren's statue on page 54.

Immediately in front of the Sphinx lie the ruins of a small temple excavated in 1936 by Selim Bey Hassan, who was able to show that its coarse limestone walls were once overlaid with granite ashlars. Its principal feature was a colonnaded court paved with alabaster. Both from the method of its construction and from its architecture it is clear that it dates from the same period as its better known neighbour situated a few paces to the south which, at one time, was thought to be a temple connected with the Sphinx. Many years ago, however, it was identified as the valley building of the pyramid complex of King Chephren, the Greek equivalent of the Egyptian name Khaef-Rē by which the builder of the second pyramid is usually known. Auguste Mariette, the founder of the Cairo Museum, discovered this building in 1853, but although he cleared the whole of the inside, considerable accumulations of sand were left against the outer walls. A further clearance was made by Mariette in 1869, when the building formed one of the principal show-places to which the distinguished visitors who attended the opening of the Suez Canal were conducted. Finally in 1909–10, the outer walls were freed of sand by the von Sieglin expedition, under the direction of Uvo Hölscher and Georg Steindorff, when excavating the whole of the pyramid complex.

Considering the very early date of the valley building, its condition is truly remarkable. No other building of the IVth Dynasty, with the possible exception of the unfinished mortuary temple of the Meidum pyramid, has survived in a comparable state of preservation. Built on a ground-plan measuring 147 feet in each direction and rising to a height of 43 feet, its immensely thick walls are composed of coarse local limestone faced, both internally and externally, with ashlars of polished red granite from Aswan. The four outer walls are not perpendicular, but have a pronounced batter – a regular feature in buildings of the period. Outside the east wall probably stood a stone kiosk containing a statue of the king. Two doorways in this wall, which may originally have been flanked by sphinxes, give entrance to the building from a terrace cut in the rock. Around each doorway was carved a band of hieroglyphic inscription giving the name and titles of the king, but only the last words, 'beloved of [the goddess] Bastet' and 'beloved of [the goddess] Hathor', are preserved; no other inscriptions or reliefs occur anywhere else in the building. Short passages lead from the doorways by way of small but lofty vestibules to a long antechamber, in the floor of which Mariette found a deep pit containing a diorite statue of Chephren – one of the finest examples of Old Kingdom sculpture hitherto recovered. Originally this statue, which is rather larger than life-size, was probably placed in the T-shaped hall leading westwards out of the antechamber; its transference to the pit, the date of which is uncertain, may have been due to a desire to preserve it from destruction. A total of twenty-three royal statues made of diorite, schist, and alabaster once stood against the sides of the hall, seventeen in the stem of the T and six facing eastwards in the cross-piece. Light entered the hall through oblique slits cut partly in the top of the walls and partly in the underside of the flat granite roof; the rays did not shine directly on the statues, but were reflected from the alabaster floor and from the massive square columns of red granite which supported the roof. Such lighting might seem inadequate for the illumination of sculptures which, to judge from the one which has remained intact, were artistic masterpieces. Egyptian sculptures, however, were not designed for display, but to provide the spirit with an imperishable substitute for the human body; dim light or even complete darkness was not thought to hinder the efficacy of the substitute – a fact which is demonstrated by the regular practice of enclosing statues in serdabs.

The precise use of the valley building in the performance of the funerary ritual is not entirely clear. Reisner, when discussing its architectural form, expressed the opinion that it was ultimately derived from a pavilion composed of matting and supported by a framework of poles lashed together with ropes. B. Grdseloff identified it with a building called in Egyptian texts *seh-netjer* (Pavilion-of-the-god). In his opinion it combined the uses of two constructions which normally stood independently when built in association

The valley building and mortuary temple of Chephren

1. thick outer walls
2. causeway
3. four chambers with shrines, possibly for the king's viscera
4. transverse section of entrance hall
5. longitudinal section of entrance hall
6. open court surrounded by a cloister
7. niches thought to have contained statues of the king
8. sanctuary
9. base of the pyramid

with mastabas of the Old Kingdom, namely the *Ibu* (Purification-tent) and
the *Wabet* (House-of-embalmment). The purification ceremonies in the
valley building of Chephren took place, Grdseloff suggested, in a temporary
pavilion built on the roof, to which a ramp paved with alabaster gave access
from a passage leading out of the north-west corner of the T-shaped hall.
Round holes, which he believed had served as sockets for the framework of
such a pavilion, are still visible in the paving of the roof. The embalming of
the body, he considered, was performed in the antechamber. The Abbé
Drioton, while agreeing with Grdseloff's interpretation in general, suggested
that his identification should be reversed and that the purification was conducted in the antechamber and the embalmment on the roof. H. Ricke,
however, thinks that the actual processes of purification and embalmment
were carried out elsewhere, probably in brick buildings, and re-enacted as
ritual ceremonies in this building. The ritual purification, he believes, took
place on the terrace in front of the building and the ritual embalmment in
the transverse part of the T-shaped hall.

Purification by washing played an important part in Egyptian ritual at all
times. The king, for instance, was ceremonially washed in the sacred lake
of the temple of Rē at Heliopolis before he entered the building. Similarly,
before his dead body could be taken into the sacred precincts of his tomb, it
was necessary that it should be purified by washing. From this purification,
moreover, it was believed that the dead king was regenerated, just as the
Sun-god was thought to be reborn each morning by bathing in the 'Lily
Lake' before embarking on his journey across the heavens. According to
Ricke it was this episode which was ritually reproduced on the terrace in
front of the valley building. Osiris too, according to one tradition, had been
revivified by the lustration of his body; the dead king therefore, when
identified with Osiris, was thought to derive equal benefit from the same
treatment.

During the funeral of the king a ritual re-enactment of the embalmment
may well have taken place in the valley building, whether or not the actual
operation was performed there. To judge from inscriptional evidence in the
tomb of Queen Meresankh III, a grandchild of Cheops, the processes of
embalmment occupied several months, two hundred and seventy-two days
being given as the interval between her death and her burial. So long a period
would not have been necessary unless either her tomb was not ready when
she died or some preservative substance with a slow action, perhaps natron
or salt, had been employed; wrapping and modelling the various physical
members, to which reference has already been made in connection with
burials in mastabas, could have been accomplished in a shorter time. The
discovery in the tomb of Hetepheres of a so-called Canopic chest containing
the viscera proves that the most decomposable organs were removed in the
embalmment of a queen at the beginning of the IVth Dynasty; in the case of
a king the practice may have existed at a much earlier date.

A third ceremony to be performed in the valley building was the so-called
'Opening of the Mouth'. Priests, at least one of whom would be a son of the
dead king, would approach each of the twenty-three statues of the king in the
T-shaped hall, sprinkle water over it, fumigate it with incense, offer
sacrifices before it, touch its mouth with various implements including an
adze and a chisel, rub milk on its mouth, and deck it with the royal regalia.
In later times these ceremonies were also performed on the dead body, but

possibly this practice was not introduced until after the Old Kingdom. By their execution it was thought that the statue or mummy would be endowed with the faculties of a living person and a statue would become an abode for the *ka* of its owner.

It is unlikely that Chephren would have placed so many statues of himself in this building merely to provide his *ka* with as many reserve 'bodies' as possible. A king required not only a continuation of life after death, but also a continuation of divine life. In order to achieve this divine existence in the Next World each of the twenty-six members of which the body was composed must be deified separately and identified with the particular deity who was associated with that member. Ricke and Schott would explain these statues as being intended for the deification of Chephren's physical members individually. Since three deities were each associated with two members, it was not necessary to have twenty-six statues, but only twenty-three, the ceremonies being repeated twice on three of the statues. While the 'Opening of the Mouth' and the deification were being performed, the coffin containing the king's body, they believe, would be placed in the hall and the viscera kept temporarily in four of a group of six long cells, arranged in two storeys and approached by a passage opening out of the south side of the hall. The two other cells, perhaps were used for storing the two crowns of Saïs.

After the completion of the three ceremonies, the embalmed body and viscera, and also the two crowns if the explanation of Ricke and Schott be correct, would have been taken out of the valley building by way of the passage which connected the hall with the causeway. On its journey through the passage the cortège would have passed the mouth of a narrow corridor leading to a small chamber built of alabaster. The purpose of this chamber is not evident, but Hölscher conjectured that a porter, whose duty it was to guard the entrance to the causeway, lived in it; Grdseloff, however, suggested that it was used for storing food-offerings required during the three ceremonies.

In order to avoid the necessity of building an embankment across a deep depression which lay directly to the east of the mortuary temple, the causeway was constructed on a ridge of rock which crossed the depression obliquely from south-east to north-west. It was more than a quarter of a mile in length and about 15 feet in breadth. Nothing of its structure is now visible except part of the rock foundation and some blocks of Tura limestone from the walls and floor of its corridor. When standing, its walls rose perpendicularly on the inside, but their outer face had a marked batter. If Herodotus is correct in his statement that the causeway of the Great Pyramid was decorated with reliefs, it must be supposed that the inner walls of the corridor of this causeway also were decorated. It was roofed with slabs of stone laid flat. Perhaps the practice of roofing causeways dates from the time when their corridors were first decorated with reliefs. The causeways of the Bent Pyramid and the Pyramid of Meidum, neither of which appears to have been decorated, were certainly not roofed; possibly, therefore, the causeway of the Great Pyramid was the first to be given a roof in order to protect the painted reliefs on its walls. Light was admitted to the corridor through horizontal slits, cut along the middle of the roof. Since rain also would enter through these slits and, unless drained, would run down into the valley building, a channel was sunk in the paving at the lower end of the causeway to conduct the water through an outlet in the side wall.

The West Cemetery at Giza, where great nobles and court officials of the IVth to VIth Dynasties were buried, is seen here from the top of the Great Pyramid.

When the body of the dead king was transferred to the mortuary temple, no one standing outside the causeway could have witnessed the ceremony. Without doubt, such screening was intentional, although the motive which prompted it cannot be deduced with certainty. The most probable explanation seems to be that it was thought necessary to protect the dead body, after its purification in the valley building, from the gaze of those who were ceremonially impure. Even the fact that the body was already enclosed within a wooden coffin was apparently not considered a sufficient protection against contamination. Persons, other than priests, who were to accompany the bier to the mortuary temple probably underwent ritual purification before joining the cortège. Priests, as their Egyptian name *wab* ('pure') implies, were ceremonially clean at all times.

The mortuary temple, now reduced to ruins, was a low, rectangular building which measured about 370 feet in length and 160 feet in breadth. Its walls were composed of local stone, in part faced on the inside with red granite. Outside, the lowest course was also faced with granite, but the remainder of the building had a facing of Tura limestone. Five pits for boats were hewn in the rock close to the north and south walls. Two of the pits still have well-preserved roofs made of limestone slabs, but no trace of the wooden boats has been found.

Not one of the mortuary temples hitherto excavated has proved to be an exact replica of any other known example. They differ, however, only in arrangement and in architectural detail. From the time of Chephren until the end of the Old Kingdom, every mortuary temple embodied five main features: an entrance hall, an open court, five niches for statues, magazines, and a sanctuary.

In Chephren's temple, the causeway did not lead directly to the entrance hall, but to a corridor, at the southern end of which were two granite chambers. According to Ricke these chambers were constructed for the crowns of Saïs, while a group of four chambers with floors and walls of alabaster situated beyond a vestibule at the northern end of the corridor were shrines for the viscera. At the funeral the first ceremonies to be performed in this building would thus commemorate two of the ancient burial rites of Saïs and Buto. A narrow passage connected the vestibule with the entrance hall, the latter consisting of two sections, one transverse and the other longitudinal. Rectangular monolithic columns of red granite, resembling those in the valley building, supported the roofs of both the vestibule and the entrance hall. At each end of the transverse section of the entrance hall, a long and narrow chamber penetrated deeply into the masonry core of the building. Since the end wall in each chamber was composed of a single block of granite Hölscher conjectured that its surface was carved into a figure of the king fashioned almost in the round. If this conjecture is correct, the chambers would have been serdabs of a kind without any known parallel in a royal mortuary temple. Ricke, however, is inclined to regard them as having been built for models of the two barques of the Sun-god, the southern for the day-barque and the northern for the night-barque.

Beyond the entrance hall lay the open court paved with alabaster. Like the court in the mortuary temple of Cheops it was surrounded by a cloister. Traces of a drain, found in the middle of the court, suggest that an altar may have stood there, the drain being required for carrying away the blood of the animals sacrificed and the liquid of the libations offered; on the other hand, the drain may have been used simply for disposing of accumulations of rain-water. Broad piers built of blocks of red granite supported the curved roof of the cloister. Twelve seated statues of the king, each about 12 feet in height, projected outwards from recesses in the outer faces of all the piers, apart from those at the four corners. A single band of hieroglyphic inscription, giving the king's names and titles, was engraved around the openings between the piers, and above each statue was carved a pair of vultures with open wings representing the protecting goddess Nekhbet. The inner walls of the cloister, above a granite dado, were decorated with limestone reliefs, one fragment of which, showing part of a bound Asiatic captive, was excavated by Hölscher, but its connection with this court was only recently recognized by Ricke. Opposite each of the five openings on the west side of the cloister was a deep niche which may have contained a statue of the king. The significance of the five statues – a number which does not vary in any of the subsequent mortuary temples – may be that each bore one of the five official names assumed by the king on his accession. It is, however, equally possible that the number was dictated by the need to represent the king in association with five different cult-symbols.

The open court marked the limit beyond which only the priests were allowed to advance. During the temple ceremonies, secular attendants must have remained in the court while the priests proceeded, by way of the corridor in front of the statue-niches, to the sanctuary. The main feature of the sanctuary was usually a false door in the west wall with a low altar at its foot. Offerings were placed on the altar daily by the priests. Since it was only the spirit of the substance provided and not the actual material which was thought to be of value to the dead, the fact that the offerings remained undisturbed until replaced would not have troubled the minds of the ancient

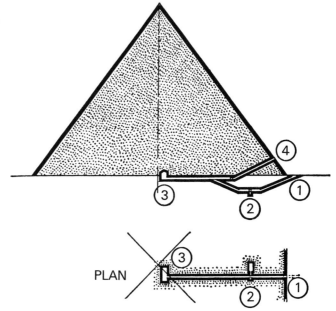

The Pyramid of Chephren, cross-section looking west, ground plan

1. entrance to lower corridor
2. abandoned burial chamber
3. actual burial chamber
4. second entrance and corridor

PLAN

Egyptians. Five magazines lay between the sanctuary and the five statue-niches – a coincidence in number which may not have been accidental. In construction also, the magazines shared with the niches the peculiarity of being the only parts of the temple not paved with alabaster. Within the magazines were stored stone vases and reserve supplies of food, which would be required by the king if the priests neglected their daily duty to provide fresh offerings.

A long ramp led from the north-west corner of the corridor surrounding the open court to the terrace on which the pyramid stood. The position of the entrance to the ramp implies that access to the pyramid enclosure was permitted to persons who were not entitled to enter the innermost parts of the mortuary temple. At the funeral service, therefore, the whole procession may have proceeded to the pyramid after the 'Opening of the Mouth' ceremony had been performed on the statues in the niches. The masons and workmen who blocked up and sealed the entrance to the pyramid must also have reached the enclosure by way of the ramp; a high wall, which surrounded the pyramid on every side, would have prevented an approach by any more direct route.

Between the pyramid and the surrounding wall there was a pavement about 34 feet in width on the north, east, and west sides and somewhat wider on the south side, where a single subsidiary pyramid stood approximately opposite the middle of the king's pyramid. The mortuary temple was separated from the east face of the pyramid by a paved alley-way. In this respect it resembles the Great Pyramid; in later enclosures the two buildings are generally contiguous, so that there is no open space between the false door and the pyramid. Borchardt conjectured that a second false door or a stela stood against the east face of the pyramid, but no trace of its existence was revealed during excavation. In the light of the discoveries at the Bent Pyramid it is perhaps more likely that if anything stood in the alley-way it was a pair of round-topped stelae and an altar.

The most distinctive external feature of Chephren's pyramid, apart from its size, is the substantial portion of its outer casing which still remains intact near the apex. Some of the casing has also been preserved at the base. The stone employed is, however, different in each place, the upper remnant being composed of Tura limestone and the lower of red granite – a material which was used only as a casing for the bottommost course. Herodotus, in his description of the pyramid, states that 'the lowest layer is of variegated Ethiopian stone',[7] apparently in the mistaken belief that granite was employed not merely as a casing but as a kind of platform on which the pyramid was built. The capstone, which has now disappeared, may also have been made of granite.

Owing to its position on somewhat higher ground, Chephren's pyramid creates the illusion of being taller than the Great Pyramid. In reality, its present height of 447 feet 6 inches falls short of that of its neighbour by 2 feet 6 inches. Originally, it rose to a height of 471 feet and was therefore about 10 feet lower than the Great Pyramid, when the latter was also undamaged. The area covered by Chephren's pyramid today is approximately 690 feet 6 inches square; formerly each side measured 707 feet 9 inches, so that the dimensions at the base were about 48 feet less in each direction than those of the Great Pyramid. The faces of the pyramid, which slope at an angle of 52° 20′, rise more steeply than the faces of the Great Pyramid – a fact which

This granite head of Userkaf, approximately two and a half feet in height, was found at Saqqara; it is a forerunner of later colossal statues. The pupils of the eyes were once painted and traces still remain.

explains the small difference in height between the two buildings when compared with the considerable inequality of their base dimensions.

Internally, Chephren's pyramid bears little resemblance to the Great Pyramid. It has two entrances, one in the north face at a height of nearly 50 feet, and the other directly below, hewn in the rock foundation of the surrounding pavement. Both entrances are situated at a distance of about 41 feet to the east of the pyramid's main north–south axis. From the upper entrance, a low and narrow corridor descends at an angle of 25° 55′ through the core of the pyramid until it enters the rock; here it becomes horizontal and continues on a level plane to the tomb-chamber. The roof, walls, and floor of the whole of the sloping section and of a small part of the horizontal section are lined with red granite. Near the end of the granite lining vertical slots have been cut in the walls to receive a portcullis, also made of granite, the damaged remains of which are still in position. The tomb-chamber has been hewn, with the exception of its roof, entirely out of the rock; the pointed gable roof consists of limestone slabs laid at the same angle as the faces of the pyramid. With its longer axis running from east to west, the chamber measures 46 feet 6 inches in length, 16 feet 6 inches in breadth, and 22 feet 6 inches in height. Rectangular cavities were cut near the top of both the north and the south walls, apparently with the intention of constructing shafts from the chamber to the outer surface of the monument, as in the Great Pyramid, but the plan was abandoned when each shaft was only about a foot in depth. Squares marked in red on the walls approximately 5 feet below these cavities suggest that an earlier plan to locate the shafts at about the same height above the floor as those in the Great Pyramid had already been discarded. On the west side of the chamber, a fine rectangular sarcophagus of polished granite has been let into the floor up to the level of its lid. The lid itself, which lies near by, is broken into two pieces – a condition in which it was found in 1818 by Giovanni Belzoni, the first European explorer to enter this pyramid in modern times. No trace of Chephren's body was discovered in the sarcophagus.

The lower corridor, at its beginning, follows a course similar to the upper corridor; it is, however, completely hewn out of the rock. After descending at a gradient of 21° 40′, it becomes horizontal for a short distance and then rises steeply to emerge in the floor of the horizontal section of the upper corridor. A granite portcullis stood also in this corridor, but the walls were not lined with granite. In the east wall of the horizontal section, there is a recess opposite which a sloping passage leads down to a chamber, measuring 34 feet 3 inches in length, 10 feet 4 inches in breadth, and 8 feet 5 inches in height. There can be no doubt that this chamber, at the time of its construction, was intended to contain the royal sarcophagus; some explanation for its abandonment must, therefore, be sought. Two exceptional features which may offer a clue in solving the difficulty immediately strike the eye: the chamber is situated very near the entrance to the pyramid and the entrance itself lies beyond the limits of the superstructure. In other contemporary pyramids, the tomb-chamber is located approximately beneath the apex and the entrance is situated in the northern face. If, however, it be supposed that, when the chamber and corridor were constructed, it was planned to build the pyramid some 200 feet further north, both the chamber and the entrance would have occupied their customary positions. A possible reason for the change in plan was the discovery of a suitable rock foundation

A schist head found in the Sun Temple of Userkaf near Abu Sir was once thought to represent the king himself. The absence of the royal beard, however, militates against this identification. Probably it represents the goddess Neith, who was regularly portrayed, as here, wearing the red crown of Lower Egypt.

for the causeway concealed beneath the sand on a line south of the one
originally chosen.

A problem for which it is more difficult to find a satisfactory solution is
the purpose of the sloping passage which connects the lower apartments
with the upper corridor. The only explanation which has been suggested
is that it was used for transferring the sarcophagus from the old chamber to
the new, but the process of cutting an additional passage through the rock
would seem unnecessarily laborious when it would have been possible to
extract the sarcophagus from the old chamber by way of the lower entrance
corridor and to introduce it into the new chamber from above, before
building the gable roof. The fact, however, remains that the passage was
constructed and that, after serving its purpose, it was blocked with limestone
boulders, many of which have never been removed. Blocking of the same
kind completely fills the lower entrance corridor so that it cannot now be
entered.

West of the pyramid, outside the enclosure wall, lies a series of galleries
which Sir Flinders Petrie identified as the barracks in which were housed the
masons and workmen employed in building the pyramid complex. These
galleries are now almost entirely concealed beneath the sand, but Petrie, who
surveyed them in 1880–2, has stated[8] that they numbered ninety-one, each
measuring about 88 feet in length, 9 feet 6 inches in width, and 7 feet in
height. The walls of the galleries are composed of rough pieces of limestone
faced with a coating of dried mud; the floor also is overlaid with a coating of
the same material. Wide pilasters of hewn limestone serve as terminals to the
walls at the entrance end. The east end of each gallery is closed by a single
wall running at right angles to the galleries and oriented almost exactly
parallel to the west side of the pyramid.

Considered in relation to its predecessors, Chephren's pyramid provides
the first recognizable example of a complex in which all the architectural
elements of the standard pattern appear in their fully developed form.
Earlier complexes, notably that of the Great Pyramid, embody many of its
salient features, but they are either not in a comparable state of preservation
or, like the mortuary temple of the Meidum pyramid, architecturally still
in embryo. In Chephren's pyramid complex, the valley building is largely
intact, the foundations of the causeway are plainly visible and enough of the
mortuary temple remains to enable its ground-plan to be determined with
certainty. Each of these structures, moreover, contains in its design all the
basic elements of the subsequent pyramid complexes; modifications in
detail and substantial decorative innovations were to be introduced, but the
essential skeleton was to remain unchanged.

The third pyramid of the Giza group stands in the south-west corner of the
wide plateau. Although it had been ascribed to Mycerinus both by Herodotus
and by Diodorus Siculus, who visited Egypt in the middle of the first century
BC, the identification was not confirmed until 1837–8, when Colonel Howard
Vyse found the name of Mycerinus written in red ochre on the roof of the
burial-chamber in the second of the three subsidiary pyramids within the
complex. Further proof was obtained by the expedition of Harvard University and the Boston Museum of Fine Arts, which excavated the site between
the years 1905 and 1927 under the directorship of G. A. Reisner.

Contemporary records shed no light on the life and character of Mycerinus. In very late times he seems to have gained a reputation for piety and

This statue of Mycerinus
and two goddesses
bearing the features of the
queen is one of four
complete triads found in
his valley building at Giza.
A detail in colour may be
seen on page 99.

justice, while Cheops and Chephren were regarded as having been wicked and tyrannical kings. Herodotus, in whose writings this tradition is preserved, speaks of Mycerinus in the following terms: 'This prince [i.e. Mycerinus] disapproved the conduct of his father, reopened the temples and allowed the people, who were ground down to the lowest point of misery, to return to their occupations and to resume the practice of sacrifice. His justice in the decision of causes was beyond that of all the former kings. The Egyptians praise him in this respect more highly than any of their other monarchs, declaring that he not only gave his judgements with fairness, but also, when anyone was dissatisfied with his sentence, made compensation to him out of his own purse and thus pacified his anger.'[9] The gods, however, had ordained that Egypt should suffer tyrannical rulers for a hundred and fifty years. The reigns of Cheops and Chephren, according to this legend, had already accounted for a hundred and six years, so that forty-four years of affliction still awaited the Egyptians when Mycerinus ascended the throne. Not to be foiled of their purpose, the gods decided that the reign of the 'just and pious' Mycerinus must be cut short, but not without warning him that this fate was impending. To quote the words of Herodotus: 'An oracle reached him from the town of Buto, which said "six years only shalt thou live upon the earth, and in the seventh thou shalt end thy days." Mycerinus, indignant, sent an angry message to the oracle, reproaching the god with his injustice – "My father and uncle," he said, "though they shut up

The Pyramid of Mycerinus, cross-section looking east, ground plan

1. original entrance corridor to burial chamber
2. burial chamber
3. final entrance corridor to burial chamber
4. chamber having groups of cells corresponding with those in Chephren's mortuary temple
5. second burial chamber

PLAN

the temples, took no thought of the gods and destroyed multitudes of men, nevertheless enjoyed a long life; I, who am pious, am to die soon!" There came in reply a second message from the oracle – "For this very reason is thy life brought so quickly to a close – thou hast not done as it behoved thee. Egypt was fated to suffer affliction one hundred and fifty years – the two kings who preceded thee upon the throne understood this – thou has not understood it." Mycerinus, when this answer reached him, perceiving that his doom was fixed, had lamps prepared, which he lighted every day at eventime, and feasted and enjoyed himself unceasingly both day and night, moving about in the marsh-country and the woods, and visiting all the places that he heard were agreeable sojourns. His wish was to prove the oracle false, by turning the nights into days and so living twelve years in the space of six.'[10]

There is certainly no reason for believing that the legend quoted by Herodotus is founded on historical fact, although evidence that Mycerinus met an untimely death is to be seen in all the buildings of his pyramid complex. Mycerinus must have intended to follow the example of Chephren by constructing his valley building and part of his mortuary temple of limestone faced with ashlars of granite and his causeway of limestone. Reisner's excavations, however, have shown that this plan was never realized and that the greater part of the work was either hastily finished in materials of inferior quality or even left incomplete. Only the foundations of the valley building were made of stone; the superstructure was composed almost entirely of crude brick. The causeway consisted of an embankment of stone, upon which was built a brick corridor overlaid, both inside and outside, with white plaster and roofed with wooden logs. In the mortuary temple the foundations and the inner core of some of its walls were composed of limestone. A beginning had also been made with laying floors of granite and with adding granite facings to the walls, but crude brick was again the material used for completing the greater part of the building.

Examples of tombs and monuments left unfinished by the owner, but completed by his son or successor, are not uncommon. It would therefore be only natural to suppose that Shepseskaf, who is believed to have succeeded Mycerinus, was the king who built the crude brick additions to the pyramid complex. Proof that Shepseskaf did, in fact, contribute towards the completion of the complex is provided by an inscription, found in the ruins of the mortuary temple, which states that he 'made it [the temple] as his monument for his father, the King of Upper and Lower Egypt [Mycerinus].' Both the valley building and the mortuary temple were, however, repaired and slightly modified in design at a later date. These repairs and alterations were attributed by Reisner to the priests who officiated in the temple during the Vth and VIth Dynasties. Their labours, he pointed out, might not have been inspired by consideration of duty alone, but also by motives of self-interest. As mortuary priests, they would have been entitled to enjoy the fruits of the rich endowments bequeathed by the dead king in return for service in his temple; they would also have been qualified to dwell in his pyramid city – a residential enclosure attached to the valley building, the inhabitants of which were exempt from the payment of certain taxes. To secure these privileges, however, it would have been necessary for them to preserve intact the fabric of the buildings and to maintain at least some show of performing the temple services. Architecturally and in their internal layout, both the

Hieroglyphic inscription and symbolic representation are combined to ornament the seat of an alabaster statue of King Mycerinus. The two plants held by the kneeling figures representing the Nile symbolize Upper and Lower Egypt and are entwined around the hieroglyph which stands for unity. The king's names are protected by two falcons, symbols of the god Horus. The designs thus signify the unity of the two lands under the king, protected by Horus, with whom he was identified.

earlier and the later forms of the buildings differed considerably from those of Chephren, but no fundamental changes in general composition were introduced.

During his excavations of the valley building and the mortuary temple, Reisner discovered a large number of statues and statuettes, most of which represented the king either alone or as a member of a group. Among those found in the valley building were some beautifully carved slate triads composed of the goddess Hathor, the king, and one of the *nome* deities. There can be no doubt that Mycerinus intended to have as many of these triads as there were nomes, each showing him with a different *nome*-god or goddess, but only four and some fragments were discovered; possibly the remainder were never carved. Another fine piece of sculpture, also found in the valley building, was a slate group-statue of Mycerinus and Queen Khamerernebty II. As works of art, these statues are worthy of comparison with the best of their kind yet known. They have all been carved in the naturalistic style typical of the Old Kingdom, with the result that a high degree of individuality in points of detail is evident. Of the eight representations of the king's face, no two are exactly alike, but the majority portray the features with slightly bulging eyes, a rounded nose, and a protruding lower lip. In many respects the face resembles that of Chephren, as portrayed in the famous diorite statue, but the cheekbones in the latter are higher and the face narrower. Fifteen statuettes of the king had been left unfinished and even the group-statue of the king and Queen Khamerernebty II had not been entirely polished – a fact which can be explained by the king's untimely death and the parsimony of his successor. While the abandonment of these sculptures before completion must be deplored on aesthetic grounds, they throw more light in their present condition on the technical processes employed by Egyptian sculptors than if they had been preserved as finished works. Reisner, who conducted a minute examination of the figures, was able to detect eight distinct stages of development, some of which corresponded with the different stages illustrated by unfinished statues in scenes of sculptors' workshops represented in the wall decorations of private tombs.

The Pyramid of Mycerinus occupies less than a quarter of the area covered by the Great Pyramid. Each side measures 356 feet 6 inches at the base. Its vertical height is now 204 feet; when complete, it was 14 feet higher. The upper portion is cased, in the normal manner, with dressed Tura limestone, but the lower sixteen courses have an outer facing of red granite, some of which has been left in the rough. It is possible that Mycerinus intended to case the whole pyramid with granite; the change of material may therefore indicate the stage reached at the time of his death. On the other hand, the combination of limestone and granite may have been deliberate, so that the only evidence of untimely death would be the undressed granite at the base.

Internally, at least one and probably two changes of plan are apparent. The first design consisted of a sloping corridor of the usual kind tunnelled through the rock and leading to a rectangular burial-chamber, the longer axis of which ran from east to west. When this design was abandoned the floor of the burial-chamber was deepened and a second sloping corridor cut beneath the first. The only reason for this change of plan seems to have been a decision to enlarge the superstructure of the pyramid and the consequent necessity for constructing the corridor at a lower level in order to preserve the position of the entrance in the new north face at about the same height

A schist group-statue, three-quarters life size, of King Mycerinus and Queen Khamerernebty, is carved in the naturalistic style of the Old Kingdom.

above the ground. As far as the point where it enters the rock, the new corridor is lined with granite. At the foot of the slope, the horizontal continuation of the corridor is enlarged into an antechamber, the rock walls of which are decorated with carved panelling. Three granite portcullises, which fitted into vertical slots in the walls, blocked the corridor between the antechamber and the burial-chamber. According to Ricke they were constructed, like the portcullises in the Great Pyramid, so that they could be lowered into position by means of ropes which passed over rollers mounted at the top of each slot.

The third and last design did not involve any alteration of the earlier plan, but only the addition of two chambers at a greater depth and an approach-ramp sloping westwards from the middle of the floor of the original burial-chamber and terminating in a short, horizontal passage. The first chamber, which lies on the right side of the passage, is entered by a flight of steps. It is a rectangular room with four deep cells in the east wall and two in the north, the entire room being hollowed out of the rock. Both in number and in arrangement the cells correspond with the two groups of cells near the entrance to Chephren's mortuary temple and, in spite of the difference of their location, it seems likely that they served the same purpose. The second chamber, designed to take the place of the original burial-chamber, is situated at the far end of the passage. Its walls, floor, and roof are composed entirely of granite. The underside of its pointed roof has been rounded, thus giving it the appearance of a barrel-vault. Within this chamber, Colonel Howard Vyse found a rectangular basalt sarcophagus, the outer faces of which were carved with a panel decoration. Unfortunately, this fine sarcophagus, which must originally have contained the body of Mycerinus, was lost when the ship which was transporting it to England foundered off the coast of Spain. In the original burial-chamber, Colonel Vyse had discovered some human bones and the lid of a wooden anthropoid coffin inscribed with the name of Mycerinus. This lid, which is now in the British Museum, cannot have been made in the time of Mycerinus, for it is of a pattern not used before the Saite Period. Radio-carbon tests have shown that the bones date from early Christian times. Borchardt, possibly influenced by the dating of the lid, believed that the whole of the third design was the work of Saite restorers who, on entering the pyramid, found the upper burial-chamber in complete disorder, and the remains of the body lying exposed. Since Borchardt expressed this view, however, excavation of the tomb of Shepseskaf has revealed that it contained both a magazine and a burial-chamber resembling in style those of this pyramid. With this knowledge there can be no reason to doubt that the third design dates from the time of Mycerinus. The Saites, it must be supposed, simply placed the body in a new inner coffin and restored it to its original sarcophagus, making no structural alterations of any kind.

South of the Pyramid of Mycerinus lies a row of three subsidiary pyramids, none of which appears to have been completed. The largest and most advanced stands at the eastern end of the row. Like the main pyramid, it was cased, in part at least, with granite. Neither of the other two pyramids had progressed beyond the construction of its inner core when the work was abandoned. Adjoining the east face of each pyramid stood a small mortuary temple composed mainly of crude brick, and therefore probably built by Shepseskaf after the death of Mycerinus.

No evidence of their owners' identity was discovered during Reisner's

Djedefrē, a IVth Dynasty king, when constructing his pyramid at Abu Roash, reverted to the open trench and vertical shaft design of the IIIrd Dynasty.

excavation of these pyramids, but the size of the first would suggest that it belonged to Khamerernebty II, the principal queen. In the second, Colonel Vyse discovered a small granite sarcophagus and some human bones, which he judged to be those of a young woman. This pyramid may therefore, have been the tomb of a younger queen or a princess. The ownership of the westernmost pyramid in the row remains completely obscure.

Apart from the three major pyramids at Giza, the Pyramid of Meidum, and the two stone pyramids at Dahshur, only one pyramid of a IVth Dynasty king has been identified with certainty. Its builder, Djedefrē, probably ruled between Cheops and Chephren. The site which he chose was a commanding eminence at Abu Roash, some five miles to the north of the Giza plateau. Of the superstructure, which seems to have been faced with granite, so little remains that it is impossible to estimate its original dimensions or even to be certain that it was ever completed. The substructure consists of an open trench which slopes downwards to the base of a vertical shaft measuring about 30 feet in depth, 30 feet from north to south, and 70 feet from east to west. It is surprising that Djedefrē should have elected to revert to the open trench and vertical shaft design of the IIIrd Dynasty, when his predecessor Cheops had succeeded in constructing the subterranean portions of his tomb by the less laborious method of tunnelling. Some difference in the quality of the rock foundation of the two pyramids may, however, account for the change in technique. Physical considerations

undoubtedly determined the line of the causeway which, instead of running from east to west, approaches the mortuary temple from the north. By
following this line, it was possible to utilize a ridge of rock and thus reduce
the amount of building necessary for raising it to the required level. Petrie,
who surveyed this causeway, estimated that it was nearly a mile in length
and, in places, 40 feet high. Nothing is now visible of the valley building, but
enough of the mortuary temple, standing as usual on the east of the pyramid,
has been preserved to enable its ground-plan to be clearly traced. Its walls
are made of mud-brick – a fact which strongly suggests that it was hastily
erected after the death of the king. Immediately south of the building lies a
deep pit, the shape of which implies that it once contained a ceremonial
boat.

Although it cannot be dated with certainty, the so-called Unfinished
Pyramid at Zawiyet el-Aryan, excavated in 1904–5 by A. Barsanti, may also
have been constructed for a king of the IVth Dynasty. Some blocks bore in
red ink a name written in cursive hieroglyphs which Jaroslav Černý has
shown should probably be read 'Nebka'. In the vicinity of the pyramid
Barsanti found a schist plaque inscribed with the name of Djedefrē. Since
the order of sequence of the immediate successors of Djedefrē for a period
of at least fifty years seems to be firmly established, it is difficult to attach
special significance to the occurrence of his name on an object at Zawiyet
el-Aryan, but it cannot be denied that the substructure of the Unfinished
Pyramid, which is the only part now visible, is essentially similar to the
substructure of the Pyramid of Djedefrē.

The main features of the Unfinished Pyramid are an open trench with
sloping floor which enters the north side of a rock-hewn vertical shaft,
85 feet in depth and measuring 82 feet from east to west and 38 feet from
north to south. The slope of the trench is broken by level stretches at two
points, the first roughly half-way along its course and the second near the
lower end. Between these level sections two parallel flights of steps, separated
by a broad raised ramp and bounded on each side by similar ramps, are cut
in the rock floor. At the lower end of the trench a pit has been cut and
partly filled with limestone blocks rising to a somewhat greater height than
the level section which immediately precedes it. The floor of the shaft has
also been built up and paved with red granite in the centre. An oval granite

The Unfinished Pyramid
of Zawiyet el-Aryan,
section looking west,
ground plan

1. two flights of steps,
separated and bounded by
ramps
2. pit partly filled with
limestone blocks
3. floor of the shaft, built
up and paved with red
granite

sarcophagus, without parallel in form, was sunk in the floor, west of the centre, but was raised from its pit by the excavator.

Shepseskaf, who completed the pyramid complex of Mycerinus, did not himself build a pyramid. His tomb, which is situated at Saqqara, was examined in 1858 by Mariette, who wrongly identified its owner first as Unas, the last king of the Vth Dynasty, and subsequently as Ity, a successor of Unas. In 1924 the Service des Antiquités conducted a thorough excavation of the site under the direction of Gustave Jéquier, and the real ownership of the tomb was established. Known to the Arabs as the *Mastabat Fara'un*, this tomb was built in the form of a huge rectangular sarcophagus resting possibly on a low platform. The sides of the sarcophagus inclined inwards at an angle of about 65°, and the square ends projected vertically above the level of the vaulted roof. Only the inner core of local stone is now visible, but originally it was cased with Tura limestone and given a skirting of granite. On the east side of the building stood a small mortuary temple, from the south-east corner of which a long causeway, with walls of crude brick, led down to the valley building.

A queen named Khentkaues, who may have been married to Shepseskaf, built on an open space lying between the causeways of Chephren and Mycerinus a tomb which was essentially similar to the *Mastabat Fara'un*. At one time it was thought to be an unfinished pyramid, but the excavations of Selim Bey Hassan on behalf of Cairo University in 1932–3 proved that, in reality, the superstructure was in the form of a sarcophagus mounted on a high, square podium. Its mortuary temple, which consists of only three rooms, has been hewn entirely out of the rock core of the podium, and is therefore not a separate construction. The causeway runs first towards the east and then turns a complete right angle southwards, finishing at a valley building which extends along the full length of the valley building of Mycerinus.

Viewing the pyramids of the IVth Dynasty as a whole, it is undeniable that they are characterized chiefly by the employment of megalithic masonry. Reisner has estimated that some of the blocks of local stone embodied in the walls of the mortuary temple of Mycerinus weigh as much as 220 tons, while the heaviest of the granite ashlars, all of which have been transported 500 miles from Aswan, may exceed 30 tons. The use of such massive blocks offered two main advantages: greater stability was attained and the number of joints to be fitted was reduced. Cheops, who may have been a megalomaniac, could never, during a reign of about twenty-three years, have erected a building of the size and durability of the Great Pyramid if technical advances had not enabled his masons to handle stones of very considerable weight and dimensions. How completely they had mastered this art may be gauged from Petrie's observation that the joints in the casing of the Great Pyramid measured only one-fiftieth of an inch in thickness.

A parallel development to the handling of heavy blocks was the progress made in the art of cutting hard stones. Even as early as the Ist Dynasty, there is an instance of the use of granite for paving a chamber, while the small burial-chambers in Zoser's step pyramid and south mastaba are composed entirely of this material. It was, however, only in the IVth Dynasty that structures of the size of Chephren's valley building and mortuary temple were faced completely or mainly with granite. Basalt also occurs sporadically long before the IVth Dynasty, but not in the quantity

The *Mastabat Fara'un*

employed in the pavement of Cheops's mortuary temple or the lost sarcophagus of Mycerinus. Petrie has even expressed the opinion that one of the subsidiary pyramids of the Great Pyramid had arris lines of basalt extending down each corner to prevent wear and weathering.

Statuary during the IVth Dynasty made a very big advance both in quantity and in quality. Reisner, after examining all the fragments of sculpture discovered in Chephren's valley building and mortuary temple, calculated that the second pyramid complex alone contained between one hundred and two hundred separate statues. A similar number may well have been made for the Great Pyramid and the Pyramid of Mycerinus, so that the aggregate of statues in the three complexes possibly reached a figure not far short of five hundred. The full effect of the stimulus to the sculptor's art given by the interest of these kings only becomes apparent in the two following dynasties, when nearly every private tomb in Giza and Saqqara included a statue of its owner. Artistically, the relatively few specimens which have survived from the three Giza pyramids bear testimony of a greater experience in portraying the human features than any earlier statues.

Until recently it was supposed that the temples and causeways of the IVth Dynasty pyramids were not decorated with reliefs. Now, however, it is known that they were employed on a large scale in the valley building, if such it be, of the Bent Pyramid and there is evidence of their employment in the mortuary temple of Cheops, in the chapel of the second of his subsidiary pyramids and in Chephren's mortuary temple. In addition to the fragments found at Giza, other fragments which are believed to have come from the temples of Cheops and Chephren have been recovered from buildings of the Middle Kingdom at Lisht whither they had been taken and re-used. All these pieces show that the art of carving in low relief, so exquisitely illustrated in the galleries of the Step Pyramid and south mastaba, was not lost during the IVth Dynasty, but, on the contrary, continued to develop and the range of subjects represented was greatly extended.

The valley building of Chephren, the best-preserved building of the IVth Dynasty, has walls faced internally and externally with polished red granite from Aswan.

1 Somers Clarke and R. Engelbach, *Ancient Egyptian Masonry*, Frontispiece.
2 E. Baldwin Smith, *Egyptian Architecture as a Cultural Expression*, p. 96.
3 J. Capart and Marcelle Werbrouck, *Memphis à l'ombre des pyramides*, p. 47.
4 *Survey of Egypt*, Paper No. 39: 'The Determination of the Exact Size and Orientation of the Great Pyramid of Giza', Cairo, 1925. The measurements in this report are given in metres and decimal fractions of a metre; they have here been translated into feet and decimal fractions of a foot for the sake of uniformity.
5 W. M. Flinders Petrie, *The Pyramids and Temples of Gizeh*, p. 72.
6 *Herodotus*, Book II, 126 (Rawlinson's translation).
7 *Herodotus*, Book II, 127 (Rawlinson's translation).
8 Petrie, *The Pyramids and Temples of Gizeh*, pp. 101–3.
9 *Herodotus*, Book II, 129 (Rawlinson's translation).
10 *Herodotus*, Book II, 133 (Rawlinson's translation).

Pyramids of the Vth and VIth Dynasties

ALTHOUGH documentary records are lacking, the character of the political events which attended the close of the IVth Dynasty may be conjectured from a number of indirect indications. The three successors of Cheops – Djedefrē, Chephren (Khaef-Rē), and Mycerinus (Men-kau-Rē) – had proclaimed their recognition of the Sun-god Rē by forming their names of compounds with his name. There is some evidence also that Chephren and Mycerinus had adopted the title 'Son of Rē' – a royal title which figures regularly from the Vth Dynasty onwards. It seems, therefore, reasonable to infer that the cult of Rē was already in the time of these kings superseding the more primitive cult of Atum in Heliopolis. At the end of the IVth Dynasty, however, Shepseskaf not only departed from the type of tomb built by his predecessors, but, so far as is known, did not follow their precedent by acknowledging unequivocally, either in name or in title, his association with Rē. Whether he was guided by motives of religious principle or political expediency cannot be deduced from the evidence available, but, in view of the caution and conservatism shown by the Egyptians at all times in matters appertaining to religion and the after-life, it is difficult to believe that Shepseskaf would have introduced such fundamental changes if he had not thought that the increasing power of the priesthood of Rē directly menaced the authority and independence of the throne. Shepseskaf's struggle, which was perhaps passive and not waged with destructive bitterness, failed to achieve any permanent success, for his death, after a reign of little more than four years, led to the accession of a line of kings who raised the cult of Rē to the position of the official state religion.

A papyrus in the Berlin Museum, known as the Papyrus Westcar, has preserved a legend concerning the origin of the Vth Dynasty which may embody a kernel of truth. The papyrus itself probably dates from the Second Intermediate Period, but it was certainly a copy of an older document. According to this legend, the first three kings of the dynasty – Userkaf, Sahurē, and Neferirkarē – were triplets begotten of Rē and born of the wife of a priest of Rē. Userkaf may well have sprung from a priestly stock, and it seems likely that he himself held the office of High Priest of Heliopolis before ascending the throne. His mother was Neferhetepes, who appears to have been a daughter of Djedefrē. Sahurē and Neferirkarē were possibly brothers, the sons of Shepseskaf and Khentkaues, whose heresy, however, they made no effort to revive.

Each of these three kings and three of their successors built special Sun-temples in honour of Rē. Contemporary inscriptions mention all six temples, but only those of Niuserrē and Userkaf have hitherto been found. Incomparably the better preserved, because it was built entirely of stone, was Niuserrē's temple, excavated in 1898–1901 by Ludwig Borchardt and Heinrich Schaefer on behalf of Baron von Bissing and the Deutsche Orient-Gesellschaft. It was erected on the summit of a low mound situated on the edge of the desert at Abu Gurab, about a mile north of Abu Sir, where Niuserrē built his pyramid. A causeway surmounted by a covered corridor led up to the mound from a large pavilion standing inside a spacious enclosure. At the upper end of the causeway, and still recognizable, is a paved court 330 feet long and 250 feet broad, in which the principal feature is a rectangular podium built to support a squat obelisk, the sacred symbol of the Sun-god. At the foot of the podium stands a low sacrificial altar composed of five massive slabs of alabaster. Channels cut in the pavement conducted the blood of the animals offered on the altar to nine large alabaster basins. A small sacrificial enclosure and a group of magazines occupy the whole northern side of the court. Outside the court, to the south, lie the brick foundations of a pit which formerly contained a model of the boat used by the Sun-god in his daily journey across the sky.

The Pyramids of Abu Sir – a reconstruction

1. Sun-temple of Niuserrē
2. Sun-temple of Userkaf
3. Pyramid of Sahurē
4. Pyramid of Neferirkarē
5. Pyramid of Niuserrē
6. valley building of Sahurē
7. causeway to Pyramid of Sahurē
8. valley building of Niuserrē
9. causeway of Neferirkarē, upper section rebuilt for Niuserrē

Temples and mortuary buildings of the Vth Dynasty were lavishly decorated with painted wall-reliefs of the highest artistic quality. In Niuserrē's Sun-temple the reliefs, later transferred to the museums of Cairo and Berlin, were found in the corridor of the causeway, in its continuation around the east and south sides of the court and in a chapel situated between the end of the corridor and the obelisk. A wide variety of subjects was represented in these reliefs, ranging from the flora and fauna created by the Sun-god to the ceremonies connected with the foundation of the temple and the *heb-sed* of the king. The representation of the *heb-sed*, if it is to be regarded as a record of an historical event, would suggest that this temple was not built until many years – possibly thirty – after the king had ascended the throne. Since it is unlikely that Niuserrē would have delayed the construction of a Sun-temple until so late in his life, the stone building may have

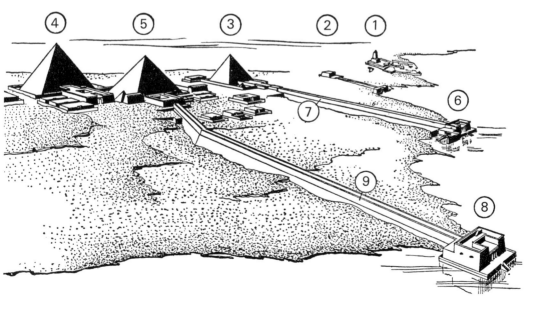

replaced an earlier temple of brick, perhaps with the intention that it should be available for his use and for the celebration of his *heb-sed* festivals in the after-life.

Although Userkaf's Sun-temple was located and partly explored by Borchardt at the beginning of this century, its site was not systematically excavated until 1955–7 when the work was carried out by a joint expedition of the Swiss and the German Institutes of Archaeology in Cairo under the direction of H. Ricke. The buildings, composed partly of limestone and partly of Nile mud and limestone chips, were set out according to the same general plan as those of Niuserrē. Complete excavation of the pavilion on the fringe of the cultivation proved impossible owing to the rise in the water-level since ancient times, and no trace was found of either a boat-pit or wall-reliefs. A fine example of sculpture in the round came to light in the form of a head of a life-size schist statue perhaps representing Neith, the goddess of Saïs, who was regularly portrayed wearing the crown of Lower Egypt. Alternatively, it may represent the king himself, but if so the absence of the royal beard is strange.

According to the Palermo Stone, a fragment of an inscription which recorded the official annals of the early kings of Egypt, Userkaf, one of the last kings named on the stone, built his Sun-temple either in the fifth or in the sixth year of his short reign of seven years. The hieroglyphic sign which represents the temple, both in the entry on the Palermo Stone and in some other inscriptions dating from the beginning of the Vth Dynasty, seems to show only a podium without an obelisk, whereas inscriptions of the time of Neferirkarē and of later times show both these features. In every probability therefore the obelisk was a later addition, and the suggestion has been made that the mastaba-like construction which eventually served as its podium was intended by Userkaf to symbolize the primeval hill. Discoveries made in the course of excavation seem to support the evidence of the inscriptions, at least to the extent of indicating that the original plan of the enclosure was altered three times and also that the later designs included an obelisk, built of blocks of granite, which stood on a podium of limestone faced with ashlars of quartzite. On the altar in front of his monument, Userkaf, so the Palermo Stone records, sacrificed two oxen and two geese daily.

The practice of building pyramids, discarded by Shepseskaf, was resumed by the kings of the Vth Dynasty. In quality, however, these pyramids were inferior to their predecessors, being composed merely of a core of small stones within a casing of Tura limestone. As a result of their poor construction, all the pyramids of this period have suffered severely, and some have been reduced to little more than mounds of sand and rubble.

Userkaf built his pyramid at Saqqara, close to the north-east corner of the Step Pyramid enclosure. By the time of the Vth Dynasty, Zoser's tomb may have acquired a particular sanctity and burial in its vicinity may have been thought to confer special benefits. Such an explanation would account for Userkaf's choice of a site which in other respects seems to have been unsuitable for a pyramid. Immediately to the east, where the mortuary temple would normally have been constructed, the ground rises steeply; only the sanctuary was therefore built against the eastern face of the pyramid, while the main temple stood exceptionally on the southern side. C. M. Firth's excavations on behalf of the Service des Antiquités in 1928–9 revealed that the temple had been destroyed in antiquity and that its site

Sahurē was the first of a line of kings who built their pyramids at Abu Sir and raised the cult of the Sun-god Rē to the position of official state religion. Like Userkaf, his predecessor, he built a temple to the Sun-god.

had been re-used in the Saite Period for building tombs, the superstructures of which were actually composed of stone taken from Userkaf's temple and from the neighbouring pyramids.

J.-P. Lauer, working intermittently between 1948 and 1955, succeeded in tracing the ground-plan of the whole enclosure with the exception of the valley building and the causeway, which still remain to be explored. The sanctuary was composed of a small hall flanked by two narrow chambers, the hall paved with basalt and the chambers with limestone. It was not possible to determine whether two emplacements in the floor of the hall were intended for rectangular granite columns or for stelae of the same material, but some fragments of quartzite found in the rubble were recognizable as having belonged to an altar. The walls of the hall, above a granite dado, were made of limestone and may have been decorated with sculptures carved in relief.

In addition to its exceptional orientation in relation to the pyramid, the main temple was abnormal in plan. The entrance lay at the upper end of the causeway near the southern corner of the eastern enclosure wall. Two oblong chambers, both partly destroyed when a large Saite tomb was constructed, stood between the entrance and the open court. A cloister with rectangular columns of granite was built on three sides of the court, no doubt for the protection of sculptured scenes on the walls, some fragments of which, showing the king fowling in the marshes of the Delta, were discovered in the course of excavation. Against the middle of the south wall, which was probably bare of decoration, stood a colossal red granite seated statue of the king facing the pyramid and giving the impression that he was gazing at it. The head of this statue, which measures about 2 feet 6 inches in height, was found by Firth and is now in the Cairo Museum. South of the court, and therefore further from the pyramid, lay a small hypostyle hall and the customary five niches with which the five magazines situated near the entrance to the temple were probably associated. Thus placed, the statues in the niches, like the statue in the court, would have faced the pyramid. The subsidiary pyramid, which in subsequent enclosures generally stood on the valley side of the main pyramid at the south-east corner, was built in the south-west corner of this complex.

While the unsuitability of the terrain to the east of the pyramid, and perhaps also the existence of earlier tombs which have not yet been found, may explain why Userkaf could not build the whole of his mortuary temple in the normal position, it is still difficult to understand why he should have chosen this site when other sites without obstruction were available near by. Perhaps the most important requirements of the mortuary cult were satisfied by having the sanctuary on the side of the pyramid facing the sun at its rising, but the inversion of the regular arrangement of the court and the five niches in relation to the pyramid seems to defy explanation. To some extent Userkaf may have been influenced by a desire not to copy too slavishly the monuments of the kings whose burial practices he had reintroduced; nevertheless architecture and religious belief in Egypt were generally complementary and it would be strange if the peculiarities of this complex did not reflect some change, albeit short-lived, in the royal mortuary creed.

Sahurē, Neferirkarē, and Niuserrē chose for their pyramids a plateau on the desert edge near the modern village of Abu Sir. While conforming with the standard layout, the complexes of Sahurē and Niuserrē surpassed in

Top: The pyramids of Abu Sir, were built during the Vth Dynasty by Sahurē, Neferirkarē and Niuserrē. Their temples and adjoining buildings surpassed in artistic magnificence all the earlier monuments. Borchardt estimated that the sculpture carved in relief in Sahurē's complex alone covered 10,000 square metres. Unfortunately, plunderers of later periods severely damaged all three pyramids and only fragments of the reliefs remain. *Bottom:* Unas, the last king of the Vth Dynasty, built his pyramid at Saqqara. Some blocks taken from Zoser's complex, which must have been falling into disrepair even then, were re-used by Unas.

The Sun-temple of
Niuserrē

artistic magnificence anything which had previously been attempted.
Ludwig Borchardt, who excavated this group of pyramids on behalf of the
Deutsche Orient-Gesellschaft in 1902–8, estimated that the area of wall-
surface covered by reliefs in Sahurē's complex alone amounted to about
10,000 square metres. Unfortunately, later inhabitants of the neighbourhood
discovered that the fine Tura limestone of the reliefs produced the best lime,
with the result that of the original total only about 150 square metres,
broken into innumerable fragments, survived their depredations. Niuserrē's
complex had suffered even more severely than that of Sahurē. The complex
of Neferirkarē was never finished, and it is probable that the work was
abandoned before many of the intended reliefs had been executed.

The valley building of Sahurē was provided with two landing-stages,
one facing towards the east and the other towards the south; ramps connected the landing-stages either with a canal or with the Nile, which, during its
annual period of inundation, may well have spread so far beyond its normal
bounds. Recessed in the east face of the building was a portico, the floor
of which was composed of black polished basalt and the ceiling of limestone,
painted blue to represent the sky and decorated with golden stars carved in
relief; the eight monolithic columns were of granite and the walls, above a
granite dado, were of limestone decorated with painted reliefs. In design,
the columns were imitations of date-palms with their leaves tied vertically
in a bunch to form the capitals. Each column bore, within a rectangular
frame, the king's name and titles carved in hieroglyphs and inlaid with green
paste. A similar, though less deeply recessed, portico was constructed in the
south face of the building; its floor, however, was of limestone and its
columns were cylindrical, lacking any form of capital. Both the porticos
were connected by passages with a small T-shaped hall, the only apartment
within the building. The reliefs in this hall probably showed the king, in the
form of either a sphinx or a griffin, trampling underfoot Asiatics and
Libyans, who were led to him bound as captives by the gods. This scene was
repeated, possibly with slight variations, on the inner walls of the causeway
at its lower end.

Sahurē's mortuary temple consisted of the five main elements seen most clearly in the temple of Chephren – an entrance hall, an open court, five niches for statues, magazines, and a sanctuary. The entrance hall is too badly damaged to allow all the details of its construction to be determined with certainty, but its floor was of limestone and its walls, above a granite dado, were probably of the same material decorated with painted reliefs. The open court was paved with polished basalt; apart from an alabaster altar standing in the north-west corner, it was completely bare. Around its four sides ran a cloister which resembled in construction the eastern portico of the valley building, except that its star-decorated roof was supported by only one row of palm-tree columns. The walls of the cloister were covered with reliefs of the king triumphing over his enemies, those on the northern side being Asiatics, and those on the southern side Libyans. One of these reliefs, found in the south-west corner, shows Sahurē in the act of slaying a captured Libyan chieftain; two of the chieftain's sons and a woman, who may be either his wife or his daughter, stand by imploringly. Other Libyan captives, some of whom are women and children, are also represented in a similar attitude. Elsewhere in the scene live animals, taken as booty, are shown; their number is given in the accompanying inscriptions as 123,440 head of cattle, 223,400 asses, 232,413 deer, and 243,688 sheep, but only the smallest fraction of this vast total is actually represented. Similar scenes, which may have amounted to eleven in number, from the remainder of the cloister were too fragmentary to be reconstructed in detail.

A wide corridor, also paved with basalt and decorated with reliefs,

The pyramid enclosure of Userkaf

1. sanctuary
2. entrance to temple
3. Saite tomb, partly destroying two chambers
4. open court
5. subsidiary pyramid

The Pyramid complex of Sahurē

1. and 2. valley building and landing stages
3. causeway
4. entrance hall
5. open court
6. five statue-niches
7. sanctuary
8. entrance corridor to pyramid
9. subsidiary pyramid and court

surrounded the outside of the court. From the surviving fragments, it is evident that these reliefs were mostly different in character from those of the court or the causeway. On the northern side were scenes of the king harpooning fish and fowling with a throw-stick. On the southern side, in a relief measuring about 30 feet in length, the king is shown hunting. Behind him stand his successor Neferirkarē and a group of courtiers. In front are antelopes, gazelles, deer, and other horned animals driven by beaters into a large enclosure where the king shoots them with arrows from his bow. Hounds seize some of the wounded beasts by the throat and dispatch them. Here

Date-palm column

and there the sculptor has varied the regularity of the scene with such lively touches as a jerboa and a hedgehog about to disappear into their holes and a hyena seizing a wounded antelope as its private quarry. The preservation of this remarkably fine piece of sculpture was due to the mere chance that this part of the corridor became in later times a sanctuary which housed a much-venerated figure of the fire-goddess Sakhmet.

Some of the most interesting reliefs in the whole temple were carved on the east wall of the western corridor. North of the door leading from the open court, the king, accompanied by his courtiers, was represented witnessing the departure of twelve sea-going ships to a land which is not specified, but which was probably Palestine or Syria. In the corresponding position on the south side of the door, the king and his retinue watched the return of the ships laden with cargo and carrying a number of Asiatics. Nothing in their appearance suggests that the Asiatics were prisoners; the ships may therefore have been employed on a commercial or perhaps a diplomatic errand. Even in the reign of Seneferu, the Egyptians had procured timber from Syria, so that if the cargo was merchandise this expedition represented no fresh enterprise initiated by Sahurē.

Access to every part of the complex could be gained directly or indirectly from the western corridor. By way of a door at the northern end, it was possible to reach either the pyramid enclosure or a staircase leading to the roof of the temple; a similar door at the opposite end of the corridor also led to the pyramid enclosure and, in addition, to the subsidiary pyramid court and a side entrance into the complex. In the middle of the corridor, on the west side, a passage followed by a short flight of steps opened into a small chamber containing the five statue-niches. A door in the southern wall of this chamber provided the only means of access to the sanctuary and five rooms lying beyond, of which at least two were used for the performance of some kind of ceremony in the temple ritual. The sanctuary measured about 45 feet in length and about 15 feet in breadth. Its floor may have been paved with alabaster – a material which was certainly used for the low altar standing at the foot of the granite false door in the west wall. Above a dado of granite, the north, south, and east walls were composed of limestone and were decorated with reliefs of gods bringing gifts of provisions to the king.

The magazines, arranged in two rows, were approached by way of passages leading from two deep recesses in the west wall of the western corridor, seventeen from the southern recess and ten from the northern recess. Supporting the roof of each recess was a granite column, 12 feet in height and shaped like a cluster of six papyrus stems tied together, the capital being formed of their buds. The magazines were constructed in blocks of two storeys, each consisting of one room, and every block had its own staircase. It seems likely that the smaller group of magazines was intended for the storage of particularly valuable objects, such as decorated vases and gilded statues, used by the mortuary priests on special occasions. Some fragments of relief from the walls of one of the rooms showed the king holding an investiture; it is possible, therefore, that this room contained specimens of the gold decorations awarded by the king to his officials in recognition of distinguished service. The magazines in the larger group were probably used for storing stone vessels and provisions.

An interesting feature in Sahurē's complex was its very elaborate drainage system. Rain falling on the roof escaped through stone spouts in the form of lions' heads which projected from the top of the outer walls. This type of gargoyle may have been chosen because rain was sometimes regarded as a manifestation of Seth and other hostile gods who were thus consumed and expectorated, after being rendered harmless, by the lion, the protector of sacred places. In the unroofed parts of the complex, the rain water flowed through apertures at the base of the outer walls, to which it was conducted by channels cut in the paving. A different method of drainage was, however, employed for removing water and other liquids used during the temple ceremonies, some of which may have become ritually impure and would therefore be dangerous to touch. Five stone basins, lined with copper and provided with lead plugs to fit the vents, stood in different parts of the inner temple, two in the rooms beyond the sanctuary, one in the sanctuary itself, another in the corridor leading to the sanctuary and the last in the smaller group of magazines. Pipes made of copper connected these basins with an underground drainage system consisting of a line of copper pipes which ran beneath the paving of the inner temple, the open court, the entrance hall, and the causeway as far as the lower end, where it terminated in an outlet in the southern side. All the metal for this piping must have been mined in Sinai or in the eastern desert; it is more than 1,000 feet in length, and the use of such a quantity of this valuable metal provides eloquent testimony of the importance attributed to its presence by Sahurē.

Papyrus-cluster column

Both externally and internally Sahurē's pyramid has suffered severely. When complete, its sides measured about 257 feet at the base and its vertical height was about 162 feet. Only a few fragments of the original Tura limestone casing have been preserved, but a considerable part of the rough inner core remains intact. The corridor leading to the burial-chamber is almost completely choked with fallen masonry so that it is virtually impassable. From its entrance in the north face, at a point a little to the east of the middle and on a level with the surrounding court, it sloped downwards at an angle of 27° for a distance of about 14 feet to continue horizontally for 27 feet, where it was blocked by a granite portcullis; from there it ascended at a gentle gradient until it entered the oblong burial-chamber. Blocks of Tura limestone lined the whole corridor, with the exception of the entrance slope, a few feet on each side of the portcullis and a short section at the end, where it was lined with granite. The burial-chamber was built entirely of Tura limestone; its pointed roof consisted of three superimposed layers of masonry. Perring, who was able to examine the roof, estimated that its largest blocks measured 35 feet in length, 9 feet in width, and 12 feet in thickness. In spite of their size and weight, however, only two of these blocks remain unbroken.

Neferirkarē, whose reign probably lasted for more than ten years, planned a pyramid complex closely resembling that of Sahurē, but on a larger scale. He was not, however, destined to see it completed. At the time of his death, the foundations of the valley building may have been laid, the causeway – but not the corridor above it – had been constructed, and work on the five statue-niches and sanctuary of the inner temple had reached an advanced stage. The pyramid, although nearer completion than the buildings in the remainder of the complex, was also unfinished; it measured 360 feet square at the base and rose to a height of 228 feet, so that it was slightly bigger than the Pyramid of Mycerinus. The few fragments surviving from the outer casing show that the lowest course at least was composed of granite, the surface of which had not been dressed. Neferefrē, Neferirkarē's short-lived successor, who may have started to build a pyramid at a short distance to the south-east, and Niuserrē continued the construction of both the pyramid and the mortuary temple after Neferirkarē's death, but not in stone. Brick and timber were used for the entrance hall and cloistered court, the roofs being supported by wooden columns standing on limestone bases. Each column was carved in imitation of a bound cluster of lotus stems and buds. The valley building and causeway were left unfinished, and were subsequently appropriated by Niuserrē. As a consequence, Neferirkarē's mortuary priests, who would otherwise, no doubt, have followed the normal practice of building their pyramid city in the vicinity of the valley building, grouped their houses of crude brick against the walls of the mortuary temple.

In order to use the causeway of Neferirkarē without any alteration, it would have been necessary for Niuserrē to build his pyramid complex immediately to the east of Neferirkarē's mortuary temple. He chose, however, a site lying to the north-east, so that the lower half of the causeway could be used as it stood. The upper half was dismantled and a large part of it rebuilt at the required angle towards the north-east. This angle was somewhat lessened by the exceptional placing of the entrance hall and cloistered court of the temple opposite the southern half of the east face of the pyramid. Unless this position was deliberately selected with a view to shortening the distance between the temple and the older causeway, the decision to depart from the normal practice of constructing the temple in line with the main east-west axis of the pyramid must have been dictated either by the presence in that area of an obstruction – possibly a tomb – or by the unsuitable configuration of the ground.

Niuserrē's complex differed from that of Sahurē in detail only, but it provides a good illustration of the extent to which the standard plan could be adapted to fit the physical requirements of any particular site. The valley building had two porticos, the larger facing eastwards and the smaller westwards; instead, however, of the palm columns found in Sahurē's valley building, these porticos were furnished with papyrus-cluster columns of red granite. Tura limestone, red granite, and black polished basalt were again used in combination for the ceilings, walls, and floors of the apartments. Basalt was also employed in the construction of a dado for the walls of the corridor of the causeway. Above this dado the walls were faced with Tura limestone and decorated with reliefs showing various scenes, which included the representation of the king as a lion or a griffin trampling his enemies underfoot. In the mortuary temple, papyrus-cluster columns supported the roof of the ambulatory surrounding the cloistered court. The magazines, owing to lack of space in the inner temple, were mostly built outside the north and south walls of the entrance hall. The sanctuary occupied its normal position due east of the burial-chamber, and therefore considerably north of the east-west axis of the temple. South-east of the main pyramid lay the usual subsidiary pyramid.

A successor of Niuserrē, Djedkarē Isesi, built his pyramid due west of the village of Saqqara. This pyramid, known formerly by its Arabic name *Haram esh-Shauwaf* – the Pyramid of the Sentinel – was excavated in 1945 by the Service des Antiquités under the direction of Abdessalam Hussein assisted by Alexandre Varille, both of whom died before the results of their work had been prepared for publication. Among the hundreds of pieces of architectural elements and sculpture found in the mortuary temple were broken palm-tree columns of red granite, fragments of limestone figures of calves and bound foreign prisoners, what appears to be a sphinx, and part of a relief showing a figure of the god Seth with eyelids inlaid with copper.

The last king of the dynasty, Unas, erected his pyramid close to the south-west corner of the Step Pyramid enclosure wall and almost diagonally opposite the Pyramid of Userkaf, the founder of the dynasty. Excavations by the Service des Antiquitiés under the direction first of Selim Bey Hassan in 1937–8 and subsequently of Abdessalam Hussein, revealed that the causeway had been preserved more completely in this monument than in any other known pyramid. It does not follow a straight line for its entire length of nearly 750 yards, but changes its direction twice in order to use the natural features to their best advantage. In spite of these adjustments, however, it was still necessary to bridge deep depressions in the ground. Some of the blocks employed in the bridging embankments were taken from the buildings of the Step Pyramid enclosure – a fact which proves that Zoser's famous monument was already falling into disrepair at the end of the Vth Dynasty. The sides of the embankment were built with a steep batter, which reduced its width at the top to about 22 feet. On this massive foundation the usual covered corridor was laid; its walls, possibly 13 feet in height, were about 6 feet 8 inches in thickness, and the central passage approximately 8 feet 8 inches in width. The flat roof was made of slabs measuring 1 foot 6 inches in depth which projected inwards from each side, leaving in the middle a gap of about 8 inches in width to admit light. South of the causeway lie two boat-pits side by side, each about 148 feet in length and lined entirely with Tura limestone.

Scenes covering a wide range of subjects were delicately carved in low relief on the inner walls of the corridor. One group of reliefs illustrated the transport by ship from Aswan of the granite date-palm columns and archi-traves used in the construction of the mortuary temple. Another series represented craftsmen hammering gold, casting copper objects, and polishing vessels made of gold and stone. Elsewhere, labourers on the royal estates were shown gathering figs, harvesting corn, and collecting honey. Long trains of servants were depicted bringing provisions of every kind to the tomb. Hunting scenes included specimens of every horned animal known to the Egyptians, as well as a giraffe, a lion, leopards, foxes, hyenas, jerboas, and hedgehogs. Possibly the most graphic scene of all illustrated the victims of a famine, whose bodies were so emaciated that they were reduced to little more than skin and bone. Unfortunately this unique scene is in-complete and it is difficult to imagine its context; even the nationality of the people cannot be identified with certainty. Since, however, tomb reliefs depicted only incidents or events which the dead owner wished to perpetuate, it must be supposed that the starving people were not Egyptians and that the missing portion contained scenes of provisions being sent to them by Unas. All these reliefs were painted in bright colours, traces of which are still clearly visible. The ceiling also was painted with golden stars carved in relief on a sky-blue background.

Unas's mortuary temple was partly excavated by Alessandro Barsanti on behalf of the Service des Antiquités in 1900. A second and more complete excavation was undertaken by the Service des Antiquités in 1929 under the

Chambers and corridors
of the Pyramid of Unas

1. square vestibule
2. chamber with three
statue-niches
3. burial chamber

direction of C. M. Firth. In plan and construction it resembled very closely the mortuary temple of Sahurē, though the layout of the corridors and magazines in the inner temple was somewhat different. Its floors also were different, alabaster having been used as paving where basalt had been employed by Sahurē. In contrast with the large number of reliefs surviving from the causeway, only a few fragments showing servants bearing offerings have been preserved from the temple.

Externally, the Pyramid of Unas presents no feature of special interest. Its original base measurement of 220 feet square and its perpendicular height of 62 feet seem modest in comparison with the monuments of the IVth Dynasty. Internally, however, many innovations are apparent. The entrance, although on the north side, is not in the face of the pyramid, but under the pavement. Three portcullises of granite formerly blocked the corridor leading from the entrance to a square vestibule. On the east side of this vestibule lies a long, narrow room, in the east wall of which are three statue-niches. The burial-chamber occupies a corresponding position west of the vestibule. At the far end of the chamber stands a rectangular stone sarcophagus which, although undamaged, had been robbed of its contents long before 1881, when it was found by Sir Gaston Maspero, the first archaeologist to clear a way into the pyramid. All the apartments are built of Tura limestone, with the exception of the west wall of the burial-chamber and the western halves of its north and south walls, opposite the ends of the sarcophagus, where the limestone is replaced by alabaster on which an elaborate panel design and a false door have been carved and painted.

More notable, however, than the structural innovations of this pyramid are the vertical columns of hieroglyphic inscription which entirely cover the walls of the vestibule and the limestone portions of the walls of the burial-chamber. Every hieroglyph has been filled with a blue pigment, so that it stands out clearly against the white background. These inscriptions are known as the 'pyramid texts'. They are found not only in this pyramid but also in the VIth Dynasty pyramids of Teti, Pepi I, Merenrē, and Pepi II, in the pyramid of a king named Ibi, whose date is uncertain, and in the pyramids of Pepi II's three queens. They do not form a continuous narrative, but consist of a collection of spells assembled in no fixed order. Although most of the spells occur in more than one pyramid, very few are repeated in all the pyramids in which the texts are found; in the Pyramid of Unas, for instance, only two hundred and twenty-eight spells are included out of a known total exceeding seven hundred.

The purpose of the pyramid texts, like that of every other element in the pyramid complex, was to secure for the king or queen a happy after-life. So powerful was the magic of the written word that its presence alone provided a sufficient guarantee that the thought expressed would be realized. Doubtless the spoken word, if delivered by a qualified person, possessed at least equal virtue, but its utterance was dependent on the goodwill or diligence of other people. A text which is generally inscribed on the north wall of the burial-chamber reproduces the ritual which the priests used to recite every day in the mortuary temple when laying the provisions on the altar in front of the false door. By having this ritual in writing and supplies of provisions in the magazines of his temple, the king believed that he would eliminate the risk of suffering hunger and thirst, even if the priests should neglect to perform their duties. Many of the texts describe the journey of the king to the Other World, situated in the sky beyond the eastern horizon, and his activities on arrival. It is clear that the king could count on little assistance from the gods when making this journey, but, armed with the magic power of the texts, he might expect to overcome successfully its many hazards. With their help, moreover, his association with the Sun-god in his daily voyage across the sky was assured. Among the texts were also collections of hymns to the gods and prayers on behalf of the dead king.

An interesting theory, which has been advanced by Siegfried Schott, is that the pyramid texts as a whole represent the spells recited at the time of the funeral in the various chambers, corridors, and courts through which the procession passed on its way to the pyramid. While this theory does not affect the explanation of the ultimate purpose of the texts already given, it attributes to them an added importance of a practical kind as furnishing a key with which the significance of many of the architectural features may be more clearly understood. Nevertheless, the identification of the physical surroundings in which a particular spell was recited is often not easy to establish from its content, but Schott and his colleague H. Ricke have produced a reconstruction which, though not acceptable to all authorities, has not yet been shown to be fundamentally unsound. Some of the results of their work have already been mentioned in connection with pyramids described in the previous chapters.

For the most part, the pyramid texts were certainly not inventions of the Vth or VIth Dynasties, but had originated in earlier times; it is hardly surprising, therefore, that they sometimes contain allusions to conditions which no longer prevailed at the time of Unas and his successors. As an example, Spell 662 includes the words 'Cast the sand from thy face', which could only refer to the burial practices of pre-dynastic times when the king was interred in a grave dug in the sand. Another anachronism of a similar kind, but referring to the brick mastabas of the Early Dynastic Period, occurs in Spell 355: 'The bricks are removed for thee from the great tomb.' A relic of even more ancient times is contained in a passage (Spells 273–4) which describes the dead king as a hunter who catches and devours the gods so that he may appropriate their qualities unto himself. On the other hand, many of the texts expressly mention the pyramid and, in consequence, may not have originated before the IIIrd to IVth Dynasties; for instance, Spell 599 states: 'They [the gods] are those who will cause this work to be enduring and this pyramid to be enduring.' It seems certain, in view of the constant references to the solar cult, that the texts were compiled by the priests of Heliopolis. When making the compilation, probably in the Vth Dynasty, they used old religious and funerary spells and added some incantations of a later date to meet contemporary needs.

Although the pyramid texts were designed to help the dead king, their presence in his tomb introduced a new complication of a very serious kind. Being written in hieroglyphs, they included many images of living creatures. Such images not only possessed the value of a particular hieroglyphic sign, but also, through the power of magic, became actual embodiments of the creatures which they represented. The lion, for instance, was simultaneously both a phonogram with the value of *ru* and the living animal itself endowed with all its attributes. Images of human beings, which form some of the most common hieroglyphic signs, likewise fulfilled a dual function. To overcome the dangers to the dead king which would have resulted from the

Religious texts in the Pyramid of Unas are shown opposite. Care was taken to avoid the use of animal and human hieroglyphs with dangerous magical properties. Texts in later tombs have these supposedly harmful hieroglyphs mutilated to neutralize their potency.

The pyramid complex of Pepi II

1. terrace of valley building reached by ramps
2. causeway
3. hall of mortuary temple
4. cloistered court
5. hall containing five statue-niches
6. sanctuary
7. entrance to pyramid
8. subsidiary pyramid
9. Pyramid of Udjebten
10. Pyramid of Iput
11. Pyramid of Neit

presence of a multitude of potentially hostile and destructive creatures in his close vicinity, the Egyptian priests and sculptors resorted to a number of different devices. Sometimes the dangerous signs were omitted or replaced by signs representing inanimate objects which possessed the same hieroglyphic value. Human beings were deprived of their legs and bodies so that they consisted of heads and arms alone. Animals could be rendered harmless by the simple expedient of mutilating their bodies and carving them in two separate halves. Serpents were represented intact, but the scorpion was deprived of its tail. One creature which, with a single exception, was never allowed to appear on the walls of the burial-chamber was the fish. This omission was not due to any fear lest the fish should molest the tomb's owner, but was the result of a belief that the fish, although innocuous to living people, would defile a dead body.

During the Middle Kingdom, the pyramid texts were retained in a modified form. The custom of inscribing the texts on the walls of the chambers and corridors of the tomb was, however, abandoned. Instead, they were written on the interior surfaces of the rectangular wooden coffins used in that period – a fact which has caused them to become known as the 'coffin texts'. By that time also they had ceased to be the exclusive property of royalty and had been usurped by the nobility, thus following the same course of democratization as so many other practices which had been designed in the first instance as a royal prerogative. Under the New Kingdom, the texts, after undergoing still further modifications, were written on papyrus, and were called the 'Book of Coming Forth by Day', better known in modern times as the 'Book of the Dead'.

Teti, Pepi I, and Merenrē built their pyramids at Saqqara, Teti choosing a site north-east of the Step Pyramid and his two successors moving southwards to sites in the neighbourhood of the mastaba of Shepseskaf. All three complexes followed conventional lines, but the full details of their construction cannot be ascertained until they have been excavated more completely. The pyramids themselves, though small in comparison with earlier works and now gravely dilapidated, are nevertheless of considerable importance on account of their texts, which include many spells not recorded in the Pyramid of Unas. One of the three pyramids – that of Pepi I – has a particular claim to be remembered for its texts because they were the first examples of their kind to be found. Before their discovery by Maspero in 1881, it was supposed that the interior walls of pyramids had at all times been left bare and uninscribed.

Pepi II, who succeeded Merenrē, ascended the throne as a child and died, according to Manetho, a centenarian. Later Egyptian historical records credit him with having ruled for ninety-four years, which if correct, would mean that his reign was by far the longest in the whole course of Egyptian history. His pyramid complex, or what remains of it after centuries of depredation, is situated a short distance to the south of those of his two predecessors and within 300 yards of the north-west corner of Shepseskaf's mastaba. It was excavated between the years 1926 and 1936 by Gustave Jéquier, who succeeded in recovering the whole of its ground-plan and not a little of its structure. As a result of his work, it is possible to see the plan of the standard pyramid complex in its final and most highly developed form.

In front of the valley building, and projecting for a considerable distance beyond its northern and southern limits, lay a broad terrace. To reach this terrace from the level of the valley, it was necessary to mount a short ramp at either end and continue by a longer ramp ascending at a right angle. A high limestone wall of great thickness bounded the terrace on its north, south, and west sides. Narrow staircases built in the masonry at each end of the wall led up to a parapet which extended along the wall for the whole of its length. In the middle of the long west wall stood a door set in a granite frame, on which the names and titles of the king were carved in large hieroglyphs. Beyond the door was a passage running through the thickness of the walls to an elongated hypostyle hall with eight rectangular pillars, probably made of limestone. As in the rest of the building, only the floor and foundation of this hall have been preserved substantially intact, but the excavator found among the debris some fragments of delicately carved and painted low reliefs which had once adorned the walls. The scenes represented appear to have been of the conventional kind, showing the king slaying his enemies, fowling in the marshes, and associating with the gods. It was undoubtedly the most important apartment in the whole building, the remainder of which consisted of magazines and two subsidiary chambers, apparently with bare walls. No trace of any sculptures in the round was revealed during the excavations, but it is not improbable that the building once housed a number of statues of the king.

Although in a far poorer state of preservation, the causeway of Pepi II resembles that of Unas in many respects. Both causeways change their direction twice, either in order to make the best use of available natural features or possibly to lessen the angle of their gradient. In their dimensions also the corridors surmounting the two causeways were approximately alike. In contrast, however, with the very substantial portions of relief which have been preserved in the corridor of Unas, only scattered fragments have been recovered from that of Pepi II. From these fragments it seems evident that the scenes at the lower end of the corridor were similar to those occupying a corresponding position in the corridor of Sahurē: the king, represented both as a sphinx and as a griffin, was shown trampling underfoot the traditional enemies of Egypt, who were led to him as captives by the gods. Accompanying this scene, as elsewhere, was another set of reliefs showing the goddess Seshat compiling a register of the victims and of the booty acquired. The scenes at the upper end of the corridor were of a purely funerary character. Long processions of servants were shown carrying produce from the royal estates to the tomb. In a neighbouring scene similar processions, but composed of gods and goddesses, advanced towards the king, who was seated on his throne. Near the top of the corridor, doors in the side-walls allowed those priests who approached the complex from the north or the south to reach the mortuary temple without being obliged to go first to the valley building and then climb up the whole length of the causeway. A porter, who was stationed in a lodge built against the wall of the corridor, guarded the southern door to prevent unauthorized persons from entering the sacred precincts. No vestiges of a similar lodge were discovered in the north side, where even the position of the door could not be accurately determined, but it must be supposed that such a building formerly existed.

The causeway in this complex was separated from the entrance hall of the mortuary temple by a transverse corridor, which can scarcely be regarded as a new architectural element, because it appears to have been intended merely for the purpose of giving access to staircases leading to the roof from rooms at either end. In shape and size the entrance hall followed the standard pattern. Its walls were decorated with reliefs, one of which showed the king hunting hippopotami from a boat made of reeds. Immediately beyond the entrance hall lay a cloistered court which, although conforming in plan with the courts of the Vth Dynasty temples, was considerably less elaborate in its architecture. The eighteen pillars of reddish quartzite supporting the roof of the ambulatory were not carved in imitation of date-palms

A relief fragment from the mortuary temple of Sahurē shows a naval expedition returning from Palestine or Syria and bringing Asiatics.

or papyrus clusters; they were rectangular monoliths decorated on the outer face only with figures of the king and one of the gods. Slabs of limestone took the place of the polished basalt or alabaster pavements of Sahurē and Unas. No brightly coloured reliefs seem to have adorned the walls of this court, which, in comparison with many of its predecessors, must have appeared plain and even monotonous.

Beyond the cloistered court lay the central transverse corridor, which not only served to separate the inner apartments of the temple from those lying outside the enclosure wall of the pyramid, but constituted the focal point of the whole complex. Although developed architecturally from the western section of the corridor, which in earlier temples surrounded the outer walls of the cloistered courts, it had now become an independent element and the southern, eastern, and western sections of the former corridor had been discarded. Doors at the northern and southern ends of this corridor gave access to the pyramid enclosure, in the south-east corner of which stood the subsidiary pyramid. East of the corridor, flanking the northern and southern sides of the cloistered court and the entrance hall, lay extensive groups of magazines. Niuserrē, apparently owing to lack of space within his inner temple, had also constructed magazines on each side of the entrance hall, so that Pepi II can certainly not be credited with having introduced an architectural innovation in this respect. West of the corridor, and approached by way of a small court or hall containing the five statue-niches, were the inner apartments of the remainder of the magazines.

Only fragments of the reliefs from the central transverse corridor have been preserved, but Jéquier's reconstructions have demonstrated that they were among the most interesting in the whole temple. At the southern end of the east wall the king was shown in the act of smiting a captured Libyan chieftain on the head with his mace. Behind the chieftain stood his wife and two sons, begging for mercy. The scene is not merely reminiscent of that in the temple of Sahurē, but is actually a replica of it, even the names of the wife and the two sons being repeated. This almost exact duplication of a scene in the temples of two kings whose reigns were separated by about two centuries furnishes conclusive proof that temple reliefs did not necessarily record historical episodes from the life of the king; all the evidence indeed goes to show that they were intended to depict the ideal life which the king wished to live in the Next World. Elsewhere on the same wall the king, wearing the crown of Upper Egypt and carrying in his hands a flail and a small rectangular portfolio, was four times represented performing a ritual ceremony which involved running between some hoof-shaped boundary stones set at a distance apart. This ceremony, an earlier example of which occurs in the Step Pyramid, formed part of the *heb-sed* and seems to have been designed, at least originally, to restore fertility to the ground. Another scene on the wall, which may also be connected with a fertility rite, shows the king standing near a high pole supported by four wooden stays. Two men, one above the other, were represented in the act of climbing the stays, while attendants held ropes attached both to the stays and to the pole. Replicas of this scene, which is a little suggestive of the medieval maypole ceremonies, occur in later times on the walls of the temples of Karnak, Luxor, Denderéh, and Edfu; in the replicas, however, the god of fertility, Min, stands facing the king on the other side of the pole and receives his homage.

From a recess in the west wall of the central transverse corridor, a short

The earliest examples of the funerary inscriptions now called the pyramid texts occur in the vestibule and burial chamber of the Pyramid of Unas. The inscriptions, filled with blue pigment, entirely cover the limestone portions of the walls. They were thought to possess magic power to help the king in his after-life.

staircase led upwards to the hall or court with five statue-niches. Nothing now remains within the niches except one badly damaged pedestal, which serves to show that the statues were made of limestone. In accordance with the regular Egyptian custom, they were probably painted and each statue may have been inscribed with one of the king's five titles and with his name. Double doors of wood concealed the statues from view when they were not required for ritual purposes. A second group of statues may have been permanently hidden, if a hollow space lying in the masonry of the building behind the five niches has been correctly interpreted as a serdab.

Passages opened from each end of the statue-hall, the northern leading to a small group of magazines and the southern to a narrow chamber which, in turn, was connected with a larger series of magazines and with a square vestibule situated next to the sanctuary. Among the reliefs which decorated the walls of the narrow chamber was one of the many examples in this temple of the king vanquishing his enemies. Only a few fragments were preserved, but they provided a clue to the reconstruction of the whole scene, for Jéquier recognized that it had survived in a copy made by Amenophis II in the temple of Karnak nearly a thousand years after the death of Pepi II. The central position in the scene was occupied by a gigantic figure of the king, who brandished a mace over the heads of a bunch of foreign captives. Behind the king was a small human figure representing his *ka*, presumably serving as his protector. Elsewhere in the scene the goddess Seshat was shown recording on a scroll the number of captives slaughtered and the amount of booty taken. The frequent occurrence of such scenes in mortuary temples suggests that periodic ceremonies were held to commemorate a victory gained in early times by the Egyptians over their foreign neighbours. A similar explanation may also account for the presence in both this temple and in certain of its predecessors of statues representing foreign captives in a kneeling position, with their arms bound. Of all these statues not one has been discovered intact, and the majority bear every sign of having been mutilated deliberately. Possibly, therefore, they were used during the commemoration ceremonies as substitutes for live captives, whose slaughter in cold blood would have been alien to the Egyptian mentality.

A single pillar, which may have been octagonal in section, supported the roof of the square vestibule. On each of its four walls, the king was shown being received by the deities of Egypt and by high sacerdotal and secular officials who had assembled to greet him as he entered the temple by way of the sanctuary from his tomb. The deities, who numbered about a hundred, stood erect, each carrying a sceptre in one hand and in the other the hieroglyph for 'life'. The officials, about forty-five in number, were bowed in an attitude of humble deference before their royal master. Butchers were shown slaughtering cattle in preparation for a feast.

The sanctuary, which measured approximately 51 feet in length, 17 feet in width, and 24 feet in height, was the largest single apartment within the inner temple. Its vaulted ceiling was decorated in the regular style with golden stars on a sky-blue background. Nothing remains of either the false door, which covered the bottom half of the west wall, or the low altar placed at its foot. The painted reliefs of the north, south, and east walls, although broken into hundreds of pieces, could be substantially reconstructed. On both the longer walls, the king was shown seated at a table laden with food.

This granite statue may represent Teti, first king of the VIth Dynasty. His pyramid at Saqqara, now sadly dilapidated, is chiefly important for its pyramid texts. A pit in the floor of the burial chamber once contained the Canopic chest holding the mummified entrails of the king.

Behind him stood his *ka*. In front of each table was a procession of about a hundred and twenty-five offering-bearers consisting of priests, provincial officials, courtiers, and other dignitaries who, by being included in these reliefs, were assured of an after-life in the service of the king. Among the offerings brought by the bearers were ducks, geese, wine, beer, fruit, bread, and vegetables. Cattle, antelopes, gazelles, and goats were led by ropes attached to their necks or front legs. Pigeons and quails were carried in cages. Above these reliefs was a deep frieze decorated with representations of provisions. This frieze was also continued on the east wall, where a scene of cattle being slaughtered took the place occupied on the north and south walls by offering-bearers.

In no other mortuary temple has it proved possible to reconstruct so much of the original decoration of the sanctuary or to see how completely it was devoted to the satisfaction of the physical requirements of the dead king. Every kind of sustenance was represented in the reliefs, so that if the priests omitted to provide daily supplies of fresh provisions on the altar he would not suffer from hunger or thirst; by the mere presence of the magic formula which accompanied the reliefs, the images would assume all the properties of their material counterparts. As a further precaution, wine and dried provisions may have been stored in a group of magazines lying to the north and connected by a passage with the sanctuary.

Before its excavation by Jéquier, a tumulus rising from the desert provided the only visible evidence of Pepi II's pyramid, which, like other pyramids of its time, had been built of small stones bonded with a mortar of Nile mud and held together by a heavy casing of Tura limestone. This method of construction had the great disadvantage that there was nothing to hinder the swift disintegration of the whole building when once a part of the outer casing had been removed. Originally, the pyramid measured about 258 feet square at the base, and its perpendicular height was approximately 171 feet; it was somewhat larger than any of its immediate predecessors. In one respect it was unique: a square girdle composed of masonry and cased with Tura limestone had been built around its entire base, broken only on the east side where the temple joined the face of the pyramid. This girdle, which measured about 21 feet in breadth, rose to the level of the second or perhaps the third course of the pyramid casing. Since it was laid directly against the casing, it follows that the girdle must have been added to the pyramid after the lower part, at least, had been completed. There is indeed every reason to believe that it was an addition to the original plan, for Jéquier discovered that the north, south, and west sides of the enclosure wall had been dismantled and subsequently rebuilt further from the pyramid, presumably in order to allow adequate space for the girdle. It is difficult to imagine why this addition was made, but it may have been necessitated by an earthquake, which had shaken the fabric of the building; the girdle would thus have been intended to increase its stability. A suggestion that the girdle might provide an explanation of the rectangular construction added to the base of the pyramid when it is used as a hieroglyph △ is hardly convincing, because the girdle is without any known parallel and its introduction in this instance seems to have been an afterthought, possibly dictated by an accident. It is far more probable that the hieroglyph represents a pyramid surrounded by its enclosure wall.

When dismantling a portion of the girdle lying outside the entrance to the pyramid, Jéquier discovered that some of the blocks in its structure were decorated with reliefs. As a rule, reliefs embodied in the inner cores of walls or buildings prove to be relics of earlier constructions which have been re-used, often after a lapse of many centuries. These reliefs, however, were undoubtedly of the same date as those in the mortuary temple near by, and the logical deduction seemed to be that they had once belonged to a building which had been pulled down when the girdle was added to the sides of the pyramid. The character of the building could be determined from the reliefs, which closely resembled those of the sanctuary in the inclusion of processions of officials bearing offerings to the king, seated at a table, and scenes of animals being slaughtered; the two buildings had evidently been designed for very similar purposes. Instances of offering-chapels standing at the entrance to the tomb are known from the pyramids of Unas and of Teti, while other examples dating from later periods have been found elsewhere. There can be little room for doubt, therefore, that Jéquier was right in his explanation that a chapel of the same kind had also been built at the entrance to this pyramid, but the addition of the girdle had necessitated its removal. Subsequently, it may have been replaced by an entirely new chapel, of which no trace has been preserved, or the plan may have been discarded.

All the pyramids of the VIth Dynasty were alike in the general design and arrangement of their internal apartments. The entrance corridor descended steeply for a short distance and then continued horizontally as far as a square vestibule lying between the serdab and the burial-chamber. At the beginning of the horizontal section, the corridor widened and also became higher, thus forming a kind of chamber. Within this chamber, in the Pyramid of Pepi II, Jéquier found some fragments of alabaster and diorite vases inscribed with the king's name and with the names of some of his predecessors. From an examination of these fragments, Jéquier concluded that the vases, which may have contained perfume, had been deliberately broken in the perform-ance of a funerary rite at the entrance to the tomb. The pyramid texts were carved on the walls of this chamber and on the whole of the remainder of the interior, with the exception of those parts of the corridor which were lined with granite, the serdab and the western end of the burial-chamber in the neighbourhood of the sarcophagus, where the walls were faced with alabaster decorated with the false door and panel design. Although less well preserved than the corresponding texts in the Pyramid of Unas, they were both more numerous and more highly developed.

Outside the enclosure wall of the king's pyramid lay three small pyramids belonging to the queens Udjebten, Iput, and Neit. A fourth queen named Ankhes-en-Pepi, whom he married in the latter part of his long reign and who survived him, was not buried in a pyramid. Each of the three pyramids possessed its own complex, which embodied in miniature the principal elements of the mortuary temple and pyramid enclosure of the king. The clearest example of their layout may be seen in the Pyramid of Neit. A narrow entrance in the south-east corner of the limestone enclosure wall gave access to a vestibule which in turn was connected with an open court surrounded on three sides by square columns. Both the vestibule and the court were decorated with reliefs which showed the queen either presenting offerings to various goddesses or receiving the homage of her family and attendants. A corridor led from the north-west corner of the court by way of a group of five magazines to the inner temple, which consisted of a long chamber or store-room, a small court with three statue-niches, and the sanctuary. Behind the long chamber and the niches lay a serdab constructed in the masonry of the building, and in that respect not unlike the serdab situated between the niches and the sanctuary in the king's temple.

Neit's pyramid, which measured approximately 79 feet square at the base and rose to a height of about 70 feet, was in all essential features only a replica of the king's pyramid on a reduced scale. In front of its entrance stood a small offering-chapel, the inner walls of which were partly adorned with reliefs showing the queen receiving provisions. An altar for the mortuary offerings rested at the foot of a false door, which formed the south wall of the chapel; since this door also covered the mouth of the pyramid corridor, it could not have been put into position until after the funeral. Inside the pyramid the side walls of the corridor, beyond a single portcullis of granite, were decorated with pyramid texts, which were continued in the burial-chamber except at its western end where the walls were faced with alabaster and ornamented with the false door and panel design. The granite sarco-phagus, when found, was empty and without a lid. By its side, sunk in the floor of the chamber, was a Canopic chest, carved of one block of the same material, which had once held four jars containing the viscera of the queen. Similar pits for Canopic chests were found in the burial-chambers of the pyramids of Djedkarē Isesi and Teti. At the opposite end of Neit's burial-chamber, a short passage led directly to the serdab without the intervening vestibule of the king's pyramid.

Perhaps the most interesting feature in each of the three complexes of the queens was the subsidiary pyramid situated near the south-east corner of the main pyramid. Subsidiary pyramids of the same kind in the complexes of the Vth and VIth Dynasty kings had been regarded by some Egyptologists as tombs of the royal consorts, on account of their resemblance to the subsidiary pyramids erected by Cheops and Mycerinus, which certainly bear every appearance of being royal tombs. This conjecture was rendered improbable, however, by the discovery that Pepi II, although incorporating the usual subsidiary pyramid in his own complex, had also built separate pyramids with independent complexes for his queens; it was conclusively disproved when it became known that each of the queen's complexes contained its subsidiary pyramid. The discovery of the Canopic chest in the burial-chamber of Neit's pyramid, moreover, showed that her subsidiary pyramid had not been used as a sepulchre for the viscera; the entire floor of its square chamber was strewn with fragments of pottery vessels and with three alabas-ter vases, one of which was inscribed with her name. While the full explana-tion of the function of subsidiary pyramids has yet to be found, it seems to have been thought, in this instance at least, that the pyramid imparted some particular efficacy to the contents of these vessels, since they could otherwise have been stored in the magazines.

In the small court outside Neit's subsidiary pyramid, Jéquier found sixteen wooden models of boats buried side by side in a shallow pit. Although instances of such models in Old Kingdom tombs are comparatively rare, they were often included in tombs of the Second Intermediate Period and Middle Kingdom as part of the furniture of the burial-chamber and were placed on the lid of the sarcophagus. The difference between the position allotted to the models in the two periods was probably not accidental, but was the result of an important distinction in their purpose. In the Middle Kingdom they were certainly designed for use by the dead person in the after-life, and it was therefore necessary that they should be preserved with the same care as the rest of the tomb equipment. The boats lying beneath the ground in the complex of Neit, on the other hand, were reproductions in miniature of the fleet employed in the funerals of kings for conveying the body to the valley building. Neit's pyramid, although built at a considerable distance from the valley, possessed neither a valley building nor a causeway, so that an approach to its precincts by water was not practicable. Nevertheless, the ceremony of transporting the body by boat had acquired such a degree of sanctity that it was thought necessary to provide a substitute for it by means of model craft. With the arrival of the body at the tomb their function had been fulfilled and they were buried in a simple pit, exposed to the ravages of ants and other destructive forces.

Pepi II appears to have been the last king of the Old Kingdom to build a pyramid complex of classic dimensions, although one of his successors, named Ibi, left an unfinished pyramid, which was no larger than the Pyramid of Neit and lacked the customary adjoining buildings. This decline did not result from any sudden change in religious ideas, but was the consequence of a cumulative loss of wealth and power on the part of the throne extending over a period of more than two hundred years. Even in the IVth Dynasty, kings had been accustomed to reward their courtiers not only with tombs, but with valuable tracts of land from the royal estates, the produce of which was intended to be used for supplying the tombs with provisions. Land so given was generally exempt from taxation, so that, in aggregate, the royal exchequer must have forfeited a very material part of its revenue. In the Vth and VIth Dynasties, moreover, the office of a nomarch, which had previously been conferred by the king for a limited period or for the lifetime of its holder, became hereditary, with the result that there soon grew up a generation of provincial nobles who were no longer conscious of owing their position to royal favour, but considered it as a right obtained in virtue of their birth. It is likely, however, that the full consequences of these developments did not become apparent until the end of the long reign of Pepi II, when his senility may also have brought about a diminution in the personal prestige formerly enjoyed by the king. Within a short time after his death, the country, possibly harassed in the north by an invasion of Asiatics, had disintegrated internally and had again split into independent principalities resembling those which Menes had conquered when uniting the Two Lands in the beginning of historical times.

To survey briefly the most distinctive artistic features of the Vth and VIth Dynasty pyramid complexes, the outstanding innovations are the plant-shaped granite columns and the great increase in the use of wall reliefs. Columns in the form of a single papyrus or lily flower had already been used by Zoser in the IIIrd Dynasty, but they were composed of limestone and were not free-standing. No comparable examples dating from the IVth Dynasty are known and Chephren's complex, if it may be regarded as representative, shows that the columns of the period, although made of granite, were rectangular and entirely without decoration. By the time of Pepi II the rectangular column had again returned to favour; it was, however, neither plain nor made of granite. In execution, reliefs of the Vth Dynasty are perhaps not equal to those of the IVth Dynasty, but they cover a far wider

Overleaf: Wall-reliefs from the tomb of Ti, a Vth Dynasty official, depict two men tying a bundle of corn in a net (*top*) and a recalcitrant ass (*bottom*).

range of subjects and are more lively in their expression. To that period belong some of the mastabas at Saqqara which are justly among the most celebrated for their reliefs, such as the tombs of Ti, Ptahhotep and Nefer. The VIth Dynasty also produced many magnificent examples of carving in relief – those in the complex of Pepi II and in the mastabas near Teti's pyramid being probably the best – but, in spite of possessing even greater liveliness and less regularity in form, the majority show an unmistakable deterioration in their technical qualities.

In contrast with the considerable quantity of reliefs found in the royal tombs of the Vth and VIth Dynasties, very few statues of the kings for whom the reliefs were made have come to light. There is no reason, however, to doubt that originally each temple housed at least the five statues in the niches, while other statues may have stood in the open courts. Those temples of the VIth Dynasty which were provided with serdabs seem also to have contained a number of statues hidden completely from view. The artistic quality of these lost sculptures may be conjectured not only from the few royal survivals, such as the colossal head of Userkaf discovered in his temple at Saqqara, but from the many statues of contemporary courtiers and officials which have been preserved in mastabas. Without doubt, the finest pieces date from the early part of the Vth Dynasty, when the lessons learnt from the sculptors who had carved the magnificent statues of Chephren and Mycerinus were still remembered. In the latter half of the Vth Dynasty and in the VIth Dynasty, the standard declined appreciably, but several pleasing specimens, including the alabaster figure of Pepi II as a child were produced.

Later Pyramids

FOLLOWING the close of the Old Kingdom, Egypt experienced one of the darkest periods in her long history. Not only was no attention paid to the development of arts and crafts, but most of the temples and tombs of the Pyramid Age, with their artistic masterpieces and untold treasures, were systematically pillaged and destroyed. According to Manetho, two dynasties of ephemeral rulers, namely the VIIth and VIIIth Dynasties, occupied the throne at Memphis, but their authority was only local, and complete anarchy prevailed throughout the greater part of the country. So great was the chaos that much of the land remained uncultivated; in a number of districts at least there was famine. At some time during the VIIIth Dynasty an attempt seems to have been made to restore order in the eight southernmost *nomes*, where a confederation was formed under the hegemony of the nomarch of Coptos. About forty years later, however, a nomarch of Herakleopolis Magna named Khety conquered the whole of Upper Egypt as far as the First Cataract at Aswan and became the founder of the IXth Dynasty (*c.* 2160). His kingdom extended northwards as far as Memphis, but may not have included the whole of the Delta, part of which was perhaps still under the control of Asiatic invaders.

Approximately a hundred years after Khety's conquest, Intef, the nomarch of Thebes, rebelled against the contemporary ruler in Herakleopolis and claimed for himself the title of King of Upper and Lower Egypt. A similar title was adopted by his two successors, both of whom were also named Intef, but it was an empty boast, for their dominion, although embracing the whole country as far as Aswan in the south, at no time extended beyond Abydos in the north. In spite of their limited realm, however, they were regarded in later times as the first three kings of the XIth Dynasty. The tombs of Intef I and Intef II were constructed at Thebes, on the western side of the river opposite Karnak in the district now called Dira Abu 'n-Naga. They were very similar in plan: each consisted of a large rectangular court, the floor sunk in the gravel of the plain and the back and sides hollowed out of the soft stone of the foothills. Doorways were cut in the face of the rock, those at the two sides leading to the tombs of courtiers and the row of about a dozen at the back being the entrances to the king's tomb. Viewed from the open front these doorways gave the courts the appearance of being colonnaded on three sides. It has generally been supposed that a brick pyramid was built either at the back of the court or on a ledge cut in the rock above the royal tomb. Mariette, who conducted excavations at this site in 1860, mentioned that the Pyramid of Intef II was about 49 feet square, but he omitted to describe its position and no trace of it or of the Pyramid of Intef I can now be seen. A recent survey by Dieter Arnold has indeed failed to find any evidence that either of these tombs was provided with a pyramid. The tomb of Intef III, which was probably constructed in the same locality as those of his two predecessors, has not yet been identified.

The three remaining kings of the XIth Dynasty were all named Mentuhotep, the first of whom – Neb-hepet-Rē Mentuhotep – was one of Egypt's greatest kings. Early in his reign of fifty-one years he recaptured Abydos, which his predecessor had lost, and then drove northwards to overcome his weaker rival in Herakleopolis and established himself as the undisputed ruler over all Egypt. If some reliefs which once decorated a chapel built by Neb-hepet-Rē Mentuhotep at Gebelein may be regarded as a record of historical events, he also conducted successful campaigns against the Nubians, Libyans, and Asiatics; evidence of such a kind, however, is not always reliable. Unlike Menes, whose achievements of a thousand years earlier he had in some degree emulated, he did not transfer his residence northwards, but continued to live at Thebes, which thus became, for the first time, the seat of government. Little exact information is available regarding his provincial administration; it seems likely, however, that the nomarchs, with perhaps a few exceptions, were again appointed by the king and that the right of hereditary succession was suppressed. The arts, after two and a half centuries of neglect, began to revive; a sculptor of the period named Irtisen has left an inscription, now in the Louvre, in which he makes the following claims: 'I was an artist skilled in my art, pre-eminent in my learning . . . I knew [how to represent] the movements of the image of a man and the carriage of a woman . . . the poising of the arm to bring the hippopotamus low and the movements of the runner. . . . No one succeeds in all this [task] but only I and the eldest son of my body.'

Sculpture was not the only branch of the arts which prospered under Neb-hepet-Rē Mentuhotep. Architecture too made remarkable progress, as is demonstrated by his singularly impressive funerary temple, which was excavated first by Edouard Naville and H. R. Hall on behalf of the Egypt Exploration Fund (1903–7) and subsequently by H. E. Winlock for the Metropolitan Museum of New York. Built at Thebes, in a deep bay in the cliffs on the west bank of the river in the region known as Deir el-Bahri, this temple embodied in its design many striking innovations. An unroofed causeway, nearly three-quarters of a mile in length and bounded at the sides by stone walls, led from the valley building at the edge of the cultivation across the desert to a large forecourt, surrounded on all sides except the west by high walls. Sandstone statues of the king, represented in the short, close-fitting garment usually worn by kings when performing the *heb-sed* ceremonies and holding in his hands the emblems of the god Osiris, were set at intervals of about 30 feet against the inner walls of the causeway. At the west end of the forecourt, a colonnade with two rows of square columns masked the eastern revetment of a broad terrace on which the temple was built. Among the painted reliefs which decorated the revetment were battle scenes depicting a campaign against the Asiatics, processions of foreign captives, companies of Egyptian soldiers armed with bows, and a fleet of ships. In front of the colonnade, planted in pits filled to a depth of 30 feet with a mixture of black soil and river sand, were rows of trees forming a kind of grove. All the trees were tamarisks with the exception of eight, arranged in two rows of four on the fringes of the avenue leading to the top of the terrace; these eight trees were sycamore figs and each shaded from the sun's rays a seated statue of the king.

The terrace, which was partly hewn out of rock and partly composed of masonry-filling, resembled an inverted T in shape, the cross-piece lying adjacent to the forecourt, and the stem being cut back into the face of the cliff. On the cross-piece stood a square building faced externally on all sides

The funerary temple of Neb-hepet-Rē Mentuhotep – a reconstruction

except the west by colonnades. Painted reliefs, of which only fragments have been preserved, adorned both the interior and exterior of its four walls. Rising from its centre was a pyramid mounted on a high rectangular podium; it was an absolutely solid structure, consisting of a rubble-core cased with dressed limestone and possessing neither corridors nor chambers. Between the podium and the walls of the building lay an ambulatory, the flat roof of which was supported by rows of octagonal columns, three rows on the north, south, and east sides and two rows on the west side. Beyond the square building, on the narrow section of the terrace, were situated a cloistered court and a hypostyle hall containing eighty octagonal columns arranged in ten rows. A small chapel built inside the hypostyle hall protected an altar and a statue of the king, placed within a niche carved out of the cliff.

Before deciding to build a funerary temple of such dimensions, Neb-hepet-Rē Mentuhotep had erected on the terrace a row of six cubical shrines made of limestone. Behind each shrine, and sunk to a considerable depth into the rock-bed, was a vertical shaft which led to a small burial-chamber lying approximately beneath the shrine. These tombs and shrines belonged to six ladies of the royal family, some of whom may have been queens and others princesses; all had died and been buried while the king still intended to confine his funerary temple to the front part of the terrace. The extension of the building westwards necessitated either the removal of the shrines – an operation which would certainly not have been undertaken without transferring the entire tombs elsewhere – or their incorporation into the new construction. The latter course was chosen and the shrines were embodied into the wall separating the square building with the pyramid from the cloistered court, three on each side of the doorway connecting these two parts of the temple. It was not an ideal solution because most of the reliefs decorating the exterior of the shrines were covered by the new wall, but, to the minds of the Egyptians, the existence of the reliefs was the first consideration; whether they were visible or invisible was less important. No disturbance of the tombs lying beneath the shrines was entailed by the extension of the temple; they had indeed gained in security, since the mouths of four out of the six shafts were now concealed beneath the paving, walls, or pillars of the cloistered court, while the two remaining shafts were also covered by a newly laid pavement. It must have been mainly due to the added protection and concealment thus afforded that all except two of these tombs had escaped being robbed more than once. Of their contents, the most valuable discoveries were undoubtedly the limestone outer sarcophagi of two of the queens named Kawit and Ashayet, both of which were decorated on their outer surfaces with beautifully carved reliefs. Among the scenes represented were incidents in the daily life of the queens, such as the performance of their toilet by a maid, drinking milk from cows which were shown accompanied by their calves, visiting a royal farm where peasants were engaged in filling the granaries with corn, and preparations for a banquet. Somewhat similar scenes were painted also on the interior of Ashayet's sarcophagus, but a band of painted inscription was the only decoration inside the sarcophagus of Kawit.

Neb-hepet-Rē Mentuhotep constructed within the temple both a cenotaph and a tomb. The entrance to the cenotaph lay at the bottom of a large pit sunk in the floor of the forecourt. From this entrance, a passage had been tunnelled for a distance of 155 yards through the subterranean rock to a point directly beneath the pyramid, where it terminated in a spacious chamber which, though it had never been opened before its excavation by Howard Carter in 1900, was found to contain nothing except the remains of offerings, a seated statue of the king wrapped in fine linen, and an empty wooden coffin. Under this chamber and connected with it by a vertical shaft was another room which yielded only a few pots and three roughly made wooden boats. To account for the existence of this cenotaph, it has been conjectured that it was used for a mock burial ceremony in the course of the *heb-sed*, which the king probably celebrated in the thirty-ninth year of his reign. Such an explanation would find support not only in the presence of the seated statue instead of the body of the king, but also in the attire of this statue, which represented the king wearing the *heb-sed* garment. The real tomb lay at the end of a tunnel even longer than that of the cenotaph. Starting in the cloistered court, it descended in a straight line under the hypostyle hall to a burial-chamber situated far beneath the cliff. This chamber, which was lined with granite, contained a shrine made of alabaster and granite, within which, it must be supposed, a painted wooden coffin holding the mummy of the king was placed. When it was opened by the excavators, the only objects discovered in the chamber, apart from the shrine, were two small boats, some broken sceptres, canes, and bows. Neither the mummy nor the coffin was found.

Ten nearly identical limestone statues of Sesostris I were found near his mortuary temple at Lisht and it is thought that twenty-four may once have existed, all of which must have been carved by a master sculptor.

No exact replica of the funerary temple of Neb-hepet-Rē Mentuhotep was ever built. His successor, Seankh-ka-Rē Mentuhotep, began to prepare a site for a similar building not far south of Deir el-Bahri, but, having ascended the throne at a ripe age, he died before the preparations for its construction had advanced beyond the initial stages, and further work was abandoned. Five hundred years later, however, a famous queen of the XVIIIth Dynasty named Hatshepsut instructed her architect, Senenmut, to build for her a mortuary temple embodying the chief architectural features of the temple of Neb-hepet-Rē Mentuhotep. In fulfilment of her command, Senenmut designed the larger and more magnificent terraced temple which stands on the north side of the ruins of Mentuhotep's building and which has justly become one of the most celebrated monuments of Egypt.

Very soon after the death of Seankh-ka-Rē Mentuhotep, the country was once again in confusion. Another Mentuhotep, who bore the name Neb-tawi-Rē, occupied the throne for part of the seven years which elapsed before order was restored, but, for reasons which are still obscure, later records do not credit him with having been a legitimate ruler. His successor was his Vizier and Commander-in-Chief, Amenemhat, now generally called Am-menemes, the Greek form of his name, who thus became the founder of the XIIth Dynasty – a dynasty composed of four kings named Ammenemes,

The pyramid enclosure of Sesostris I

1. entrance hall
2. cloistered court
3. inner temple with five statue-niches
4. sanctuary
5. offering chapel and entrance to pyramid
6. subsidiary pyramid

The nine small pyramids between the inner and outer enclosure walls belonged to female members of the royal family.

three kings named Sesostris and a queen named Sebekneferu. It was one of the greatest dynasties in Egypt's history. The name of the founder, which means literally 'Amun-is-at-the-head', shows that he was born in Thebes where the god Amun was already established; his forebears, however, may have lived in El-Eshmunein, the earlier home of this god. He did not follow the example of the kings of the XIth Dynasty by making Thebes his capital, but, profiting from their experience and perhaps from his knowledge of the difficulty which they had found in maintaining control over Lower Egypt from such a distance, he transferred his seat of government northwards and established it at a place called It-tawi, 'Seizer of the Two Lands'. The exact location of It-tawi has not been determined with certainty, but it must have been situated in the vicinity of Lisht, where the tombs of both Ammenemes I and Sesostris I, his successor, have been found.

Influenced by the funerary monuments of the Old Kingdom, some of which could be seen from Lisht, Ammenemes I constructed his tomb on a plan conforming in its main features with the standard pyramid complex. In one respect, however, its design resembled that of the Deir el-Bahri temple of Neb-hepet-Rē Mentuhotep: it was erected on rising ground with its buildings on two different levels. On the upper terrace stood the pyramid, surrounded by a stone wall. West of the pyramid, also on the terrace but outside the stone wall, lay a row of tombs belonging to members of the royal family, all of which were found, when excavated in 1920 by an expedition of the Metropolitan Museum, to have been robbed in antiquity of their entire contents. On the lower and smaller terrace east of the pyramid stood a mortuary temple, near which, to the north and south, were the tombs of a few particularly favoured courtiers. Both the terraces and the adjacent tombs were enclosed by a rectangular wall of brick. Outside this wall lay a cemetery containing the mastabas of about a hundred nobles and officials.

When constructing the inner core of his pyramid and the walls of the mortuary temple, Ammenemes I employed a large number of limestone blocks taken from the Old Kingdom tombs at Dahshur, Saqqara, and Giza. Many of these blocks had been decorated with reliefs or inscribed with texts and, since it is likely that the buildings to which they originally belonged were already falling into ruin when the blocks were removed, their re-use has preserved a number of interesting fragments of sculpture which might otherwise have been lost. In consequence, however, of the complete desolation to which this pyramid and its complex had been reduced by the time of their excavation, it was sometimes difficult to distinguish the re-used Old Kingdom blocks from those which had been prepared in the XIIth Dynasty for the decoration of this temple. The difference in style, which might have been expected between reliefs of the two periods, was not always very marked, because Ammenemes I deliberately reproduced some of the technical characteristics of Old Kingdom reliefs and occasionally made actual facsimiles of scenes from Old Kingdom tombs.

The entrance to this pyramid occupied its normal position on ground-level in the middle of the north face. In front stood an offering-chapel of the kind found in the pyramids of Teti and Pepi II with a red granite false door, 11 feet 6 inches in height, built into the back wall. Behind the false door lay a granite-lined corridor leading towards the burial-chamber. Enormous plugs of granite were used for blocking this corridor after the king's funeral. Very little is known about the internal arrangement of the pyramid apart from the corridor because, owing to a considerable rise in the level of the Nile bed, the burial-chamber is now permanently flooded and the seepage of water is so rapid that all efforts to reach it have hitherto failed.

Sesostris I built his pyramid at a distance of about a mile to the south of the pyramid of his predecessor. Its ownership was first determined in 1882 by Sir Gaston Maspero, who found some fragments of alabaster objects bearing the name of Sesostris I inside the pyramid. Twelve years later, J.-E. Gautier and Gustave Jéquier excavated a considerable part of the site, and the remainder, together with the surrounding cemetery, was cleared by successive expeditions of the Metropolitan Museum, working intermittently from 1908 to 1934 under the direction of A. M. Lythgoe, A. C. Mace, and Ambrose Lansing. Fundamentally, it resembled closely the complex of Ammenemes I. Whereas only the general outline of the latter can be ascertained with certainty, however, the greater part of the original plan of Sesostris I's complex has been established, and the extent to which its mortuary temple was copied from the mortuary temples of the VIth Dynasty, as illustrated by that of Pepi II, is clearly evident.

A corridor 8 feet wide, built on top of the causeway, linked the valley building – scarcely a trace of which was discovered – with the entrance hall of the mortuary temple. Above a dado stippled red and black in imitation of granite, the limestone walls were decorated with scenes of a conventional kind. At intervals of about 33 feet on both sides of the corridor were statues of the king represented as the god Osiris, each one standing in a recess. Similar statues, six of which were discovered in a pit near the pyramid, originally stood against the walls of the entrance hall, thus emphasizing that this apartment was essentially a continuation of the corridor on the causeway. In the cloistered court there were also statues of the king, probably one against each of the twenty-four rectangular pillars supporting the roof of the ambulatory. Ten of the number, made of the finest Tura limestone, were found by Gautier and Jéquier lying side by side in a pit where they had been concealed in antiquity, like the Osiride figures, by someone who was anxious to preserve them from impending destruction. Although displaying slight differences in facial expression, they are really duplicates, each statue being a life-size representation of the king seated on his throne and wearing the customary regal attire. Other statues, no doubt representing the king standing, were placed behind the wooden doors of the five niches within the inner temple. The remainder of the inner temple contained only the usual magazines, antechambers, and the sanctuary; no serdab for a further group of statues seems to have been constructed in the masonry between the niches and the sanctuary. Two remarkable wooden portrait figures of the king, each about 2 feet in height, were however found in 1914 by the expedition of the Metropolitan Museum concealed in a small chamber which had been constructed in the thickness of the enclosure wall of a mastaba lying north of the causeway and close to the east wall of the pyramid enclosure. The mastaba belonged to a high official of the court named Imhotep, who, like his more famous namesake, was also a High Priest of Heliopolis. It is difficult to imagine why the figures, which were probably part of the funerary equipment of the king, should have been placed in this position and not in the pyramid itself. With them in the chamber was a wooden shrine containing the fetish of the god Anubis – the skin of a headless animal wrapped like a mummy and suspended on a rod mounted in an

The head of Pepi I, a detail from a life-size copper statue which has suffered from oxidation, appears to have been made by hammering the metal over a wooden core, although some casting may also have been employed. This statue and a much smaller one of Merenrē are the only surviving examples of VIth Dynasty royal sculpture in copper.

alabaster jar of ointment. Both the figures, each of which was made of sixteen pieces of cedar wood carefully joined, show the king clad in a short kilt and holding in the left hand a long sceptre in the shape of a shepherd's crook. The only significant difference between them is the white crown of Upper Egypt worn in one and the red crown of Lower Egypt worn in the other.

The arrangement of the enclosure walls in this complex was almost identical with the plan of the walls in the complex of Ammenemes I. An inner wall of stone, decorated at regular intervals with panels, about 14 feet in height, and inscribed with the king's names, enclosed the pyramid, the inner apartments of the mortuary temple and the subsidiary pyramid. Between this wall and a mud-brick outer wall lay a wide court in which were situated the cloistered court and the entrance hall of the mortuary temple and nine small pyramids belonging to female members of the royal family. Inscriptions found in the easternmost pyramid in the southern row and in its immediate neighbour to the west enabled their owners to be identified respectively as the principal queen, Neferu, and a princess named Itakayt. Each of these nine pyramids was provided with its own miniature mortuary temple, offering-chapel, and enclosure wall. Beneath the floor of the offering chapel, a shaft was sunk vertically downwards to a considerable depth. A second shaft of the same kind was constructed, usually at a short distance to the east of the first, and was connected with it by a subterranean passage. It is not easy to account for the presence of the second shaft, but it may have been intended to enable the sarcophagus to be introduced at a stage in the construction of the tomb when the small offering-chapel had already been built. The body and probably the wooden inner coffin would be lowered down the first shaft and thence conveyed to the burial-chamber by way of a corridor which was subsequently blocked at intervals by portcullises sliding to the side.

In the burial-chamber of one of the small pyramids lying at the western end of the southern row, the excavators of the Metropolitan Museum found a fine, but empty, quartzite sarcophagus. So closely did it fit the chamber that the ancient plunderers, when searching for hidden treasure, had been compelled to break through its sides and floor in order to reach the walls of the chamber; their destructive work, however, appears to have yielded no reward. A Canopic chest, composed of the same material as the sarcophagus and made with equal care, lay in a niche in the south-east corner of the burial-chamber. Neither the sarcophagus nor the Canopic chest bore any inscription by which the name or title of the royal owner could be identified.

The king's pyramid occupied an area of approximately 352 feet square and rose to a height of about 200 feet. Its superstructure consisted of a framework of eight massive stone walls radiating from the centre outwards to the four corners and to the middle of each side. The eight compartments so formed were further divided into two sections of unequal size by walls built parallel to the sides and about half-way between them and the centre. These sixteen compartments were filled with rough pieces of limestone laid in white sand, the whole mass being held together by a heavy casing of well-cut blocks of Tura limestone. The entrance was not in the face of the super-structure, but under the paving of the offering-chapel. From there a corridor, which measured only 3 feet 1 inch square in section, sloped downwards in the direction of the burial-chamber. For a distance of about 36 feet it was

Pepi II ascended the throne very young and died a centenarian, possibly having reigned for ninety-four years. This alabaster statuette portrays him as a child.

lined with slabs of dressed limestone, but beyond that point the lining was
composed of granite. Although the body and the inner coffin were probably
taken to the burial-chamber by way of this corridor, it seems unlikely, in
view of its small dimensions, that the outer sarcophagus was similarly
conveyed. Perhaps it was taken by a separate shaft which may still lie
concealed beneath the ruins of the superstructure. Nothing is known
about the burial-chamber which, like its counterpart in the Pyramid of
Ammenemes I, is now under water.

Three of the four successors of Sesostris I built pyramid complexes at
Dahshur, on the edge of the cultivation east of the two pyramids built during
the Old Kingdom. The earliest of these complexes, which belonged to
Ammenemes II, embodied no important innovations in design or in
method of construction. It acquired, however, a particular distinction at
the end of the last century as the provenance of part of the so-called 'Dahshur
treasure' – a remarkable collection of jewellery and personal accoutrements
discovered by J. de Morgan and now preserved in the Cairo Museum. The
owners of this part of the treasure were two princesses named Khnumet and
Ita, whose graves were included among the group of royal tombs lying close
to the king's pyramid on the west side. In technical skill and artistic taste
the whole treasure demonstrates the work of the Egyptian goldsmith and
lapidary at the highest stage of its development.

Sesostris II, who succeeded Ammenemes II, discarded the most persistent
of all the conventions of pyramid architecture, namely the location of the
entrance on the north side. The supposed advantages of an entrance corridor oriented towards the circumpolar stars must, therefore, have counted
for less in his eyes than the increased security likely to result from an
approach starting in a more unexpected quarter. It certainly added to the
difficulties of the archaeologist, for Petrie, who excavated his pyramid –
situated at Illahun on the edge of the Faiyum – worked for some months in
1887–8 without being able to find a way inside. After a considerable expenditure of time and labour in the following year, he succeeded in discovering
to the south of the pyramid a shaft which descended vertically to a passage
tunnelled at a depth of 40 feet below the ground and leading by a devious
course to a burial-chamber built entirely of granite. Subsequently he found,
still further south, a second and larger shaft which also descended to the
passage. By this shaft, as Petrie observed, the magnificent red granite
sarcophagus found in the burial-chamber must have been lowered to the
passage, because the first shaft was about 1 foot 7 inches narrower than the
width of the sarcophagus. Commenting on the workmanship of this
sarcophagus, Petrie declared that it was one of the finest pieces of mechanical
work ever executed in such hard and difficult material. The parallelism,
according to his calculations, was almost perfect, and the errors in regularity
amounted to no more than one hundredth of an inch in a cubit. Apart from
the sarcophagus, the chamber contained an offering-table made of alabaster.

In its superstructure also, the Pyramid of Sesostris II differed in many
respects from its predecessors. To a height of 40 feet from the ground, the
inner core consisted of a knoll of rock; above that level, in place of rock, there
was a framework of retaining walls with the intervening spaces filled with
mud-bricks. This core was cased in the normal manner with blocks of fine
limestone, the lowest course being embedded in the rock foundation to
counter the outward thrust of the structure. Around the base on each side lay

This dark grey granite statue of Sesostris III is one of six which were found in the temple of Mentuhotep at Deir el-Bahri.

a shallow trench filled with sand, the purpose of which was to absorb rain
water flowing off the face of the pyramid. Such a trench, Petrie estimated,
could easily hold the volume of water resulting from the heaviest downpour
likely to occur in Egypt. Two walls encompassed the pyramid, one of stone
bordering the trench and one of brick standing further back. Beyond the
outer wall was a single row of trees planted in pits which had been sunk
in the rock and filled with earth.

Between the two enclosure walls on the south side of the pyramid lay
four shaft-tombs made for members of the royal family. When excavating
the easternmost of these tombs in 1913, Petrie and his assistant, Guy Brunton, discovered a collection of jewellery and personal possessions belonging
to a princess named Sat-Hathor-Iunut, the owner of the tomb. It was a
collection which rivalled in every respect that previously found at Dahshur.
Among the most important pieces were a magnificent gold diadem, two
gold pectorals inlaid with glass and precious stones, one bearing the name of
Sesostris II and the other the name of Ammenemes III, necklaces consisting
of beads made of gold, amethyst, carnelian, lapis lazuli and felspar, a gold
collar composed of beads in the shape of double lion heads, bead girdles of
gold and precious stones, bracelets, and rings. Toilet objects included
razors with copper blades and gold handles, alabaster vases for unguents
and cosmetics, other vases designed for the same purpose but made of
polished obsidian partly overlaid with gold, and a silver mirror with a handle
of obsidian and gold. The whole collection had originally been placed in three
ebony caskets, at least one of which was inlaid with gold, ivory, carnelian,
and blue faience. All these objects, with the exception of a small number retained by the Cairo Museum, are now in the Metropolitan Museum of Art,
New York.

Sesostris III and Ammenemes III, whose pyramids at Dahshur lie to the
north and south respectively of the Pyramid of Ammenemes II, followed
the example set by Sesostris II, both in the employment of brick for the
inner core of the superstructure and in the elaboration of the substructure
into a kind of maze of chambers and corridors. In the same way also the
entrance to the substructure was not placed on the north side, but at a point
outside the body of the pyramid, which could only be discovered either by
chance or by exhaustive search, with the result that J. de Morgan, when
excavating these pyramids in 1894–5, spent many months of fruitless labour
before finding a way to the burial-chamber. Ultimately he located the
entrance to Sesostris III's pyramid in the court on the west side of the building, and the entrance to the Pyramid of Ammenemes III in a similar
position opposite the southern corner of the east face. In spite of this
subterfuge, the architects of the pyramids had failed to defeat the ancient
plunderer, and de Morgan reaped only a meagre reward for his efforts. He
was, however, more fortunate when excavating the tombs of the royal family
on the north side of each pyramid, finding in the tombs of the princesses
Sat-Hathor and Merit (in the enclosure of Sesostris III) and in the tomb
of the princess Nubhotep (in the enclosure of Ammenemes III) jewellery of
the same character as the treasure buried with the princesses of Ammenemes
II and Sesostris II. Like the earlier treasures also, this jewellery had not been
laid on the mummies of the princesses, but had been concealed in a separate
place within the tomb – a fact which has given rise to the theory that a
different, and possibly inferior, set of jewellery was prepared specifically for

Jewellery which belonged
to Princess Sat-Hathor-
Iunut includes a
collar with double
lion-head beads, an
amethyst necklace with
gold claw-pendants (*top*)
and a diadem of gold.

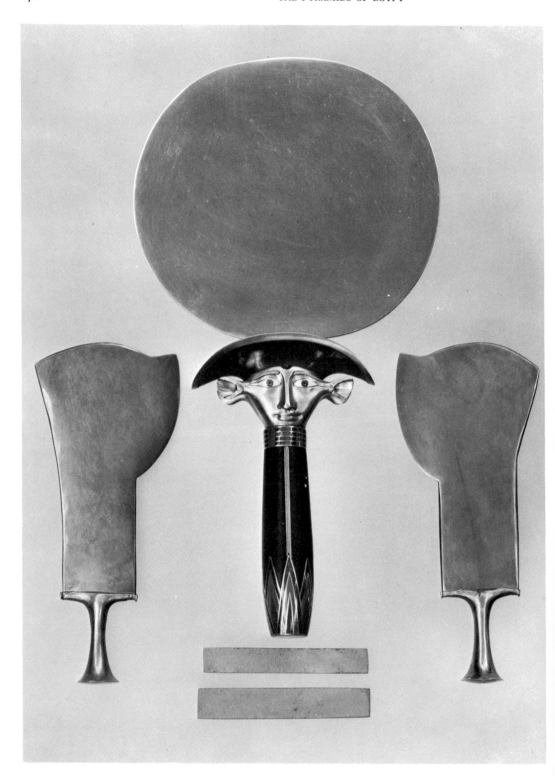

each mummy, while the jewellery found consisted of the objects actually worn by the princesses in their lifetime. Another interesting discovery by de Morgan, south of the enclosure wall of the Pyramid of Sesostris III, was an underground chamber containing two wooden boats. No emblems of a solar nature were buried with the boats and consequently it seems more likely that they were used to convey the body of the king and some of his personal possessions to the pyramid than that they were intended to represent the day- and night-barques of the Sun-god.

Reigning for at least forty-six years, Ammenemes III ranks as one of the outstanding monarchs of Egyptian history. His fame rests not on military achievements or administrative prowess – though a more complete knowledge of the political and social conditions of his time might well reveal that in these respects also he deserved recognition from posterity – but on the works of art and monumental constructions, including two pyramids, with which his name has been associated. Undoubtedly, the surviving portraits of this king are among the finest pieces of sculpture ever produced by the ancient Egyptians; they mark the culmination of the renascence in the arts which originated in the time of Neb-hepet-Rē Mentuhotep and continued to develop without noticeable interruption until the end of the XIIth Dynasty. But long before excavation had brought to light any of these sculptural masterpieces, Ammenemes III had been immortalized by the classical historians as the constructor of Lake Moeris in the Faiyum and as the builder of a labyrinth in the neighbourhood of the lake, which was considered to bear comparison with the older labyrinth of Minos at Knossos in Crete. Diodorus, who visited Egypt in the middle of the first century before the Christian era, describes the lake in the following terms:

'Moeris . . . dug a lake of remarkable usefulness, though at the cost of incredible toil. Its circumference, they say, is 3,600 stades, its depth at most points fifty fathoms. Who, then, on estimating the greatness of the construction, would not reasonably ask how many tens of thousands of men must have been employed, and how many years they took to finish their work? No one can adequately commend the king's design, which brings such usefulness and advantage to all the dwellers in Egypt.

'Since the Nile kept to no definite bounds in its rising, and the fruitfulness of the country depended upon the river's regularity, the king dug the lake to accommodate the superfluous water, so that the river should neither, with its strong current, flood the land unseasonably and form swamps and fens, nor, by rising less than was advantageous, damage the crops by lack of water. Between the river and the lake he constructed a canal 80 stades in length and 300 feet in breadth. Through this canal, at times he admitted the water of the river, at other times he excluded it, thus providing the farmers with water at fitting times by opening the inlet and again closing it scientifically and at great expense. No less than 50 talents had of necessity to be expended by anyone who wished to open or shut this sluice. The lake has continued to serve the needs of the Egyptians down to our own days, and it has its name from its constructor, being still called the Lake of Moeris.'[1]

Personal possessions found buried with Princess Sat-Hathor-Iunut include razors, a silver mirror with a handle of gold and obsidian, and two whetstones.

Although Ammenemes III may well have undertaken some irrigation or land-reclamation schemes in the neighbourhood of this lake, Diodorus and the classical writers were probably mistaken in ascribing its actual creation to him, for it was almost certainly in existence before his time, and its name was undoubtedly derived not from his pre-nomen – possibly pronounced

Nemare – which was known to the Greeks colloquially as Mares, but from a town on the lake called Mi-wer (possibly identical with the modern Ghurab) or from the canal linking the Nile with the lake, which was also called Mi-wer.

Happily, Ammenemes III's connection with the labyrinth has been proved to be based on a firmer historical foundation, as Petrie was able to show in 1888–9 when he excavated this king's second pyramid at Hawara and discovered that its mortuary temple was, in fact, designed as a kind of labyrinth. It was a large construction, covering an area of about 1,000 feet in length and 800 feet in breadth. In plan, it differed from every other known mortuary temple, consisting not of a series of courts and corridors leading to a sanctuary, but of a large number of separate courts arranged in rows. Few architectural details could, however, be recognized by Petrie, so complete had been its destruction. Some conception of its former appearance may be gained from Strabo's description, written at about the beginning of the Christian era:

'We have here [besides Lake Moeris] also the labyrinth, a work equal to the pyramids, and adjoining to it the tomb of the king who constructed the labyrinth. After proceeding beyond the first entrance of the canal about 30 or 40 stadia, there is a table-shaped plain, with a village and a large palace composed of as many palaces as there were formerly *nomes*. There are an equal number of aulae, surrounded by pillars, and contiguous to one another, all in one line and forming one building, like a long wall having the aulae in front of it. The entrances into the aulae are opposite to the wall. In front of the entrances there are long and numerous covered ways, with winding passages communicating with each other, so that no stranger could find his way into the aulae or out of them without a guide. The [most] surprising circumstance is that the roofs of these dwellings consist of a single stone each, and that the covered ways through their whole range were roofed in the same manner with single slabs of stone of extraordinary size, without the intermixture of timber or of any other material. On ascending the roof – which is not of a great height, for it consists only of a single storey – there may be seen a stone-field, thus composed of stones. Descending again and looking into the aulae, these may be seen in a line supported by twenty-seven pillars, each consisting of a single stone. The walls also are constructed of stones not inferior in size to these.

'At the end of this building, which occupies more than a stadium, is the tomb, which is a quadrangular pyramid, each side of which is about four plethra in length and of equal height. The name of the person buried there is Imandes. They built, it is said, this number of aulae, because it was the custom for all the *nomes* to assemble there together according to their rank, with their own priests and priestesses, for the purpose of performing sacrifices and making offerings to the gods, and of administering justice in matters of great importance. Each of the *nomes* was conducted to the aula appointed for it.'[2]

The pyramid to which Strabo refers stood on the north side of the labyrinth. Its superstructure, in keeping with the practice of its time, was composed mainly of mūd-brick overlaid with a casing of limestone. In its substructure, the intricacies of design already embodied in its immediate precursors were further developed, with the result that Petrie was able to force a way into its passages only after weeks of toil extending over two seasons. From the entrance, situated about 80 feet west of the middle of the

The paint is well preserved on this statue of Mentuhotep which had been carefully wrapped in fine linen and placed for safe-keeping in a cenotaph in his funerary temple at Deir el-Bahri. Mentuhotep is wearing the costume of the *sed* festival.

Overleaf: Hatshepsut, the famous XVIIIth Dynasty Queen, so admired the mortuary temple of Mentuhotep that she ordered her architect, Senenmut, to build one for her based on it. The result was the magnificent building which can be seen on the right. Mentuhotep's smaller temple, reduced to ruins, is on the left. Beyond the cliff lies the Valley of the Kings.

south face, a flight of steps descended to a small chamber, beyond which lay a short passage leading to a dead end. Concealed in the roof of this passage, was a block of stone 20 tons in weight which slid sideways, thus forming a trap-door through which access could be gained to a second chamber and to the passages lying beyond. One of these passages was intended solely to delude any plunderer who might succeed in penetrating past the first trap-door, for although it had been carefully blocked, it was blind. The other passage, which had been closed only by a wooden door, led by way of two right-angle turns and two further roof trap-doors – neither of which had been closed after the funeral – to a large antechamber. At each end of the antechamber, a false well had been sunk into the floor and subsequently blocked with stone so that plunderers, labouring under the delusion that the entrance to the burial-chamber lay beneath, might be tricked into wasting time and effort in removing the filling. Another stratagem intended for the same purpose was the blocking of the entire northern half of the ante-chamber, although nothing but a solid wall was concealed behind.

In order that the real way of approach to the burial-chamber should be intelligible, it is necessary first to describe the method by which this chamber was constructed. Before the superstructure was built, a large rectangular shaft was sunk into the rock at a point somewhat to the west of the centre of the area ultimately to be covered by the base of the pyramid. Into this shaft, after it had been lined with stone, the burial-chamber, composed of a single block of yellow quartzite and shaped like a box without a lid, was lowered. The length and breadth of this monolith, Petrie calculated, were about 22 feet and 8 feet respectively and the height was about 6 feet; its weight must have amounted to about 110 tons. Notwithstanding the hardness of the material, it was exquisitely cut and polished, while the inner corners were so sharp that, at first sight, Petrie supposed them to be jointed. The roof of the chamber consisted of three slabs of yellow quartzite lying side by side, each measuring about 4 feet in thickness.

These slabs did not rest directly on the walls of the monolith, but were laid on a course of stone blocks placed on top of the walls in order to heighten the ceiling of the room. Above the burial-chamber were two relieving chambers, the lower with a flat roof, and the upper with a pointed roof composed of limestone blocks, each weighing nearly 50 tons. Lastly, an enormous arch of brick, 3 feet thick, was built over the pointed roof to support the core of the pyramid.

Until the tomb had been finally closed, the roof-slab which lay nearest to the antechamber was propped up, leaving a gap between it and the course of blocks on which it was ultimately to rest. A cross-trench in the floor of the antechamber led directly to this gap. The king's mummy was, therefore, taken by way of this trench to the gap and then let down into the burial chamber, where a large quartzite sarcophagus had already been placed in position before the roof-slabs were lowered into the shaft. A second, smaller sarcophagus, made of the same material and intended for the princess Neferu-Ptah, had been built into the chamber, probably at the same time. Canopic chests, also made of quartzite, were included with the sarcophagi. After the funerary ceremonies had been completed, the raised roof-slab of the burial-chamber weighing about 45 tons was lowered and the trench in the antechamber filled and covered with a pavement, so that no outward sign of its existence remained. In spite of all the precautions taken, however, this

Elaborate gold jewellery inlaid with amethyst, carnelian, felspar and lapis lazuli was worn by ancient Egyptian princesses. The top pectoral was found in the tomb of Merit at Dahshur while the one at the bottom, which bears the name of Ammenemes III, is from the tomb of Sat-Hathor-Iunut at Illahun.

N

The Pyramid of Ammenemes III
at Hawara

1. entrance and flight of steps
2. small chamber and dead-end
passage with trap-door
3. second chamber
4. and 5. two further trap-doors
6. antechamber
7. burial-chamber

pyramid suffered the same fate as all its predecessors, and Petrie, when at length he succeeded in reaching the burial-chamber, found that all the movable objects had been plundered and the bodies, together with the wooden inner coffins, had been burnt.

Nothing is known about the circumstances which led Ammenemes III to build two pyramids. Since only one pyramid could have been his tomb, the second – presumably that of Dahshur – must have been left empty. Sesostris III may also have constructed, besides his pyramid at Dahshur, a cenotaph of mastaba form at Abydos, thus providing his soul with a second tomb, which it could occupy when so inclined, near the traditional tomb of Osiris. Religious motives could hardly have governed the choice of either Dahshur or Hawara, and therefore it can only be assumed that Ammenemes decided to replace his first tomb at Dahshur by the more elaborate pyramid and mortuary temple at Hawara.

With the death of Ammenemes III, the Middle Kingdom virtually came to an end. A fourth Ammenemes and a queen named Sebekneferu (or Sebekneferurē) figure at the end of the XIIth Dynasty in the later historical records, but the evidence of contemporary inscriptions suggests that Ammenemes IV never reigned independently; he was probably co-regent with Ammenemes III – a position sometimes occupied by the heir apparent when the reigning king became advanced in years – and was deprived of his succession to the full title by premature death. Sebekneferu was subsequently appointed co-regent, and she may well have continued as the sole occupant of the throne for a short time after the demise of Ammenemes III. Neither Ammenemes IV nor Sebekneferu has left a pyramid which can be identified from written evidence, but E. Mackay, when working under Petrie in 1910–11, found at Mazghuna – about three miles south of Dahshur – the remains of two ruined pyramids which resembled more closely in plan the Hawara Pyramid of Ammenemes III than any other pyramid at that time known. Some technical improvements in the devices for sealing the Maz-

The burial-chamber of Ammenemes III at Hawara

1. three roof-slabs of yellow quartzite

2. stone blocks placed on top of the walls to heighten the room

3. lower relieving chamber

4. upper relieving chamber

5. arch of brick 3 feet thick

ghuna pyramids indicated that they were later than the Pyramid of Hawara, and Mackay therefore ascribed one to Ammenemes IV and the other to Queen Sebekneferu, without attempting to identify the actual owner of each pyramid more precisely. If more recent discoveries have shown that Mackay failed to understand fully an important innovation in the method of closing the sarcophagus chamber, which is not otherwise known to have been employed before the next dynasty, it does not necessarily follow that his deduction regarding the ownership of the pyramids was incorrect. This innovation, which will be described later in this chapter, may have been introduced at the end of the XIIth Dynasty.

During the two centuries occupied by the XIIIth–XVIIth Dynasties, Egypt passed through the second dark period in her dynastic history. Ruled by a succession of weak and ephemeral kings, the country gradually lapsed into a state of anarchy only comparable with the disorder which followed the end of the Old Kingdom. By an unfortunate chance, this period of chaos coincided with a vast ethnic movement which affected the whole of western Asia and ultimately reached Egypt. At about the end of the XIIIth Dynasty or the beginning of the XIVth Dynasty, a host of Asiatics, the majority of whom were probably Semites, invaded the country, bringing with them a weapon of which the Egyptians had previously had no experience. These invaders were known as the Hyksos – a name which Manetho explained as meaning 'Shepherd Kings', but which probably means 'Rulers of Foreign Countries' – and their new weapon was the horse-drawn chariot.

The Pyramid of Khendjer, plan

1. rectangular well with walls of brick constructed outside entrance

2. passage ending in a blank wall

3. portcullis

4. and 5. corridors leading to the shafts

6. burial chamber

7. subsidiary pyramid

N

With the help of this weapon, their army gained not only in quality of arms, but also in power of manoeuvre. Having overcome whatever resistance they may have encountered, the Hyksos established their capital at Avaris, the site of which has not yet been located with certainty; it lay in the north-east of the Delta and may have been identical with the city later known as Tanis – the Zoan of the Old Testament. From there they governed the whole of the Delta and Middle Egypt at least as far as Cusae, which lay about thirty miles north of Asyut. Further south, a native Egyptian dynasty continued to rule at Thebes, but probably only as vassals rendering tribute to their Hyksos overlords. At length however, one of these vassals named Kamose, possibly the last king of the XVIIth Dynasty, revolted and drove the Hyksos out of Middle Egypt, and may even have recovered Memphis. The complete expulsion of these foreign oppressors followed in the beginning of the sixteenth century BC when Amosis I, the founder of the XVIIIth Dynasty, captured Avaris and pursued the invaders back into southern Palestine.

Royal funerary monuments dating from the so-called Second Intermediate Period (i.e. the XIIIth–XVIIth Dynasties) are rare – a fact which is no doubt partly to be explained by the unsettled political conditions of that time. Nevertheless, the ruined remains of three pyramids belonging to kings of the XIIIth Dynasty have been found. One of these pyramids, each side of which measured about 165 feet at the base, was partly excavated in 1957 at Dahshur. Its owner, whose sarcophagus and Canopic jars were found in the tomb-chamber, was a king named, surprisingly, Ameny the Asiatic (Ameny-Aamu). The two other pyramids, both of which were excavated by Jéquier between the years 1929 and 1931, are situated in the neighbourhood of the *Mastabat Fara'un* at Saqqara. The builder of the earlier of these two pyramids bore the name Khendjer, but the owner of the second, which was probably never finished, has not been identified. Both pyramids demonstrate in plan and execution a further elaboration of the devices intended to render them impregnable, the development of which was certainly the main preoccupation of the architects of the pyramids of the Middle Kingdom.

Khendjer's pyramid, from which its neighbour differs only in detail, consisted of an inner core of brick measuring about 140 feet square at the base and an outer casing of Tura limestone, approximately 15 feet in thickness, of which almost nothing has been preserved. The entrance to the substructure lay beneath the outer casing on the west side. In order that sufficient space should be available for manoeuvring the coffin and other large pieces of funerary equipment, a rectangular well with walls of brick was constructed outside the entrance. After the funeral the well was filled with rubble and paved with slabs of limestone so that, in appearance, the surface was indistinguishable from the rest of the corridor between the pyramid and the inner enclosure wall. From the entrance a ramp with fourteen shallow steps leads downwards to a short horizontal passage ending in a blank wall. At this point a large rectangular portcullis of quartzite still remains lodged in its recess on the south side of the passage. The floor of the recess slopes towards the passage, but apparently the angle of incline was not sufficiently steep to enable the block to be moved into position. An opening in the end wall 5 feet above the floor of the passage, which the portcullis was intended to cover, gives access to a second ramp set on the same axis as the first but having thirty-nine steps. At the bottom of this ramp stood a wooden door with two leaves which, when open, fitted into recesses

A seated sandstone statue of Ammenemes III, of which the upper part is shown, was found while a canal was being dug near his funerary temple at Hawara in 1895.

in the side-walls. Beyond the doorway, still resting in its recess, is another portcullis identical in design with the first. The next section of the passage continues without change in direction and runs almost horizontally, but at a higher level than the bottom of the second ramp, to a rectangular pit, the floor of which was no doubt raised after the funeral to the level of the floor of the passage and thus concealed the entrance to the last section of the passage, which runs northwards to emerge in the floor at the eastern end of a wide antechamber lying north of the burial-chamber.

Before describing the method of entry into the burial-chamber, it is necessary to explain that the whole of the substructure must have been completed before the lowest course of the superstructure could have been laid. The sequence of the operations probably corresponded with the order followed by the builders of the Pyramid of Hawara. First, a rectangular pit measuring about 43 feet square and 36 feet deep was excavated mostly south-east of the middle of the site on which the pyramid was to be built. Into this pit the burial-chamber, its walls and floor carved of a single block of quartzite, was lowered by way of a trench with a temporary ramp which entered the pit at the south-west corner. The burial-chamber occupied only a small part of the whole area of the pit and as soon as it had been placed in position work was started on the construction of the antechamber and the passages in the pit, each at its proper level. While this work was in progress, the temporary ramp was dismantled and replaced by the two stepped ramps. Finally the portcullises were lowered into their recesses and the filling necessary to provide a level surface for the base of the pyramid was laid in the pit and in the trench of the stepped ramps, not however directly on the flat ceilings of the various constructions, but on brick vaults which had been built above them. Over the burial-chamber alone a pointed roof, composed of two pieces of limestone, was placed between the brick vault and the flat ceiling.

Entry into the burial-chamber at the time of the funeral would have been impossible if the two heavy ceiling-blocks of quartzite had already been laid on the walls. The block nearer to the antechamber was therefore propped up in the void between the ceiling and the pointed roof, leaving a gap above the northern wall to which a trench in the centre of the antechamber and a short corridor gave access. Two props of granite supported the block which projected on both sides about 1 foot 6 inches beyond the walls of the chamber. The props did not, however, stand on the floor of the pit but on deep beds of sand encased in vertical shafts built of stone, each shaft rising to the height of the walls and the upper part serving as a kind of socket for its prop. After the coffin, the Canopic chest, and some of the king's personal possessions had been placed in the chamber, a stone at the base of each shaft was removed and the sand allowed to escape, no doubt gradually, until the props rested on the floor and the block on the walls. In order to enable this operation to be carried out, corridors leading to the shafts had been built in the pit, one from a trench in the east passage and the other from a trench at the west end of the antechamber. When the ceiling-block, which measured about 5 feet in thickness, had been lowered the gap at the end of the corridor of approach to the burial-chamber was completely closed. Nevertheless, as a further measure of protection the trench connecting this corridor with the ante-chamber and the two trenches of the corridors leading to the shafts were filled with masonry and paved.

The Pyramid of Khendjer, burial-chamber, cross-section looking north and plan of surrounding passages (*see also page 181*)

3. portcullis
4. and **5.** corridors leading to the shafts
6. burial chamber

Although this ingenious method of lowering a heavy block of stone in a confined space had not been recognized in any earlier pyramid, it may not have been an invention of the architect of this pyramid. Jéquier, to whom the credit for its discovery belongs, believed that it was employed by the builders of the pyramids of Mazghuna, but while the precise date of these monuments remains uncertain their chronological position in relation to the Pyramid of Khendjer cannot be determined. It was not used in Khendjer's subsidiary pyramid, a building situated north-east of the king's pyramid and somewhat similar in plan, but exceptionally having two burial-chambers, each made of quartzite. These burial-chambers were however smaller than the burial-chamber of the king and the stone blocks supporting the raised portions of their lighter ceilings, which had never been lowered, could have been removed if the weight of the ceiling-slabs had been eased by means of levers while the blocks were being extracted. In every probability some unexpected turn of events prevented the execution of the plan for burying two queens in these chambers, but there is nothing to suggest that the king was not interred in his pyramid. How long his body remained undisturbed is not known, perhaps only until the Hyksos invasion. By means of a hole cut immediately beneath the ceiling and only large enough to admit a child, the robbers succeeded in gaining possession of the entire contents of the chamber, leaving behind nothing of any kind, not even a fragment of wood, stone, or pottery.

In the unfinished pyramid, Jéquier estimated that the burial-chamber weighed as much as 150 tons. One new feature was introduced into the fashioning of this monolith, namely that the lower portions of both the sarcophagus and the Canopic chest were carved in one piece with the floor of the chamber; the two lids were composed of separate pieces. The same method for lowering the raised ceiling-slab had been planned in this pyramid as in the Pyramid of Khendjer, but it was never used. No doubt in the hope of finding treasure, the robbers had released the sand from the shafts, with the result that the quartzite props slid downwards; the ceiling-slab however still rests on supporting blocks placed on the walls.

Not a single tomb of the Hyksos kings has yet come to light, and, in consequence, it is impossible to know whether they adopted the Egyptian practice of building pyramids or whether they were buried in some other kind of tomb. References to the pyramids of the XVIIth Dynasty kings occur in the Leopold-Amherst Papyrus and its congener the Abbott Papyrus, now in the British Museum. Both papyri report the findings of a committee appointed by a vizier of the XXth Dynasty to investigate certain allegations of neglect of duty, resulting in tomb robbery, laid by the Mayor of Thebes against the Mayor of the Necropolis on the west bank, where these pyramids were situated. Although material evidence is scant, it seems clear that the superstructures, built of crude brick, covered an area of only about 25 feet square; the four faces sloped inwards at an angle of about 65°, which gave the buildings the appearance of being tall and slender. At the apex was a capstone made, at least in some instances, of limestone and engraved with the name and titles of the king. The burial-chamber was carved out of the rock foundation of the pyramid chapel.

Perhaps the last Egyptian king to build a pyramid was Amosis I. His real tomb lay at Thebes, the capital, but a cenotaph which he built at Abydos was in the shape of a pyramid. He also constructed at Abydos a dummy pyramid for his grandmother, Tetisheri, whose actual tomb, although not yet found, is stated in an inscription discovered at Abydos to have been situated at Thebes. These two pyramids were, however, exceptional; the remaining kings of the XVIIIth Dynasty and their successors for many generations built neither tombs nor cenotaphs of pyramidal form. Experience must by that time have shown that the pyramid gave unnecessary prominence to the location of the tomb and that, even after the adoption of every stratagem which human ingenuity could devise, plunderers were ultimately able to force their way into the burial-chamber, and not only to despoil the contents but also to violate the body. A different method of countering these evils was now attempted. Instead of constructing their mortuary temples and tombs together in one place, the Pharaohs of the New Kingdom built their temples in the Nile Valley and hollowed out deep caverns in the western cliffs for tombs. By this method it was hoped that the knowledge of the actual location of the tomb would be shared only by those who had assisted in its construction, by a small number of officials, and by members of the royal household. The architect of the first tomb of this kind to be constructed in the famous 'Valley of the Kings' – a valley running parallel with the Nile behind Deir el-Bahri – describes the secrecy with which the work was carried out in the following words: 'I supervised the excavation of the cliff-tomb of His Majesty [Tuthmosis I] alone, no one seeing and no one hearing.' Neither Tuthmosis I nor his architect, however, could possibly have known that the lonely valley they had chosen was destined to become the regular burial-place of the Pharaohs for many generations to come; inevitably the secret of the whereabouts of the royal tombs became common knowledge. Robbery was bound to follow sooner or later, and Tutankhamun alone of the sixty or more royal persons buried in this valley was left virtually undisturbed until modern times. His tomb was only spared by the fortunate chance which guided Ramesses VI to excavate his own tomb in the cliffs immediately above the tomb of Tutankhamun, with the result that the entrance to the latter became deeply buried under rubble thrown out from the upper tomb, and must clearly have been forgotten. Fifty-three mummies from the other tombs in the valley, including those of such famous Pharaohs as Tuthmosis III, Sethos I, and Ramesses II, were ultimately transferred to an unfinished tomb at Deir el-Bahri, and to the tomb of Amenophis II, where they remained without further disturbance until their discovery at the end of the last century.

Although scarcely meriting comparison with the royal pyramids, private tombs of pyramidal form or incorporating a pyramid in their architectural design were built from the Middle Kingdom until Roman times. The earliest examples at present known – found by Mariette at Abydos – consisted of a small brick pyramid mounted on a rectangular podium, both parts being covered with a coat of mud-plaster and whitewashed. Within the pyramid lay a burial-chamber, conical in shape and corbelled in construction. A second chamber was sometimes built in the podium to serve as a serdab. Most of these tombs had no external chapels, but some were provided with a two-storeyed chapel projecting from the side. Each storey consisted of one chamber only, the upper containing a niche for the stela and the lower affording the only means of access to the serdab.

During the New Kingdom, a more elaborate type of private tomb, outwardly resembling the upper-class dwelling-house of the time, came into

By the end of the XIIth Dynasty sculpture tended to show a more natural portrayal of features and garments, a development which can be detected in the face of this statue of Ammenemes III. His long kilt-type garment has been executed as a separate unit, rather than as an integral part of the sculpture as, for example, in the earlier statues of Mycerinus (*see pages 114 and 118*).

fashion. Tombs of this kind were built in Thebes and at other places even as far away as Aniba, about 130 miles south of Aswan. Some of the best examples, however, were found by the excavators of the French Institute of Archaeology when digging at Deir el-Medina, near the Valley of the Queens. Their owners were the scribes, artists, and artisans who had been employed on the construction of the royal tombs of the XVIIIth-XXth Dynasties. Each tomb consisted of two parts, a superstructure and a sub-structure. Above ground lay a court enclosed on three sides by a wall of brick or stone. On the fourth side of the court stood a chapel, usually masked by a colonnade. Internally, the chapel consisted of a single room decorated with painted scenes and having a stela recessed in the back wall. Mounted on the roof was a hollow brick pyramid, capped with a block of limestone. Figures of the owner adoring the Sun-god, together with short inscriptions, were carved on all four sides of the capstone. A niche in the side of the pyramid facing the court contained a statuette of the owner, who was sometimes represented kneeling and holding a miniature stela. The burial-chamber, which lay deep in the rock, was a room with a vaulted ceiling of brick connected with either the court or the chapel by a shaft and an underground staircase. In the XVIIIth Dynasty only the owner and his wife were buried in the chamber. In the XIXth-XXth Dynasties, however, several generations of the same family regularly shared the same tomb and additional chambers were constructed when necessary. The walls of the chambers, after the XVIIIth Dynasty, were usually decorated with religious scenes and inscriptions.

More than eight hundred years after the last royal pyramid had been constructed in Egypt, pyramidal tombs suddenly made their appearance in the Sudan. The builders were a line of kings whose capital – known in ancient times as Napata – was situated on the banks of the Nile in the province of Dongola, a short distance downstream from the Fourth Cataract. Concerning the racial origin of these kings, very little information has yet come to light, but an inscription found by Reisner during his excavation of their tombs suggests that they were of south Libyan stock. Napata offered no rich pasturage to attract the settler; on the contrary, it lay in one of the most barren parts of the Nile Valley, and its importance was principally due to its geographical position on the main trade route between Central Africa and Egypt, which enabled its rulers to control the passage of slaves and supplies of ivory, ebony, myrrh, resin, incense, and other products required by the Egyptians. The rich gold-fields of the eastern desert were also included in their domain. To ensure an uninterrupted flow of these commodities, the kings of Egypt during the Middle Kingdom and again during the XVIIIth-XXth Dynasties had incorporated the northern Sudan into their empire. In the latter period in particular, temples were built in honour of the Egyptian gods at many places between the First Cataract and the Fourth Cataract. The largest of these temples stood at Napata, where a high table mountain, now called Gebel Barkal, acquired the reputation of being the dwelling of the god Amun. At the end of the XXth Dynasty (c. 1080 BC), internal weakness forced Egypt to relax her grip on the northern Sudan and, little more than a century later, the ancestors of the kings who were to build the pyramids gained possession of the country, without, however, causing its people to discard the Egyptian religion or to abandon the fund of technical knowledge which they had learned from the Egyptians.

The divine nature of the king made him a link between men and gods. This unusual statue of Ammenemes III shows him wearing the garments of a priest. In theory, but not in function, the king was the high priest of every major god.

Nothing is known concerning the relations between the early rulers of Napata and the Libyan kings who formed the XXIInd and XXIIIrd Dynasties of Egypt. The XXIVth Egyptian Dynasty consisted of one king only, Bocchoris by name, whose reign did not exceed six years in length and whose authority over the country was at best extremely tenuous and may have been purely nominal, for Egypt had disintegrated politically into a number of independent districts, each governed by a petty despot. At that time Kashta, king of Napata, and his Ethiopian army advanced northwards beyond the First Cataract and conquered Egypt as far as Thebes. His successor, Piankhy, completed the conquest, to establish himself in about 721 BC as the first king of the XXVth Dynasty – a dynasty consisting, apart from Piankhy, of four kings named Shabaka, Shabataka, Tirhaqa, and Tanutamun, one of whom, Tirhaqa, is mentioned in the Bible as helping Hezekiah[3] to resist the Assyrians. These kings, although of foreign blood, were not true aliens like the Hyksos invaders; they were already thoroughly Egyptianized, and Piankhy, at least, regarded his conquest of Egypt as a crusade to restore to the god Amun some of that pre-eminence of which he had been deprived by years of political dissension.

Perhaps as a result of seeing the pyramids of the early Egyptian kings at Saqqara, Giza, and elsewhere, Piankhy abandoned the mastaba type of tomb built by the kings of Napata who preceded him and erected a pyramid. The site which he chose was at Kuru, about five miles downstream from Napata, in the midst of a large cemetery already containing the tombs of his ancestors. Scarcely a stone of the superstructure of this pyramid still remains in position, but it is evident that it occupied an area of only about 40 feet square. Subsequent pyramids in a better state of preservation suggest that its four sides inclined inwards at an angle of about 68°. Beneath this structure lay a pit, roofed with a corbel vault, which served as a burial-chamber. To enable the chamber to be entered after the pyramid had been built, an open stairway was cut from a point east of the superstructure to a door in the east wall of the chamber. After the funeral, this stairway was filled with rubble, and a mortuary chapel, consisting of a single room decorated with reliefs, was erected on top. Shabaka, when constructing his pyramid, added a short tunnel to the end of the stairway and cut his burial-chamber out of the rock. The mortuary chapel was built against the east side of the pyramid, directly above the tunnel, and the stairway – filled after the funeral like the trench of Piankhy – lay outside the east wall. In this way, the chapel stood on a rock foundation, and its construction could be completed during the lifetime of the king. Tirhaqa, in his pyramid at Nuri on the opposite bank of the Nile to Kuru, developed the tunnel into a small antechamber and enlarged the burial-chamber into a hall divided by rock pillars into three aisles; he also cut a corridor which surrounded both apartments and gave access to the hall by a staircase at its western end. Some of his successors increased the number of underground chambers in their pyramids to three by interposing between the antechamber and the burial-chamber a room inscribed on its walls with the so-called 'Negative Confession' from the Book of the Dead. In spite of these modifications in matters of detail, however, the general pattern of the tomb as first developed by Shabaka was never radically changed.

In addition to the king's pyramids, Reisner found in the cemetery of Kuru a row of five pyramids built for the queens. Close to this row lay twenty-four graves of horses, four of which belonged to the horses of

The Nile from Aswan to
Khartoum

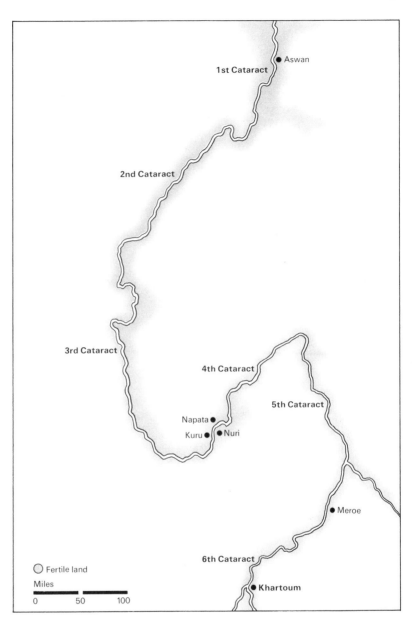

Aswan

1st Cataract

2nd Cataract

3rd Cataract

4th Cataract

5th Cataract

Napata

Kuru   Nuri

Meroe

Fertile land

Miles

6th Cataract

Khartoum

0   50   100

Overleaf: The North
Cemetery at Meroe
contains the pyramid-
tombs of the rulers of
that kingdom dating from
about 300 BC until its
collapse in about AD 350.

Piankhy and four to those of Tanutamun, while the remainder were equally
divided between the horses of Shabaka and Shabataka. Each horse was richly
caparisoned with silver trappings and strings of beads. They were, without
doubt, sacrificed at the time of the king's death, in order that they might
accompany him to the Next World. Only one instance of a horse-burial is
known from Egypt, although chariots were included in the tombs of royalty
and some nobility during the New Kingdom. The sacrifice of the royal
steeds was therefore probably an innovation by Piankhy, whose affection
for horses is witnessed by a passage in his famous Victory Stela. In this

Private tombs at Deir
el-Medina — a
reconstruction

graphic account of his conquest of Egypt, he describes his indignation at the
discovery that Namlat, the despot of El-Eshmunein, had allowed his horses
to starve during the siege which he himself had laid to the city. Namlat was
ultimately pardoned, but he came near to paying with his life for his neglect
of the horses.

In about the year 661 BC, the Assyrian king Ashurbanipal brought to an
end a number of inconclusive encounters between Assyria and the kings of
the XXVth Dynasty by defeating Tanutamun and conquering the whole of
Egypt as far as Thebes. Tanutamun retreated to Napata, where he and his

The Pyramid of Tirhaqa

successors continued to rule without serious interference for about 350 years. Their kingdom was bounded on the north by the First Cataract and on the south by the swamps of the White Nile. With only two exceptions, these kings, of whom there were twenty-one including Tanutamun, were buried at Nuri in pyramids of the standard size and shape; the two exceptions were Tanutamun himself and a later king, both of whom erected their pyramids at Kuru. In addition to the kings' pyramids, the Nuri cemetery contained fifty-three smaller pyramids belonging to queens and princesses.

From about 300 BC until AD 350, when the kingdom was finally over-whelmed by the Abyssinians, the capital was situated at Meroe, 130 miles north of Khartoum. Twice during this period rival claimants to the throne endeavoured, with some measure of success, to re-establish the capital at Napata, but on each occasion the dissident faction ultimately succumbed and the authority of Meroe remained unchallenged. Both the kings of Meroe and their rivals at Napata continued to be buried in pyramids, nearly fifty in Meroe and eighteen in Napata; all these pyramids, like their predecessors, were of stone except those built at Meroe after AD 200, when brick coated with plaster was employed.

A barbarous custom, already practised during the Middle Kingdom in northern Sudan, was revived by the kings of Meroe. This custom was the burial of his servants with the king in his tomb, so that their spirits might continue to serve him in the Next World. Whether they were actually buried alive or were put to death before burial is still open to conjecture. The queens were not subjected to this treatment, but were buried, also in pyramids, in a separate cemetery on the west side of the city. In this con-nection, Strabo makes the following statement: 'It is still the custom in Ethiopia that when the king, by accident or otherwise, has lost the use of a member, or a member itself, all his usual followers (those who are destined to die at the same time as himself) inflict on themselves a similar mutilation, and that explains the extreme care with which they watch over the person of the king.'[4] Strabo may have been misled in matters of detail, but the excava-tions of Reisner at Meroe suggest that the general accuracy of his assertion need not be doubted.

1 Diodorus Siculus, *The Historical Library*, Bk. I, LI and LII (W. G. Waddell's translation).
2 Strabo, *Geographica*, Book XVII, I, 37 (Bohn's Classical Library).
3 II Kings xix. 9.
4 Strabo, *Geographica*, Book XVII, II, 3.

Construction and Purpose

EXTANT Egyptian records, whether written or pictorial, throw no light on the methods employed by the builders of the pyramids either in planning or in constructing their monumental works. Close study of the buildings, combined with an ever-increasing knowledge of the implements available to the builders, has, however, made it possible to determine many details of construction with certainty and the likely limits of practicability can often be deduced where positive evidence is lacking. Nevertheless, several problems remain to be solved, and in such cases it is only possible to suggest an answer without any pretence of support other than the belief that the means proposed would achieve the results which can be observed.

When choosing the site for a pyramid, it was necessary that certain overriding considerations should be borne in mind: it must be situated west of the river – the side of the setting sun; it must stand well above the level of the river, but not be too remote from its west bank; the rock substratum must be free from any defect or tendency to crack; it should be situated not far from the capital and possibly even closer to a palace which the king may have built as a residence outside the capital. Of the sites chosen by the kings of the Old Kingdom, Saqqara and Abu Sir lay in sight of Memphis, Abu Roash about seventeen miles distant to the north, and Dahshur only five miles away to the south. Thirty-three miles separated Memphis from Meidum, where one pyramid alone was built. Proximity to the river was an important factor, because much of the stone used for the pyramid and its adjacent buildings must be conveyed from the quarries by ship. Thus, during the season of the inundation, an expanse of desert only 250 yards in width lay between the river and the pyramid at Meidum, while at Giza the interval was about a quarter of a mile; at Dahshur and Abu Roash, however, the most practical routes for hauling the building materials measured about a mile.

A suitable site having been found, the first task of the builders was to remove the thick surface layer of sand and gravel so that the buildings might stand on a firm foundation of rock. Levelling and smoothing of the rock were then begun, the pieces removed being either used to fill up depressions or placed on one side for subsequent employment. How accurately this operation could be performed is demonstrated by the Great Pyramid, in which the perimeter of the bed deviates from a truly level plane by only a little more than half an inch – the almost imperceptible amount by which the south-east corner stands higher than the north-west corner. Such a high degree of accuracy in the technique of levelling was undoubtedly the outcome of accumulated experience gained by generations of Egyptians, dating back to the pre-Pyramid Age, when preparing their lands for irrigation by means of water conducted through channels and canals from the river. To level an area like the bed of a pyramid it would have been necessary to surround it on all four sides with low banks of Nile mud, fill the enclosure so formed with water, and cut a network of trenches in the rock in such a manner that the floor of each trench lay at the same depth beneath the surface of the water; the intervening spaces could have been levelled after the water had been released. In actual practice the whole area to be covered by the pyramid was not always reduced to the same level as the perimeter; as the Great Pyramid shows, a mound of rock might be left in the centre to be used at a later stage in the work of construction.

The last of the preliminaries to be accomplished on the site was the execution of an accurate survey in order to ensure that the base of the pyramid should form as nearly as possible a perfect square, each side of which would be so oriented as to face directly one of the four cardinal points. The unit of measurement was the Royal Cubit (20·62 inches in length) consisting of seven *palms* or twenty-eight *digits*, one *palm* being equal to four *digits*. Measuring cords were made either of palm-fibre or flax-fibre, both of which would certainly have stretched when used; it is therefore hardly surprising that there should be a difference of 7·9 inches in length between the longest and shortest sides of the Great Pyramid – indeed, it seems remarkable that on sides exceeding 9,000 inches in length so small an error should have occurred, especially when it is remembered that the central mound of rock would have rendered impracticable any measurement of the diagonals to check the accuracy of the square.

An exact orientation of the pyramid on the four cardinal points could only have been achieved with the aid of one or more of the celestial bodies, since the magnetic compass was certainly unknown to the ancient Egyptians. The results of the method, as exemplified by the Great Pyramid and the Pyramid of Chephren, left little to be desired, the errors in the four sides of the former being the following fractions of one degree:

North side   2′ 28″ south of west
South side   1′ 57″ south of west
East side   5′ 30″ west of north
West side   2′ 30″ west of north

According to Petrie's survey, the mean error of the east and west sides of Chephren's pyramid was about 5′ 26″ west of north. Among other pyramids surveyed by Petrie were three, in the orientation of the east and west sides of which he observed the following significantly greater errors:

Meidum Pyramid: 24′ 25″ west of north
Bent Pyramid: 9′ 12″ west of north
Pyramid of Mycerinus: 14′ 3″ east of north

Which or how many of the celestial bodies were employed to attain these results cannot be deduced with certainty, but it was clearly only necessary to fix one axis; the other axis could be determined by the use of a set-square; contemporary buildings with corners forming a perfect right angle prove that an accurate instrument for this purpose must have been available to the pyramid-builders. East and west could have been discovered approximately by observing the rising and setting of the sun on the two equinoctial days every year, and north by an observation of the Pole Star, but in each case the resultant error (even after allowance has been made for a change in the position of the Pole in relation to the Pole Star in the course of about 4,500 years) would have been greater than the amount revealed by at least the two main pyramids of Giza.

Egyptian texts giving information on the method of orienting buildings are few in number, late in date, and formal in character. They refer invariably to the foundation ceremonies of temples performed by the king. According to the most instructive of these texts, which are inscribed on the walls of the Graeco-Roman temples of Dendereh and Edfu, the king marked out the line of the four outer walls after observing the position of the stars in the Great Bear. In conducting the observation he was assisted by a priest, impersonating the god Thoth, who was in charge of an instrument called the *merkhet*. As long ago as 1899 Borchardt was able to identify as a *merkhet* a bone object dating from Saite times in the Berlin Museum which consisted of a narrow horizontal bar with a small block at one end rising above the level of the bar; a transverse hole bored through the block and a perpendicular groove cut beneath each aperture of the boring were no doubt intended to hold the upper end of a plumb-line. The word *merkhet* means literally 'instrument of knowing' and may be translated 'indicator'. It was used, as the Czech Egyptologist Z. Žába has shown, to express 'shadow-clock', 'water-clock', and 'astral-clock', an instrument for measuring nocturnal hours by determining the height of a star above the horizon. All three instruments also possessed individual names; the general term *merkhet* would refer to their common function as indicators of time by means of measurement. The *merkhet* used in astral observations and the *merkhet* used in sunlight for registering the hours of the day by measuring the length of shadow cast by the block on the horizontal bar were, however, identical apart from the addition of a plumb-line to the former and the calibration of the bar in the latter.

As an astral gauge the *merkhet* was employed in conjunction with another instrument which the Egyptians called the *bay* (*en imy unut*) 'palm-rib (of the observer of hours)'. Borchardt recognized an example of this instrument also in the Berlin collection and its inscription revealed that it had belonged to the same priest as the *merkhet* previously mentioned. It was a straight palm-rib with a V-shaped slot cut in the wider end. How these two instruments (neither of which is mentioned in Egyptian texts before the XVIIIth Dynasty) may have been used for surveying will shortly be described.

In spite of the relatively late date of the inscriptions referring to the episodes of the foundation ceremonies, there is no reason to doubt that they preserve an ancient tradition. Some indication that similar ceremonies were already current in the Pyramid Age is provided by a fragmentary relief found in the Vth Dynasty Sun-temple of Niuserrē, which shows the king and a priestess impersonating the goddess Seshat, each holding a mallet and a stake to which a measuring cord is attached. The scene is in complete agreement with the text in the temple at Edfu which represents the king as saying: 'I take the stake and I hold the handle of the mallet. I hold the [measuring] cord with Seshat.' Nevertheless, it is necessary to bear in mind that actions performed in a religious ceremony would be symbolical and would not reproduce fully the various measures laboriously taken beforehand to secure the desired results. Thus a text in the temple at Dendereh which describes the king as 'looking at the sky, observing the stars and turning his gaze towards the Great Bear' should not be regarded as more than a record of a formal ceremony in which the king was credited with having himself determined the orientation of the temple, although in reality he merely went through the motions, as is done at the present day in laying a foundation-stone.

The *merkhet*

Wedge-slots (*opposite*) left by the men who quarried for granite to build the ancient monuments of Egypt can still be seen at Aswan.

A simple method of determining true north, which would have been consistent with the evidence of the later texts, was by sighting on a star in the northern heavens and bisecting the angle formed by its rising position, the position from which the observation was made, and its setting position. To achieve the degree of accuracy needed, it would have been necessary either to be able to see the true horizon at the points where the star rose and set or to create an artificial horizon at a uniform height above those two points.

Since an observation of the true horizon would be precluded anywhere on land by irregularities, however slight, in the ground, an artificial horizon would be required. This end could have been secured by building a circular wall with a diameter of a few feet on the already levelled rock-bed of the pyramid. The height of the wall must be sufficient to prevent a person standing within the circle from seeing anything outside other than the sky, but, subject to this single reservation, it should not be higher than such a person could reach. For the whole of its circumference, the top of the wall must be on an absolutely even plane – a requirement which again could easily have been attained by means of water, temporary mudbanks on the inner and outer peripheries of the top surface providing the support necessary to prevent the water from flowing away. The observation would be made by one person sighting over a short perpendicular rod or through the slot of the *bay* at the centre of the circle; a second person standing within the circle would receive directions from the first and, at the moment when the star appeared above the wall, would place a mark or the *merkhet* on the wall directly in line between the observer and the star. This operation would first be performed towards the east, and subsequently, some hours later, perhaps with a second *merkhet*, towards the west, the same star being sighted on both occasions. If the *merkhet* had not been invented at this period a plumb-line (which the Egyptians of the Pyramid Age are known to have possessed) would have been suspended from the two marks on the wall and corresponding marks made on the ground at points perpendicularly below. The first of these two operations would have been unnecessary if the *merkhet* with a plumb-line attached to the block were available to the pyramid-builders. By bisecting the angle pOq, true north would be obtained and the bisecting line N–O would run due north and south. As a check, the operation could have been repeated by sighting several different stars in the same way before dismantling the wall in readiness for the foundation ceremonies.

The *bay*

At the same time as the preliminary work was being conducted on the pyramid site, other preparations for building were being made elsewhere. The foundation of the causeway, composed of stone quarried in the locality, was being laid so that it could be used for the passage of material when constructional work on the pyramid began. Fine limestone blocks for the outer casing of the building were being quarried on the east bank of the Nile at Tura in the Mukattam hills. The men employed on this work painted the names of their gangs in red ochre on the blocks before they were taken from the quarry; although these names were very often erased in the course of subsequent operations, enough remain to perpetuate many of the gangs. As examples, the following names, found by Alan Rowe, occur on casing-blocks of the Meidum pyramid:[1] 'Stepped Pyramid Gang', 'Boat Gang', 'Vigorous Gang', 'Sceptre Gang', 'Enduring Gang', 'North Gang', and

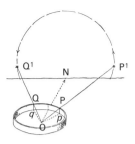

A method of discovering
true north

O centre of circle

*P*¹ position of star in the
east

P siting towards the east

*Q*¹ position of star in the
west

Q siting towards the west

p and *q* marks made
perpendicularly below *P*
and *Q* to determine the
angle *pOq*

line *NO* bisecting line of
angle *pOq* running due
north and south

'South Gang'. A block in the Great Pyramid bears the name: 'The Craftsmen-gang. How powerful is the White Crown of Khnum Khufu!' Why these names were placed on the stones is not evident, unless it was with the intention of facilitating the task of keeping a tally of the work done by each gang. Far away to the south, at Aswan, another group of men were quarrying granite for columns, architraves, door-jambs, lintels, casing-blocks, and sometimes the outer sarcophagus.

Limestone, whether obtained from the surface of the rock, as at Giza, or extracted by tunnelling, as at Tura, presented the pyramid-builders with no serious difficulties in its quarrying. A discovery by W. B. Emery in the early dynastic cemetery of Saqqara has shown that even in the Ist Dynasty the Egyptians possessed excellent copper tools, including saws and chisels, which were capable of cutting any kind of limestone. As an aid to sawing, a wet abrasive material such as moistened quartz sand, which is plentiful in Egypt, may have been employed, but there is no positive evidence either of the material used or of the practice. Chisels and wedges were, however, the tools most favoured for quarrying limestone, the former for cutting the blocks away from the rock on every side except the bottom and the latter for detaching the blocks at the base. In a tunnel-quarry, for instance, a deep hollow resembling a shelf and extending across the whole breadth of the passage was first cut between the roof and the block to be detached. The purpose of this hollow was to allow a quarryman to crawl across the top of the block and separate it from the rock behind by chipping vertically down-wards with a chisel struck by a wooden mallet. At the same time other quarrymen made similar vertical cuttings down the two sides. Finally, wedges were inserted into holes cut at the bottom in order to make a horizontal split in the rock, which freed the block entirely. Sometimes the wedges were composed of wood, and the split was achieved by wetting the wood and so causing it to expand. The process was afterwards repeated on the rock below, without the necessity of cutting the initial hollow, until floor-level had been reached; a new series of cuttings, started at roof-level, was then begun deeper in the tunnel.* Surface-quarrying was carried out by exactly the same method. It possessed a great advantage over tunnel-quarrying, in so far as the space for working was not so confined and a greater number of men could therefore be employed at one time. On the other hand, the finest limestone often lay in strata buried deeply beneath the surface, and tunnelling offered the only practical means of access.

The methods employed in the Pyramid Age for quarrying granite and other hard stones are still a subject of controversy. One authority even expressed the opinion that hard-stone quarrying was not attempted until the Middle Kingdom; before that time, the amount needed could have been obtained from large boulders lying loose on the surface of the ground.[2] It seems difficult, however, to believe that a people who possessed the degree of skill necessary for shaping the colossal monoliths built into the granite valley building of Chephren were not able to hew rough blocks of this stone out of the quarry, particularly since tunnelling was never adopted. Further-more, on the backs of the slabs roofing Mycerinus's burial-chamber marks made by the insertion of wedges may still be seen, and the natural inference appears to be that the operation denoted by these wedge-marks was the splitting of the slabs from the rock in the quarry. This method of quarrying was certainly practised in later times, as is demonstrated by the countless

* Many soft-stone quarries in the United Kingdom are worked at the present time in the way described above, the only important difference being the substitution of steel tools and the greater use made of the saw. The mason's pick, now used instead of chisels, may also have been known to the ancient Egyptians, but no specimen has yet been found.

The transport of a colossus

rows of wedge-slots still visible today in the Aswan quarries; there is nothing to suggest that quarrymen were not detaching blocks by the same device in the Old Kingdom. The slots may have been made either by rubbing an abrasive powder with stone or by a metal tool. Since copper is the only metal for tools known to have been available in Egypt before the Middle Kingdom, it has been supposed that the Egyptians had mastered a process, now lost, of giving copper a very high temper, but this surmise has not yet been proved.

An alternative and more laborious method of quarrying granite was by pounding the rock around the block to be detached with balls of dolerite – a hard greenish stone found over a wide area of the eastern desert near the Red Sea. An unfinished obelisk dating from the New Kingdom, which still lies at Aswan, was undoubtedly quarried by this method, and there is no inherent improbability in the supposition that quarrymen were already acquainted with the technique in pyramid times.

By whatever method of quarrying the granite blocks were obtained, the procedure for reaching stone of the quality required, if it were not available in the uppermost stratum would have been similar. Granite, like many other stones, if heated to a high temperature, and then suddenly cooled, will develop superficial cracks, and the face, when subjected to the slightest friction, will immediately crumble away. A fire lit on the rock to be pared down would soon raise its temperature to the requisite degree, and the application of cold water would cause the disintegration of the surface, which could then be rubbed away with the aid of a small stone scraper. If necessary, the process could be repeated many times until stone of the desired hardness had been reached.

By no means the least remarkable achievement of the pyramid-builders was the transport of the blocks from their quarries to the site of the pyramid. Some of the heaviest pieces of local limestone embodied in the mortuary temple of Mycerinus, according to Reisner's estimate,[3] weigh about 200 tons. In comparison with this amount, the casing-blocks of the Great Pyramid, which average only about $2\frac{1}{2}$ tons, and the 50-ton granite roof-slabs of the King's Chamber may seem trivial, but it must be remembered that the latter required not only to be loaded on barges and subsequently unloaded, but also, for the most part, to be raised at the end of their journey to a very considerable height above ground-level. The navigation of these megaliths, probably undertaken in the main during the inundation season, may well have been the least formidable part of the whole task, though the control of heavily laden barges on a fast-flowing river must always have been a hazardous operation requiring great skill. Moreover, the journey from Aswan, although free from cataracts, involved negotiating the difficult waters and shifting sandbanks near Gebel Abu Foda, about ninety miles south of Saqqara. For transport over land, the method employed was probably the same whether the weight to be moved was 200 tons or $2\frac{1}{2}$ tons, the number of men being regulated by the amount of the weight. What was this method? It is highly improbable that wheeled vehicles were used, because although some of the carrying possibilities of the wheel had been realized at least as early as the Vth Dynasty,[*] scenes in tombs of the XVIIIth Dynasty demonstrate that, even after a lapse of a thousand years, statues and heavy blocks of stone were not moved by wheeled transport. Instead, sledges were employed, and there can be little doubt that the pyramid-builders also used this method. Each block was probably levered on the sledge either directly from the ground or by way of a low ramp composed of brick or stone. Both sledge and block, lashed together by ropes, may then have been raised again by means of levers, in order that wooden rollers might be placed underneath. The loaded sledge would subsequently be dragged over a way paved with baulks of timber by men pulling on ropes attached to the sledge. An illustration of the actual process of transport was included by Djehutihotep, a nobleman of the XIIth Dynasty, in his tomb at El-Bersheh. In this scene an alabaster statue of Djehutihotep, which probably weighed about 60 tons, is mounted on a sledge pulled by 172 men.[†] Water or some other liquid is poured on the ground to lessen the friction and thus facilitate haulage.

With his material close at hand and the site prepared, two difficult problems still confronted the pyramid-builder: he must raise the stones to the height required and must lay them so that the monument gained internal cohesion and regularity of outward form. Before attempting to explain how these problems were overcome, it may be worth while to stop and consider the main internal and external features of the structures to be built, disregarding, for the present, the chambers and corridors.

When describing the Pyramid of Meidum it was stated that its core consisted of several coatings of masonry diminishing in height from the centre outwards and leaning on a central nucleus at an angle of about $75°$. Each layer was cased from top to bottom with Tura limestone, and its outer surface dressed smooth. The step pyramid so formed was subsequently converted into a true pyramid by filling the steps with packing-blocks and adding an outer casing of dressed Tura limestone. Borchardt has shown that

* A relief in the Vth Dynasty tomb of Kaemheset at Saqqara shows a scaling-ladder mounted on wheels. (See Somers Clarke and R. Engelbach, *Ancient Egyptian Masonry*, Fig. 83).
† Reliefs from the Palace of Sennacherib at Nineveh, now in the British Museum, show that the Assyrians of the seventh century BC transported their sculptures by a very similar method.

the same method, modified only to the extent of leaving the faces of the
internal casing-stones rough, was still practised by pyramid-builders in the
Vth Dynasty,[4] and it may well have continued until an even later date in the
Old Kingdom. The Pyramid of Sahurē at Abu Sir, for example, was composed of upright layers of core-masonry, internal casings of fine limestone,
packing-blocks of stone, and lastly the usual smooth outer casing of Tura
limestone. Whether the three main pyramids at Giza were also built in this
fashion is uncertain and, without dismantling substantial portions of their
superstructures, no examination seems likely to yield conclusive results.
Borchardt considered the presence of the 'girdle-stones' in the ascending
corridor as proof that the Great Pyramid followed the standard pattern,
each 'girdle-stone' being part of an internal casing,[5] but two equally eminent
authorities, Somers Clarke and R. Engelbach, refused to accept Borchardt's
arguments;[6] even if the 'girdle-stones' are not internal casings, however, it
need not follow that such casings do not exist elsewhere in the pyramid.
It is, moreover, irrefutable that all the surviving subsidiary pyramids at Giza
were built with internal casings, and it would be strange if the main pyramids
were composed in a different way. Externally, all pyramids built after the
Bent Pyramid at Dahshur were alike, except in size and in such small details
as the angle of incline and the kind of stone used for the lower courses of the
outer casing. The normal angle of incline was about 52° – a slope which, in
the Pyramid of Meidum and in the Great Pyramid, would have resulted if the
height had been made to correspond with the radius of a circle the circumference of which was equal to the perimeter of the pyramid at ground-
level. The Northern Stone Pyramid at Dahshur, with its gradient of 43° 36',
provides the only striking exception to this rule.

Herodotus, who was presumably quoting the tradition current in
Egypt during his time, makes the following assertions with regard to the
building of the Great Pyramid: 'The pyramid was built in tiers, battlement-
wise, as it is called, or, according to others, stepwise. When the pyramid was
completed in this form, they raised the remaining stones to their places by
means of machines formed of short beams of wood. The first machine raised
them from the ground to the top of the first step. On this there was another
machine, which received the stone upon its arrival, and conveyed it to the

The Pyramid of Sahurē, cross-section
looking east

1. upright layers of core masonry
2. internal casings of fine limestone
3. packing-blocks of stone
4. smooth outer casing of Tura
limestone

second step, whence a third machine advanced it still higher. Either they had as many machines as there were steps in the pyramid, or possibly they had but a single machine, which, being easily moved, was transferred from tier to tier as the stone rose – both accounts are given and therefore I mention both. The upper portion of the pyramid was finished first, then the middle, and finally the part which was lowest and nearest the ground.'[7] Archaeological discovery, while tending to confirm the concluding sentence, has so far revealed little evidence in support of Herodotus's statements as a whole, but it must be admitted that pyramid construction is a subject on which the last word has certainly not yet been written.

In the absence of the pulley – a device which does not seem to have been known in Egypt before Roman times – only one method of raising heavy weights was open to the ancient Egyptians, namely by means of ramps composed of brick and earth which sloped upwards from the level of the ground to whatever height was desired. If, for instance, a short wall were to be built, the stones for each course after the lowest would be taken to the required level on a ramp constructed against the wall for the whole of its length and projecting outwards at right angles to the line of the wall. With the addition of each successive course of masonry, the ramp would be raised and also extended so that the gradient remained unchanged. Finally, when the wall had been built to its full height, the ramp would be dismantled and the outer faces of the stones, which had not previously been made smooth, dressed course by course downwards as the level of the ramp was reduced. A late example of such a ramp could, until very recently, be seen against the unfinished first pylon of the temple of Karnak,[8] and proof that the method was already practised in earlier times has been furnished by the discovery of the remains of ramps at the Pyramid of Meidum, in the unfinished mortuary temple of Mycerinus, and at the Pyramid of Ammenemes I at Lisht. The gradient of a ramp probably depended on the weight of the material to be conveyed. A papyrus in the British Museum dating from the XIXth Dynasty gives the following approximate measurements for a hypothetical ramp: length 415 yards, width 32 yards, and maximum height 35 yards. By arithmetical calculation it may be deduced that the gradient of this ramp would have been about 1 in 12. The gradient of the ramp in the mortuary temple of Mycerinus was about 1 in 8.

If it be conceded, as the evidence would appear to demand, that ramps were employed by the builders of the pyramids, how were these ramps set out? No difficulty would arise in the construction of a step pyramid, because each step could serve as a platform on which four ramps could be built sideways, one against each face of the monument. Narrow foothold embankments built of brick against the portions of the faces which were not partly or entirely covered by the ramps would enable the builders to manoeuvre more easily the stones of the outer casing. By a progressive reduction in the height of the embankments they could subsequently begin work on dressing the exposed surface of the casing while the upper part of the pyramid was still under construction. The operation could not have been completed until the last stone had been taken to the top and the ramps had been dismantled.

It has been suggested that a similar method, but without the addition of foot-hold embankments, was employed in building the true pyramid.[9] According to this suggestion one ramp would begin at each corner of the monument and continue its upward course in zigzag fashion around all four faces until it reached the summit. Ramps of this kind, built in tiers, would depend for their support, beyond the first stage, on the casing-blocks which, it is maintained, would be laid in steps and cut back to the correct angle after the work of building was finished. In order to demonstrate the feasibility of this method a model of a pyramid with tier-ramps was constructed at the Museum of Science, Boston, Mass., in 1950, and no practical difficulties in putting the theory into effect were discovered. Nevertheless, it is hard to believe that this was in reality the method employed by the ancient Egyptians for three reasons: it does not accord with the traces of ramps found at Meidum and elsewhere; undressed casing-blocks, such as may be seen at the base of the Pyramid of Mycerinus, though rough, are not step-like and would not have provided support for a ramp; if, as observation suggests, the casing-stones were laid from in front it is questionable whether the widest possible step would have allowed sufficient space for blocks of the weight of those at Giza to be unloaded from their sledges and placed in position. It may perhaps be argued that the rough granite casing-blocks in the Pyramid of Mycerinus represent an intermediate stage after the steps had been cut away, but support for the ramps would have been almost completely lacking in the Bent Pyramid, the casing-blocks of which, being laid on beds inclining downwards towards the centre, required very little trimming and would have presented an almost unbroken surface at every stage in construction.

A more plausible solution seems to be that a single supply-ramp was constructed to cover the whole of one side of the pyramid. As the pyramid rose in height, so the ramp was increased both in height and in length; simultaneously the top surface would become progressively narrower to correspond with the constantly diminishing breadth of the pyramid face. If the angle of incline of the pyramid were 52°, the two side faces of the ramp would also slope at an angle of 52°, so that any risk of collapse would be eliminated. The three sides of the pyramid which were not covered by the supply-ramp would have foot-hold embankments of sufficient width at the top to allow for the passage of men and building material, but, since they were not required for raising the stones from the ground, their gradient on the exposed outer surface could be as steep as would be compatible with firmness. Wooden baulks, some of which were actually found *in situ* by the American excavators at Lisht, would be placed on the top surface of both the supply-ramp and the foot-hold embankments in order to provide a firm roadway for the passage of sledges bearing the stone blocks.

As an illustration of the practical application of the method suggested, let it be imagined that a pyramid has been built to half its final height.[10] Nothing of the stonework already laid would be visible from the ground, because three of the outer faces would be entirely covered by the foot-hold embankments and the fourth face would be screened by the supply-ramp. The top surface of the pyramid would resemble a square platform and would be ready to receive the next course of masonry. The first stones to be hauled up to the platform would be core-blocks from the local quarries; their sides and top surfaces would be left rough, but the bottom surfaces – the so-called 'bedding joints' – would be smooth. These stones would be taken to the centre of the platform and laid against each other, the gaps caused by the irregularities in their sides being often left unfilled. Care would be taken to extend the new course evenly in all four directions, so that it always remained approximately in the form of a square, and at regular intervals its sides would be made absolutely equal in length by the addition of an internal casing composed of Tura limestone laid directly above the corresponding casing in the floor of the platform; the outer face of the casing would be cut so as to incline inwards at an angle of about $75°$, but it would not be dressed smooth. At length, the area of the course being laid would have been enlarged until only a narrow margin at the outer edges of the original platform remained uncovered. At that stage the packing-blocks of local limestone would be added and considerably greater attention would be given to securing close joints. In the Great Pyramid the packing-blocks were laid in such a way that they sloped slightly inwards towards the centre of each course, with the result that a noticeable depression runs down the middle of each face – a peculiarity shared, as far as is known, by no other pyramid.

The core having been completed, only the outer casing of Tura limestone remained to be added. It was a delicate operation and imperfections in the setting of the stones would not only mar the outward appearance of the monument, but, unless counteracted, would lead to irregularity in the pyramidal form. The joints, moreover, must be as close as possible. In order to save time and to achieve the highest possible degree of accuracy, the fitting of the rising joints – those between neighbouring blocks on the same course – was probably carried out by highly skilled masons working on ground-level. Only by such a method could the results to be observed in the so-called 'oblique rising joints' – those cut either not at right angles to the bedding joint or not parallel with the central axes of the pyramid – have been attained. Possibly the joints between the backs of the casing-stones and the front faces of the packing-blocks were also fitted on the ground so that, when each block finally reached the men who were to lay it, only the upper surface and the front – already cut to the pyramid angle but not dressed – needed further attention from the masons.

Even after making such careful preparations, the laying of a casing-block was still a difficult task, especially if it were a large block weighing perhaps more than 10 tons. Doubtless it would be carried on its sledge to the furthest possible point, namely on the embankment directly opposite the place in the structure which it was ultimately destined to occupy. The block would then be levered sideways off the sledge until it rested on battens placed ready to receive it on top of the casing-stone in the course below; in order to enable levers to be used, bosses were left by the masons on the outer face of every casing-block. While it stood in that position, a thin layer of mortar would be spread over both the bedding joint and the rising joint about to be formed. The main purpose of the mortar was to provide a kind of lubricant so that the casing-block, after being lowered to its bed, might be slid first into contact with the block of casing previously laid and then back against the packing-blocks. How this last operation was performed is not clear, but it is possible that it could have been achieved by pulling on ropes attached to a baulk of timber laid across the free outer corner of the casing-block and then pressing it back into line by levering from in front. The few remaining casing-blocks at the foot of the Great Pyramid offer the best examples of such jointing hitherto discovered; the credit for being the first to bring their excellence to the notice of the modern world belongs to Petrie, who wrote of them: 'Several measures were taken of the thickness of the joints in the casing-stones. The mean thickness of the joints of the north-eastern casing-stones is 0·02 inches, and therefore the mean variation of the cutting of the stone from the straight line and from a true square is but 0·01 on a length of 75 inches up the face, an amount of accuracy equal to the most modern opticians' straight-edges of such a length. Though the stones were brought as close as $\frac{1}{50}$ inch, or, in fact, in contact, the mean opening of the joint was but $\frac{1}{100}$ inch.'

When the casing-stones on all four sides of the course had been placed in position, it would be necessary to make a survey in order to ascertain whether the correct form had been retained. Small deviations were almost inevitable and, if detected in time, could be counteracted in the laying of the next course. While this work was in progress, the main supply-ramp and the foot-hold embankments would be raised to the new level of the pyramid and masons would be employed on the task of dressing the tops of the stones just laid – the bedding joints of the course about to be added. So the building would continue to grow course by course until lastly the capstone, generally made of granite, would be placed on the apex. As a means of securing the stone firmly to its bed, a projection resembling a disk would be carved in the centre of the base to fit like a tenon into a mortise cut to receive it in the middle of the top course of masonry. It may therefore be deduced that the capstone, already shaped but still in the rough, was taken to the top of the pyramid on its sledge, and then supported on levers while the sledge was being removed. Battens would be inserted underneath and a thin layer of mortar be spread over the bed; finally, after the removal of the battens, it would be lowered by means of levers placed under the side-bosses. An inscription found by Jéquier at the Pyramid of Queen Udjebten refers to the gilded capstone on her pyramid, which suggests that these stones were, at least sometimes, overlaid with gold. No early example has yet come to light, but six specimens have been found, the finest, now in the Cairo Museum, having belonged to the Pyramid of Ammenemes III at Dahshur; it is made of grey granite, and on its four faces are carved inscriptions containing invocations addressed to the Sun-god and to three other deities.

The laborious process of assembling the pyramid was now finished, and work could be started on dressing the four outer faces, beginning with the capstone. As the work proceeded, the supply-ramp and the foot-hold embankments would be lowered, thus making fresh courses of casing-stones accessible for dressing. In order to complete the task more quickly, it is possible that the reduction of the ramp and embankments was not carried out gradually, but in layers of several feet; wooden scaffolding would then be erected in their place so that a large number of men could be employed on different levels at the same time. Scaffolding was certainly known to the Egyptians, and the time saved by its use when dressing the five acres of casing on each face of the Great Pyramid, for example, would have been very considerable. When at length the whole operation had been completed, the builders would be free and the ground clear for erecting the mortuary temple, the corridor of the causeway, and the valley building, some of which had certainly had their foundations laid before the construction of the pyramid had been begun.

No mention has yet been made of the method whereby corridors and chambers would have been incorporated into pyramids. In one respect, the task resembled that of building the internal casings; both operations necessitated the introduction of closely fitting stones into a core otherwise composed of rough masonry. Since, however, the corridors and chambers occupied so small a portion of the whole pyramid, they may have been built almost independently of the rest of the work. Subsidiary ramps, capable of being dismantled in a few hours, could have been erected at any stage convenient, so that blocks could be taken to a considerably greater height than the level of the course under construction. In this way, the men employed would have time to complete their work on the interior of the pyramid before the surrounding courses of core-masonry had risen to such a height that it would become necessary to roof the corridor and chambers; afterwards, access to the interior would not be possible until the foot-hold embankment or supply-ramp covering the northern face of the pyramid had been lowered to the level of the entrance. As a further aid, the stones would be carefully prepared before they were required by the builders; the roofing-slabs of the King's Chamber in the Great Pyramid, for instance, were fitted together on the ground and numbered so that, when they were taken to their final position, they could be reassembled with the minimum delay. The sarcophagus, portcullises, and, in the Great Pyramid only, the plug-blocks, would be introduced before the walls of the chamber, slots, or gallery in which they were to rest had been fully built.

The capstone from the Pyramid of Ammenemes III at Dahshur, made of grey granite, is inscribed with invocations to the Sun-god and three other deities.

It must be emphasized that the foregoing attempt to reconstruct the methods used by the pyramid-builders differs in many important respects

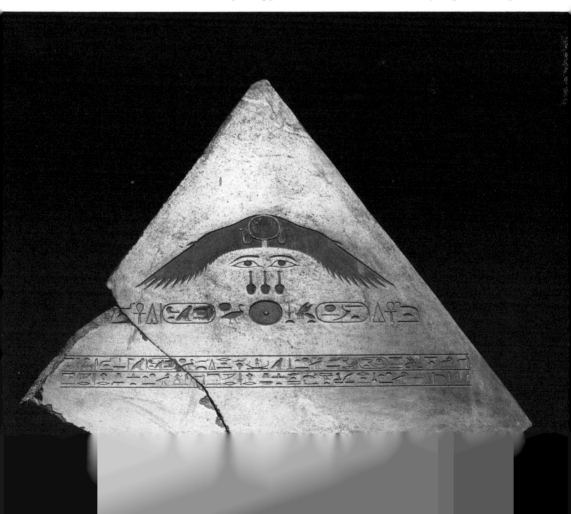

not only from the explanation previously mentioned but also from the views expressed by some other authorities.[11] The main divergence of opinion arises in connection with the number and arrangement of the ramps – a problem on which archaeological investigation has not yet revealed sufficiently clear evidence to enable positive deductions to be made. Petrie, in one of his last essays on this subject, stated his belief that the casing-stones of the Great Pyramid had been taken to their respective courses with their outer faces already dressed, and that they were laid in position from the inside. The casing would thus have been laid first in every course, and the core have been filled in afterwards. By such a method, as Petrie pointed out, only one ramp would have been required and three faces of the pyramid would have been finished as soon as their casing-stones had been laid. In support of his views Petrie wrote: 'There is small difference of angle between the [casing-] blocks at their junction, proving that the faces have not been even smoothed since being built together.'[12] There is certainly no good reason for doubting the accuracy of Petrie's observations or his deductions in so far as they apply to the method adopted for laying the few casing-stones of the Great Pyramid which have survived to the present day, but his general conclusion that the same procedure would have been followed when laying all the casing-stones of the building is open to grave objections. All the stones in question stand on the lowest course; beneath them lies a smooth pavement of Tura limestone which also projects outwards beyond the pyramid to a width of about 2 feet. It would have been impossible to lay these stones from the outer side without damaging the fringe of the pavement which was to remain exposed. Likewise, it would have been undesirable to dress the lower edge of stones after they had been placed in position: the surface of the pavement would inevitably have been chipped and scratched. Moreover, these particular casing-stones may well have been laid before the core in order to define the size and orientation of the pyramid base. Slight adjustments in the setting of the stones could so much more easily have been made if they were free at both back and front; any error at the base would result in the faulty orientation of the whole monument, and might destroy its regularity of form. If Petrie could have shown that casing-blocks on a higher level than the bottom course in any pyramid were laid at an angle to each other, his argument would have carried greater weight. Furthermore, the evidence in favour of the method of laying casing-stones from the front is very considerable. Several unfinished works testify that it was the technique employed by Egyptian builders from the inception of megalithic masonry until the latest times. An example exists even in a pyramid, namely the Pyramid of Mycerinus, where the limestone which cased the upper portion was completely dressed, but the granite casing lower down was left partly in the rough, thus marking the point where work on the monument came to a premature end. Laying masonry from the front, however, necessitated both leaving the outer faces of the stones in the rough until they had been placed in position and the erection of embankments against the outer face of the course previously laid, which would have involved, in the case of a pyramid, building embankments against all four faces.

A suggestion regarding the construction of pyramids which owes its origin to Richard Lepsius was that their size was determined by the length of their owner's reign – the so-called 'accretion theory'. Undoubtedly, some

Copper implements dating from the Ist Dynasty, found by W. B. Emery at Saqqara, prove that even at that early date the Egyptians had tools capable of cutting limestone.

pyramids, notably the Step Pyramid of Zoser and the Meidum pyramid, underwent successive enlargements and some, probably including the Great Pyramid and the Pyramid of Mycerinus, were altered internally while under construction, but changes in the original design were, on the whole, exceptional. If length of reign had possessed any direct bearing on the dimensions of a pyramid, it might have been expected that Pepi II, who occupied the throne for about ninety-four years, would have built a pyramid several times larger than that of Mycerinus, who reigned only about eighteen years, or that Cheops in a reign of about twenty-three years would have failed to build a pyramid equal to that of Unas, who is believed to have ruled for thirty years. Clearly, therefore, the length of a king's reign did not necessarily affect the size of his pyramid; the determining considerations seem rather to have been his personal inclinations, his power, and the religious beliefs current in his time.

Divergent opinions have been expressed by chemists on the question whether the pyramids were painted. Tests carried out by A. Pochan on fragments of the outer casing of the Great Pyramid and of the Pyramid of Chephren revealed traces of chemical elements which were not naturally present in the stone, but which he believed could be explained on the assumption that the monuments had been coated with a thin layer of siliceous gypsum plaster and painted with a pigment of red ochre. That the casing-stones of pyramids show coloration varying from brownish red to greyish black is not disputed. There is, however, disagreement on the cause of this coloration. A. Lucas, who accepted in the main Pochan's chemical analysis, maintained that no coating of plaster had been applied and that the colour was merely the result of desert patination brought about gradually by atmospheric conditions. Both these authorities have received independent support for their contentions, but a valuable piece of evidence which seems to have been overlooked is that the pyramid, when employed as a hieroglyphic sign on the painted walls of Old Kingdom mastabas, is usually represented white with a band of brownish red stippled with black at the base and sometimes a blue or yellow capstone. The stippled band is clearly intended to indicate pink granite, as exemplified in the two lowest courses of the casing of the Pyramid of Chephren, the blue signifies grey granite and the yellow must represent the gold overlay which was sometimes placed on the capstone. If the main body of the casing of pyramids had normally been painted, it would surely not have been depicted, when reproduced as a hieroglyph, in white, the natural colour of Tura limestone.

In the face of so many unknown or unconfirmed factors, speculations regarding the number of men required for building one of the larger pyramids and the time needed for the work may perhaps appear vain. Certainly, any estimate based on the evidence now available must lack precision and can only serve to convey an approximate idea. Herodotus claims to have been informed that the Great Pyramid was built in twenty years. Levies numbering 100,000 men, he says, were employed for 'periods of three months' on transporting the stones from the quarry to the pyramid.[13] Herodotus seems to have intended his readers to understand that the aggregate of men engaged annually was 400,000 – four separate groups of 100,000, each group being employed for three months in the year. Such a number would, however, have been unnecessarily large, as a simple mathematical calculation will demonstrate. If the estimated total of 2,300,000

Two painted wooden statues of Sesostris I were found in the mastaba tomb of an official named Imhotep. This example shows the king wearing the red crown of Lower Egypt; the companion piece shows the white crown of Upper Egypt. The crown and kilt are covered with gesso. Both statues seem to represent the king as a young man at the beginning of his long co-regency.

Overleaf: Egyptian artists excelled at two-dimensional relief. They portrayed the after-life as a mirror image of life as they knew it and left an invaluable social history in visual form. These scenes from the tomb of Nefer indicate the wide variety of occupations pursued by people in the time of the pyramid-builders; gathering papyrus, fowling in the marshes, dancing and mock-fighting are only a few of the activities depicted.

separate blocks in the pyramid is approximately correct, the average number of blocks to be transported annually for twenty years would have been 115,000. The mean weight of the blocks is about $2\frac{1}{2}$ tons, a weight which Petrie believed could have been handled by a gang of eight men.[14] Assuming that Petrie was right and that only 100,000 men were employed in a year, each gang would have been required to move ten blocks in twelve weeks. Such a task would almost certainly have been within the ability of a gang, bearing in mind that the distance to be traversed, especially by the core-blocks, was not very great. Moreover, as Petrie pointed out, the work could have been done during the inundation season, between the end of July and the end of October, when the land could not be cultivated and the majority of the population would have been idle.

There can be little doubt but that, in addition to the men levied annually for the special purpose of transporting the blocks of the Great Pyramid, a large number of whole-time workers must have been engaged in building the pyramid. These men, consisting of skilled masons and an attendant body of labourers, were continuously employed preparing and laying the blocks and erecting or dismantling the ramps and foot-hold embankments. They lived, it may be presumed, in the buildings found by Petrie lying west of the Pyramid of Chephren. About 4,000 men, according to Petrie's estimate, could have been housed in these barracks, and that figure would therefore represent the total number of permanent workers. The chips of stone cast away by the masons were dumped over the side of the cliffs both north and south of the pyramid. Commenting on the size of the dumps, Petrie wrote: 'They are probably equal in bulk to more than half of the Pyramid.'[15]

Although the period of twenty years quoted by Herodotus does not seem unreasonable for building a monument of the size of the Great Pyramid, it is necessary to observe that this figure is not in accord with the evidence offered by the dates inscribed in red ink on two casing-blocks of the Northern Pyramid at Dahshur. One of these blocks bears a date which has been read as the twenty-first year of the reign of Seneferu and, being situated at the north-east corner, it should indicate the year in which the work of construction was begun; the other block, seen by Richard Lepsius half-way up the face of the pyramid, was dated in the following year. In view of the time required for building the Bent Pyramid and at least part of the Pyramid of Meidum, it is probable that the Northern Pyramid was not built until late in Seneferu's reign of twenty-four years, but it is hard to believe that it would have been possible to construct this pyramid in three years if twenty years were required to build the Great Pyramid, a monument only about one-third greater in volume. Perhaps further excavation around the base of the northern pyramid will reveal other examples of dated blocks *in situ*; if they confirm the date read on the single block now available a considerable revision in the hitherto accepted estimates of time spent in building the larger pyramids will clearly become necessary.

A complete solution to such problems as the methods used by the pyramid-builders, the number of men employed, and the time required for the task would undoubtedly shed a very valuable sidelight on technical development in ancient times, but it would hardly be likely to provide an answer to an even more interesting question, namely why the early Egyptian kings should have chosen to construct their tombs in the pyramidal form. Before this question is considered, however, the derivation of the name is

Khendjer, whose head in granite is shown at the left, ruled at the beginning of the Second Intermediate Period – a time of weakness and political unrest. It is not surprising that the main innovations in his pyramid were devices intended to make it impregnable.

worth examining. In Egyptian, this type of tomb, at least in the geometrically true form, was called *m(e)r*, a name which has not been suspected of concealing any descriptive significance. The word 'Pyramid' owes its origin to the Greek *pyramis*, plural *pyramides*, for which a satisfactory Egyptian derivation has often been sought, but in vain. A geometrical term *per-em-us* (literally 'what goes [straight] up from the *us*' – a word of uncertain meaning), which embodies the requisite consonants, is used to indicate the vertical height of a pyramid in an Egyptian mathematical treatise.[16] To suppose, however, that *pyramis* was derived from *per-em-us* would imply that the Greeks either mistook the meaning of the Egyptian term or, for reasons unknown, deliberately named the whole structure after a part, by the linguistic process known as 'synecdoche'. In the absence of any more convincing explanation, it seems better to regard *pyramis* as a purely Greek word which had no etymological connection with the Egyptian language. An exactly similar word exists with the meaning 'wheaten cake', and the suggestion has been made that the early Greeks used this word humorously as a name for the Egyptian monuments,[17] possibly because, when seen from a distance, they resembled large cakes. The word *obeliskos*, which in addition to meaning an obelisk also means a 'little spit' or 'skewer', furnishes another example of the same kind of process of thought whereby the Greeks, instead of borrowing a foreign word, jocularly adapted a descriptive word of their own to name an object which had no exact parallel in their own country.

Two important factors, one constant and the other variable, which influenced the development of early Egyptian sepulchral architecture were the need to provide sufficient protection for the body and the belief that the tomb, in its general character, should supply the owner with the basic requirements of the after-life. Within the limits thus imposed the architect could exercise his artistic talents and introduce structural innovations. Although it follows as a corollary that a major change in the design of the tomb probably signified a change in the prevailing conception of the after-life, it does not also follow that previous architectural elements were immediately discarded; if possible the architect tried either to superimpose the new on the old or, alternatively, to combine the new with the old as separate constructions within one complex. The results of the two methods are seen most clearly in the brick mastabas of the Ist Dynasty at Saqqara which embodied the pre-dynastic mound, the Step Pyramid of Zoser, and the pyramids of Meidum and Sahurē. It is true that the mastabas at Saqqara were not, at least exclusively, royal tombs and that the two examples chosen were the only mastabas in which at the time of excavation the mound could be recognized, but in the light of the knowledge gained by this discovery its presence has been suspected in other mastabas previously excavated. It must also be conceded that no account is taken of the Early Dynastic royal 'tombs' at Abydos, the superstructures of which were completely destroyed. Nevertheless, the evidence available, though manifestly incomplete for the early period, is capable of interpretation as a connected sequence of architectural developments which reflected progressive changes in the nature and location of the royal after-life and in the apparatus considered necessary for its realization.

Burial customs in Upper and Lower Egypt before the unification under Menes were certainly not identical. One important difference concerned the type of grave. In Upper Egypt the dead were buried in cemeteries situated on the edge of the desert and separated from the settlements of the living. Their graves, though sometimes lined with brick and roofed with timber, were outwardly marked only by mounds of sand. In Lower Egypt, however, if the practice exemplified at Merimde Benisalame (about thirty miles north-west of Cairo) may be regarded as typical, the dead were buried within the settlement and occasionally under the floors of dwelling-houses. Perhaps the original intention of the house-burial was merely to give the dead greater protection than would have been possible in isolated cemeteries, but it can easily be imagined that in the course of time the belief would grow that the dead required houses as part of their burial equipment. It would certainly explain why the Upper Egyptian conquerors, who undoubtedly adopted other Lower Egyptian customs, should suddenly have begun to build tombs in the shape of houses (mastabas), made, moreover, of mud-brick, a material which had been used for houses in Lower Egypt for centuries, but not in Upper Egypt. Among the customs of their own people which they continued to observe were the separation of the cemeteries from the settlements and, at least in some instances, the construction of the mound above the actual grave. It is hardly conceivable that a feature so adventitious in origin as the mound should have been retained if it had not acquired some magico-religious significance which gave it too great an importance to permit of its general abandonment. Only one explanation suggests itself, namely that it had already come to be regarded as a symbol of the primeval mound which emerged from the waters of chaos, as patches of high ground emerged annually from the Nile when the waters of the inundation receded. On this mound Atum, the god of creation, was believed to have first manifested himself and to have created the universe. It was thus the symbol of existence, as opposed to non-existence, and consequently, when placed above the grave or embodied in the tomb, it was imagined that it could serve as a potent source of magic from which the dead might hope to receive a renewal of existence.

The suggestion has been made that the pyramid, in both its designs, was only a monumental representation of the primeval mound, but although this conception may have been present in the minds of the Egyptians it seems more probable that a different motive inspired its development. Just as the mastaba had been superimposed on the mound in the Ist Dynasty, so was Zoser's step pyramid, at the beginning of the IIIrd Dynasty, superimposed on a solid box-like structure which has generally been regarded as a mastaba. But was it really a mastaba? If so the squareness of its plan would be difficult to understand. Nothing, however, seems to rule out the possibility that the structure represents the mound which, in the simple form but not in the stepped form, was nearly square (34 feet 6 inches × 30 feet 3 inches) whereas the mastaba (123 feet 3 inches × 52 feet) was oblong. The existence of an independent mastaba (the south mastaba) is not decisive. On the one hand it may be explained as a substitute for the central structure conceived as a mastaba, and, on the other hand, if the central structure be regarded as a mound, it may be considered as having no connection with an original plan to build a mastaba tomb which was superseded when it was decided to build a pyramid. Whichever explanation is correct, its position in the core of the southern enclosure wall would be in accord with the regular practice of concealing the older type of tomb.

If the step pyramid is not itself a monumental mound and not, as has

sometimes been supposed, a mere architectural development achieved by superimposing one mastaba on another, how is its form to be explained and what was its purpose? The pyramid texts suggest an answer to these questions. One of the many different ways by which the deceased king, or more probably his spiritualized body, could approach the celestial heaven was by a staircase. Spell 267 reads: 'A staircase to heaven is laid for him [i.e. the king] so that he may mount up to heaven thereby.' The same thought is repeated almost verbatim in Spell 619. It is not difficult to imagine that the same process of imitative magic as had inspired the inclusion of the mound in the mastaba was again responsible for the choice of the step pyramid. As models, both were credited with embracing the magical properties ascribed to the objects which they represented. Through the possession of the pyramid the king would be able to mount up to heaven at will and to return to his tomb in order to enjoy the offerings brought to him by his priests and relations. The nature of this heavenly life will be discussed after the significance of the true pyramid has been considered.

Perhaps some support for the explanation of the step pyramid as a staircase may be seen in the writing of the Egyptian word 'r meaning 'to ascend'. It was the regular practice of the Egyptians to add a sign, the so-called 'determinative' or 'sense-sign', to the consonantal spelling of a word, in order to define its meaning; vowels were never written. The determinative of the word 'r is ⌂, which has generally been regarded as a double staircase, but it could equally well have been a representation of a step pyramid, for the Egyptians, when depicting an object, always gave a full view, either from the front or from the side. The technique of drawing a three-quarter view was unknown to them. Thus the determinative of the word for a true pyramid – the word for a step pyramid has not yet been identified – is always written △ which represents the front view of a true pyramid and of one side of the surrounding wall. If ⌂ does represent a step pyramid it must have been chosen as the determinative of the word 'r because step pyramids were particularly associated with the idea of ascending.

Step pyramids (apart from a brief revival in the time of the XVIIIth Dynasty at Soleb in the Sudan, about which little is yet known) remained in favour for perhaps less than a century. At the beginning of the IVth Dynasty Seneferu built the Bent Pyramid at Dahshur, the first tomb planned from the beginning as a true pyramid. In doing so he made the task of the builders incomparably more difficult and laborious; the true pyramid required for its construction long and high embankments and at least one ramp of immense length and height, whereas a step pyramid needed only a small number of low ramps. Whether or not a step pyramid was embodied within the Bent Pyramid has never been ascertained, but if Seneferu had already built a step pyramid at Meidum he may not have thought it necessary to build a composite pyramid. His successors however certainly followed the practice of superimposing the new type of tomb on the old and thereby no doubt hoped to profit from the magical properties ascribed to both types. What were the supposed advantages offered by the true pyramid at the cost of so much additional labour in comparison with the step pyramid?

J. H. Breasted, writing about the importance of the pyramid, stated: 'The pyramidal form of the king's tomb was of the most sacred significance. The king was buried under the very symbol of the Sun-god which stood in the holy of holies in the Sun-temple at Heliopolis, a symbol upon which,

This pit, lined with limestone, once contained a barque for use by Cheops in the after-life.

from the day when he created the gods, he was accustomed to manifest himself in the form of a Phoenix; and when in mountainous proportions the pyramid rose above the king's sepulchre, dominating the royal city below and the valley beyond for many miles, it was the loftiest object which greeted the Sun-god in all the land and his morning rays glittered on its shining summit long before he scattered the shadows in the dwellings of humbler mortals below.'[18] Although it now seems probable that the stone symbol of the Sun-god at Heliopolis, the *benben*, was conical and not pyramidal in shape, Breasted was undoubtedly right in associating it with the true pyramid. The construction of a conical building of pyramidal dimensions would surely have defeated the ancient Egyptian builders, and moreover it could not easily have been superimposed on a step pyramid. But what did the *benben* and its architectural derivative, the true pyramid, represent? Only one answer suggests itself: the rays of the sun shining down on earth. A remarkable spectacle may sometimes be seen in the late afternoon of a cloudy winter day at Giza. When standing on the road to Saqqara and gazing westwards at the pyramid plateau, it is possible to see the sun's rays striking downwards through a gap in the clouds at about the same angle as the slope of the Great Pyramid. The impression made on the mind by the scene is that the immaterial prototype and the material replica are here ranged side by side.*

Is it necessary to suppose with Breasted that the true pyramid was intended merely as a copy of the solar symbol in the temple of Heliopolis? Could it not, like the step pyramid, also have possessed a supposed practical purpose? The pyramid texts often describe the king as mounting to heaven on the rays of the sun. Spell 508 of these texts, for instance, reads: 'I have trodden those thy rays as a ramp under my feet whereon I mount up to that my mother, the living Uraeus on the brow of Rē.' Again, Spell 523 reads: 'Heaven hath strengthened for thee the rays of the sun in order that thou mayest lift thyself to heaven as the eye of Rē.' The temptation to regard the true pyramid as a material representation of the sun's rays and consequently as a means whereby the dead king could ascend to heaven seems irresistible. Such an explanation would give the true pyramid a practical purpose in keeping not only with the step pyramid but also with the other elements in the royal mortuary complex. Moreover, the pyramid would not be the only material representation of an intangible object included in the king's funerary equipment; the wooden boats placed near the pyramid in pits lined with Tura limestone were representations of the immaterial boat in which the dead king would traverse the sky in company with the Sun-god. The underlying conception in each case was the principle of creation by imitation: a model, whether it were a stone statue of a person or a scene carved in relief, was thought to possess all the virtues of the actual object which it represented. Size was not a matter of primary importance to the efficacy of the substitute, and herein may be one reason for the rapid decline in the dimensions of the pyramid after the time of Cheops and Chephren.

Although the two types of pyramid admit of interpretations which are similar, at least in their broad conception, it seems unlikely that the change in design occurred merely because doubts were felt about the efficacy of the staircase method of approach to heaven. The transition was accompanied by the construction of a complex of a very different kind in which the mortuary temple was placed not on the north side but on the east side

* Alexandre Moret, *Le Nil*, p. 203, makes the following observation: 'These great triangles forming the sides of the pyramids seem to fall from the sky like the beams of the sun when its disk, though veiled by storm, pierces the clouds and lets down to earth a ladder of rays.'

facing the rising sun. This position would be natural in a solar cult, whereas a northern orientation would seem to be inexplicable. If the same principle governed the choice of position for the temple of the step pyramid it should be indicative of the cult with which it was associated.

Turning again to the pyramid texts, it may be seen that the dead king was frequently considered to have ascended to the stars, and particularly to the circumpolar stars, the so-called 'Indestructibles'. As an example, Spell 269 reads: 'He [Atum] assigns the king to those gods, who are nimble [?] and wise, the Indestructible Stars.' On the ground of internal evidence alone it has been deduced that the pyramid texts which refer to the stars had an independent origin from the solar spells and that eventually they were merged into the Heliopolitan doctrine. Imhotep's title 'Chief of the Observers', which became the regular title of the High Priest of Heliopolis, may itself suggest an occupation connected with astral, rather than solar, observation. Here, therefore, may be the difference between the underlying purpose of the true and the step pyramid, the latter being a product of the stellar cult and intended to enable the king to reach the astral heaven.

In the light of the foregoing explanations, it may be worth while to glance again at the Egyptian word for a pyramid; perhaps it may yet possess some significance. The Egyptians frequently designated the constituent parts of their temples and sacred enclosures by names which were indicative of their particular functions. In the temple of Heliopolis, for example, the building which housed the *benben* was named the 'House of the Benben'. The tomb, it has already been remarked, was called the 'Castle of Eternity'. Some of the elements within the pyramid complex also possessed descriptive names: the causeway was called the 'Entrance of the Haul' (*ra-sta*), meaning the way along which the sledges bearing the body of the dead king and his personal possessions would be hauled; the stone false door in the sanctuary was named the 'Entrance of the House' (*ra-per*). *M(e)r*, a pyramid, could belong to the same class of name if it could be established that it was a compound consisting of the prefix *m*, found in Egyptian to convey the meaning 'instrument' or 'place', and the verb '*r*, 'to ascend', already mentioned: *m(e)r* would then mean the 'Place of Ascension'. The disappearance of the ' (which corresponds with the *ayin* of the Semitic languages) thus postulated however constitutes a formidable objection to this derivation. In order to conform with known philological laws it would be necessary to suppose that the *ayin* had first been weakened into an *i* and then become assimilated with the *m*. No parallel to such a twofold development of one word has yet come to light and, in its absence, the likelihood that it occurred in *m(e)r* must be open to justifiable doubt.

The Egyptians were not the only ancient people of the Middle East who believed that heaven and the gods might be reached by ascending a high building; a kindred trend of thought prevailed in Mesopotamia. At the centre of any city in Assyria or Babylonia lay a sacred area occupied by the temple complex and a royal palace. Within the temple complex was a high brick tower known as the 'ziggurat'. Describing the Ziggurat of Babylon – the supposed origin of the Biblical Tower of Babel – Herodotus states:

'In the middle of the precinct there was a tower of solid masonry, a furlong in length and breadth, upon which was raised a second tower, and on that a third, and so on up to eight. The ascent to the upper towers is made on the outside, round all the towers. . . . On the topmost tower there is a spacious temple, and inside the temple stands a great bed covered with fine bedclothes, with a golden table by its side. There is no statue of any kind set up in the place, nor is the chamber occupied of nights by any one but a single native woman who, as the Chaldeans, the priests of this god, affirm, is chosen for himself by the deity out of all the women of the land. They also declare – but I for my part do not credit it – that the god comes down in person into this chamber, and sleeps upon the couch.'[19]

Ziggurats, like the Pyramids, were given individual names; the Ziggurat of Sippar, for example, was called the 'House of the Staircase of the bright Heaven' – a name which itself emphasizes that the building was considered as a link between heaven and earth. The resemblance between the two edifices does not, however, extend to sepulchral realms, for the ziggurat was certainly not a tomb, whereas every pyramid was intended for that purpose.

In contrast with the short chronological span of step pyramids, the history of the true pyramid extends over a thousand years, without taking into account its lineal successors in the Sudan. Only one king during this long period, Shepseskaf of the IVth Dynasty, is known to have possessed a tomb of a different pattern, but doubtless the ephemeral kings, of whom there were many in the two Intermediate Periods, were seldom able to command the resources necessary for constructing pyramids, certainly not of monumental dimensions, even when their tenure of the throne might have allowed sufficient time. It is difficult to believe that Shepseskaf, whose example was followed by Queen Khentkaues, probably his wife, was not trying to break away from the influence of Heliopolis and its powerful priesthood. Some suggestion of the same motive, or at least of incomplete confidence in the value of the true pyramid, may perhaps be detected in the pyramids of two other kings of the IVth Dynasty, Djedefrē and Nebka. Not only do they resemble the step Pyramid of Zoser in the location of the burial-chamber at the base of a deep vertical shaft, but the name of one of these pyramids – Djedefrē is a *sehed*-star – and the name of a quarry-gang connected with the building of the other pyramid – Nebka is a star – clearly associate their owners with an astral after-life.

Apart from these apparent aberrations, the changes and developments follow a course which suggests at least the tacit acceptance of a well-established creed. Sceptics there may have been among the royal builders, but the prospect of achieving immortality – even though time has shown that this ambition could not have been realized without the services of the archaeologist – may itself have proved a sufficient inducement to maintain a custom long after confidence in its value had been lost. How little could these kings have imagined what opportunities for speculation they were providing for posterity! Centuries before John Taylor in 1859 had published his theory that the Great Pyramid had been built by a divinely chosen race of non-Egyptian invaders acting directly under God's guidance, Arab writers had associated the pyramids with the Biblical narrative of the Flood, claiming that they had been built as a result of a dream to serve as repositories for all the wisdom and scientific knowledge of the Egyptians which would otherwise have been lost. Julius Honorius (pre-fifth century AD) quoted a legend that the pyramids were Joseph's granaries which had been used for storing corn during the years of plenty, a legend which was still current in the Middle Ages and has been preserved in the decoration of a dome in the Church of Saint Mark at Venice. Speculation only began to assume a more scientific appearance in 1864 when the Astronomer Royal of Scotland, Charles Piazzi Smyth, propounded his theories regarding the Great Pyramid based on a unit of measurement which he called the 'pyramid inch' (equal to 1·001 inches). His prestige no doubt gave the movement in search of mystery a powerful impetus which, after a century of theory and counter-theory, shows no sign of reaching exhaustion.

1 Alan Rowe, *The Museum Journal*, Philadelphia, Vol. XXII (1931), p. 21 (Pl. VI).

2 A. Lucas, *Ancient Egyptian Materials and Industries* (1962), p. 65.

3 G. A. Reisner, *Mycerinus*, p. 70.

4 L. Borchardt, *Das Grabdenkmal des Königs Sahure*, Vol. I, p. 29.

5 L. Borchardt, *Einiges zur dritten Bauperiode der grossen Pyramide bei Gise* (Cairo, 1932).

6 Somers Clarke and R. Engelbach, *Ancient Egyptian Masonry*, pp. 123–4.

7 *Herodotus*, Book II, 125 (Rawlinson's translation).

8 Somers Clarke and R. Engelbach, op. cit., Fig. 87.

9 Dows Dunham, 'Building an Egyptian Pyramid', in *Archaeology*, Vol. 9, No. 3 (1956), pp. 159–65.

10 In the following descriptions, as elsewhere in this chapter, liberal use has been made of the conclusions contained in *Ancient Egyptian Masonry* by Somers Clarke and R. Engelbach (Oxford 1930).

11 Petrie, 'The Building of a Pyramid' in *Ancient Egypt*, 1930, Pt. II, pp. 33–9; N. F. Wheeler, 'Pyramids and their Purpose' in *Antiquity*, Vol. IX (1935), pp. 172–4.

12 Petrie, op. cit., p. 34.

13 *Herodotus*, Book II, 124 (Rawlinson's translation).

14 Petrie, *The Pyramids and Temples of Gizeh*, p. 210

15 Ibid., p. 213.

16 The Rhind Mathematical Papyrus in the British Museum.

17 W. G. Waddell, *Herodotus*, Book II, p. 139.

18 J. H. Breasted, *The Development of Religion and Thought in Ancient Egypt*, p. 72.

19 *Herodotus*, Book I, 181–2 (Rawlinson's translation).

MAJOR PYRAMIDS OF THE OLD AND MIDDLE KINGDOMS

Name of King	Dynasty	Location	Dimensions	Name of Pyramid
Zoser (Step Pyramid)	3rd (*c.* 2686 BC)	Saqqara	411 ft E.-W. by 358 ft N.-S.	—
Sekhemkhet	3rd	Saqqara	395 ft sq	—
Khaba (?) (Layer Pyramid)	3rd	Zawiyet el-Aryan	276 ft sq	—
Seneferu (?)	4th (*c.* 2600 BC)	Meidum	473 ft sq	—
Seneferu (Bent Pyramid)	4th	Dahshur	620 ft sq	The Southern Pyramid: 'Seneferu gleams' (?)
Seneferu (?) (Northern Stone Pyramid)	4th	Dahshur	719 ft sq	'Seneferu gleams'
Cheops (Great Pyramid)	4th	Giza	756 ft sq	'Cheops is one belonging to the horizon'
Djedefrē	4th	Abu Roash	320 ft sq	'Djedefrē is a *sehed*-star'
Chephren	4th	Giza	708 ft sq	'Great is Chephren'
Mycerinus	4th	Giza	356 ft sq	'Mycerinus is divine'
Nebka (?) (Unfinished Pyramid)	4th (?)	Zawiyet el-Aryan	—	—
Userkaf	5th (*c.* 2490 BC)	Saqqara	247 ft sq	'Pure are the places of Userkaf'
Sahurē	5th	Abu Sir	257 ft sq	'The *Ba* of Sahurē gleams'
Neferirkarē	5th	Abu Sir	360 ft sq	'Neferirkarē has become a *Ba*'
Neferefrē	5th	Abu Sir (?)	197 ft sq	'The *Bas* of Neferefrē are divine'
Niuserrē	5th	Abu Sir	274 ft sq	'The Places of Niuserrē are enduring'
Isesi	5th	Saqqara	265 ft sq	'Isesi is beautiful'
Unas	5th	Saqqara	220 ft sq	'Beautiful are the places of Unas'
Teti	6th (*c.* 2345 BC)	Saqqara	210 ft sq	'Lasting are the places of Teti'
Pepi I	6th	Saqqara	250 ft sq	'Pepi is established and beautiful'
Merenrē	6th	Saqqara	263 ft sq	'Merenrē gleams and is beautiful'
Pepi II	6th	Saqqara	258 ft sq	'Pepi is established and alive'
Ibi	8th (*c.* 2170 BC)	Saqqara	102 ft sq	—
Neb-hepet-Rē Mentuhotep	11th (*c.* 2130 BC)	Deir el-Bahri	70 ft sq	'Glorious are the places of Neb-hepet-Rē'
Seankh-ka-Rē Mentuhotep	11th	Western Thebes	Unfinished	—
Ammenemes I	12th (*c.* 1990 BC)	Lisht	296 ft sq	'Ammenemes is high and beautiful'
Sesostris I	12th	Lisht	352 ft sq	'The one who is associated with the places of Sesostris'
Ammenemes II	12th	Dahshur	263 ft sq	'Ammenemes is strong'
Sesostris II	12th	Illahun	347 ft sq	'Sesostris is strong'
Sesostris III	12th	Dahshur	350 ft sq	—
Ammenemes III	12th	Dahshur	342 ft sq	'Ammenemes is beautiful' (?)
Ammenemes III	12th	Hawara	334 ft sq	'Ammenemes lives'
Queen Sebekneferu (?)	12th	Mazghuna	—	—
Ammenemes IV (?)	12th	Mazghuna	—	—
Khendjer	13th (*c.* 1777 BC)	Saqqara	170 ft sq	—

Bibliography

Abbreviations

A.J.A.	*American Journal of Archaeology.*
A.J.S.L.	*American Journal of Semitic Languages and Literatures.*
Anc. Egypt	*Ancient Egypt.*
Ann. Serv.	*Annales du Service des Antiquités de l'Égypte.*
Bull. F.A.C.	*Bulletin of the Faculty of Arts, University of Egypt, Cairo.*
Bull. Inst. d'Ég.	*Bulletin de l'Institut d'Égypte.*
Bull. Inst. fr.	*Bulletin de l'Institut français d'archéologie orientale.*
Bull. M.F.A.	*Bulletin of the Museum of Fine Arts, Boston.*
Bull. M.M.A.	*Bulletin of the Metropolitan Museum of Art, New York.*
Chron. d'Ég.	*Chronique d'Égypte.*
C.-R. Ac. Inscr. B.-L.	*Comptes-Rendus de l'Académie des Inscriptions et Belles-Lettres.*
J.E.A.	*Journal of Egyptian Archaeology.*
J.N.E.S.	*Journal of Near Eastern Studies.*
J.R.A.S.	*Journal of the Royal Asiatic Society.*
M.D.A.I.K.	*Mitteilungen des deutschen archäologischen Institute, Abteilung Kairo.*
P.R.S.H.S.	*Proceedings of the Royal Society of Historical Studies, Cairo.*
W.Z.K.M.	*Wiener Zeitschrift für die Kunde des Morgenlandes.*
Z.Ä.S.	*Zeitschrift für ägyptische Sprache und Altertumskunde.*

When several works by one author appear they are listed chronologically.

General

BADAWY, A. *A History of Egyptian Architecture*, Vols. I–III. Cairo, Berkeley and Los Angeles, 1954–68.

CAPART, J. and WERBROUCK, M. *Memphis à l'ombre des Pyramides.* Brussels, 1930.

HELCK, W. 'Pyramiden', Pauly-Kroll-Ziegler, *Real-Encyclopädie der classischen Altertums-Wissenschaft*, XXIII, 2, cols. 2167–2282.

LAUER, J.-P. *Le Problème des Pyramides d'Égypte.* Paris, 1948.

LAUER, J.-P. *Observations sur les Pyramides.* Cairo, 1960.

LAUER, J.-P. *Histoire monumentale des Pyramides d'Égypte*, Vol. I. Cairo, 1962.

MARAGIOGLIO, V. and RINALDI, C. A. *L'Architettura della Piramidi Menfite*, Vols. II–VII. Turin and Rapallo, 1963–70.

RICKE, H. *Bemerkungen zur ägyptischen Baukunst des Alten Reichs*, 2 vols. (*Beiträge zur ägyptischen Bauforschung und Altertumskunde*, Vols. IV and V). Zurich and Cairo, 1944–50.

RÜHLMANN, G. *Kleine Geschichte der Pyramiden.* Dresden, 1962.

SCHOTT, S. *Bemerkungen zum ägyptischen Pyramidenkult* (*Beiträge zur ägyptischen Bauforschung und Altertumskunde*, Vol. V). Cairo, 1950.

SMITH, W. S. *The Art and Architecture of Ancient Egypt* (*The Pelican History of Art*). London, 1958.

VANDIER, J. *Manuel d'archéologie égyptienne*, Vols. I and II. Paris, 1952–5.

VYSE, H. and PERRING, J. S. *Operations carried out on the Pyramids of Gizeh*, 3 vols. London, 1840–2.

Introduction

ANTHES, R. 'Egyptian Theology in the Third Millennium B.C.', in *J.N.E.S.*, XVIII (1959), pp. 169–212.

BREASTED, J. H. *The Development of Religion and Thought in Ancient Egypt.* New York, 1912.

ČERNÝ, J. *Ancient Egyptian Religion*. London, 1952.

DRIOTON, É. and VANDIER, J. *Les Peuples de l'orient Méditerranéen*, Vol. II, *L'Égypte* (4th edn.). Paris, 1962.

ERMAN, A. *A Handbook of Egyptian Religion* (English translation by A. S. Griffith). London, 1907.

ERMAN, A. *Die Religion der Ägypter*. Berlin, 1934.

GARDINER, A. H. *The Contendings of Horus and Seth* (*The Chester Beatty Papyri*, No. I). Oxford, 1931.

GARDINER, A. H. *The Attitude of the Ancient Egyptians to Death and the Dead*. Cambridge, 1935.

GRIFFITHS, J. G. *Plutarch's De Iside et Osiride*. Cardiff, 1970.

HAYES, W. C. *The Scepter of Egypt*, 2 vols. New York and Cambridge, Massachusetts, 1953–9.

JUNKER, H. *Pyramidenzeit, Das Wesen der altägyptischen Religion*. Zurich, 1949.

KEES, H. *Der Götterglaube in alten Aegypten*. Leipzig, 1941.

KEES, H. *Totenglauben und Jenseits-Vorstellungen der alten Ägypter* (2nd edn.). Berlin, 1956.

MEUNIER, M. *Plutarque, Isis et Osiris*. Paris, 1924.

SETHE, K. *Übersetzung und Kommentar zu den altägyptischen Pyramidentexten*, 4 vols. Glückstadt.

SETHE, K. *Urgeschichte und älteste Religion der Ägypter*. Leipzig, 1930.

STEINDORFF, G. in Baedeker, K. *Guide to Egypt and the Sudan* (8th edn.). Leipzig, 1929.

VANDIER, J. *La Religion égyptienne* (2nd edn.). Paris, 1949.

Chapter One   DAVIES, N. de G. *The Mastaba of Ptahhetep and Akhethetep*, 2 vols. London, 1900–1.

DUELL, P. *The Mastaba of Mereruka*, 2 vols. Chicago, 1938.

EDWARDS, I. E. S. *The Early Dynastic Period in Egypt*. Cambridge, 1964.

EMERY, W. B. *The Tomb of Hemaka*. Cairo, 1938.

EMERY, W. B. *The Tomb of Hor-Aha*. Cairo, 1939.

EMERY, W. B. *Great Tombs of the First Dynasty*, 3 vols. Cairo and London, 1949–58.

EMERY, W. B. *Archaic Egypt*. Harmondsworth, 1962.

HASSAN, S. 'Excavations at Saqqara, 1937–38', in *Ann. Serv.*, XXXVIII (1938), pp. 503–21.

JUNKER, H. *Giza, Grabungen auf dem Friedhof des Alten Reiches bei den Pyramiden von Giza*, 12 vols. Vienna, 1929–55.

LAUER, J.-P. 'Évolution de la tombe royale égyptienne jusqu'à la pyramide à degrés', in *M.D.A.I.K.*, XV (1957), pp. 148–65.

PETRIE, W. M. F. *The Royal Tombs of the First Dynasty*, Part I. London, 1900.

PETRIE, W. M. F. *The Royal Tombs of the Earliest Dynasties*, Part II. London, 1901.

QUIBELL, J. E. *The Tomb of Hesy*. Cairo, 1913.

REISNER, G. A. *The Development of the Egyptian Tomb down to the Accession of Cheops*. Cambridge, Massachusetts, 1935.

RICKE, H., *see under* General.

SMITH, G. E. and DAWSON, W. R. *Egyptian Mummies*. London, 1924.

STEINDORFF, G. *Das Grab des Ti*. Leipzig, 1913.

VANDIER, J., *see under* General.

Chapter Two   BARSANTI, A. 'Ouverture de la pyramide de Zaouiét el-Aryān', in *Ann. Serv.*, II (1901), pp. 92–4.

BORCHARDT, L. 'Die Pyramide von Silah', in *Ann. Serv.*, I (1900), pp. 211–14.

DRIOTON, É. and LAUER, J.-P. *Sakkarah, The Monuments of Zoser*. Cairo, 1939.

FIRTH, C. M., QUIBELL, J. E. and LAUER, J.-P. *The Step Pyramid*, 2 vols. Cairo, 1935–6.

GONEIM, M. Z. *The Buried Pyramid*. London, 1956.

GONEIM, M. Z. *Horus Sekhem-khet, The Unfinished Step Pyramid at Saqqara*, Vol. I. Cairo, 1957.

HELCK, W., *see under* General.

HERMANN, A. *Führer durch die Altertümer von Memphis und Sakkara*. Berlin, 1938.

HURRY, J. B. *Imhotep*. Oxford, 1926.

LAUER, J.-P. *La Pyramide à degrés*, 3 vols. Cairo, 1936-9.

LAUER, J.-P. *Études complémentaires sur les monuments du roi Zoser à Saqqarah*. Cairo, 1948.

LAUER, J.-P. 'L'apport historique des récentes découvertes du Service des Antiquités de l'Égypte dans la nécropole memphite', in *C.-R. Ac. Inscr. B.-L.*, 1954, pp. 368-79.

LAUER, J.-P. 'À propos de la nouvelle pyramide à degrés de Saqqarah', in *Bull. Inst. d'Ég.*, XXXVI (1955), pp. 357-64.

LAUER, J.-P. Reclassement des rois des IIIe et IVe dynasties égyptiennes par l'archéologie monumentale', in *C.-R. Ac. Inscr. B.-L.*, 1962, pp. 290-310.

LAUER, J.-P. 'Les petites pyramides à degrés de la IIIe dynastie', in *Revue Archéologique*, 1962, pp. 5-15.

LAUER, J.-P. 'Nouvelles remarques sur les pyramides à degrés de la IIIe dynastie' in *Orientalia*, 35 (1966), pp. 440-8.

LAUER, J.-P. 'Au complexe funéraire de l'Horus Sekhem-khet. Recherches et travaux menés dans la nécropole de Saqqarah au cours de la campagne 1966-67', in *C.-R. Ac. Inscr. B.-L.*, 1967 (Nov.-Dec.), p. 493ff.

LAUER, J.-P. 'Recherche et découverte du tombeau sud de l'Horus Sekhem-khet dans son complexe funéraire à Saqqarah', in *Revue d'Égyptologie*, 20, (1968), pp. 97-107.

LAUER, J.-P. 'Recherche et découverte du tombeau sud de l'Horus Sekhem-khet à Saqqarah', in *Bull. Inst. d'Ég.*, XLVIII and XLIX (1969), pp. 121-31.

MARAGIOGLIO, V. and RINALDI, C. A. Part II, *see under* General.

PETRIE, W. M. F. and QUIBELL, J. E. *Nagada and Ballas*. London, 1896.

RICKE, H., *see under* General.

STIÉNON, J. 'El-Kôlah, Mission de la Fondation Égyptologique Reine Élisabeth; 1949', in *Chron. d'Ég.*, 49 (1950), pp. 43-5.

VANDIER, J., *see under* General.

WEILL, R. 'Fouilles à Tounah et à Zaouiét el-Maietin', in *C.-R. Ac. Inscr. B.-L.*, 1912, pp. 484-90.

Chapter Three   ABD ES-SALAM MOHAMMED HUSSEIN. 'Pyramids' Study Project', in *P.R.S.H.S.*, I (1951), pp. 27-40.

BARSANTI, A. 'Fouilles de Zaouiét el-Aryân (1904-6)', in *Ann. Serv.*, VIII (1907), pp. 201-10.

BATRAWI, A. 'A Small Mummy from the Pyramid at Dahshur', in *Ann. Serv.*, XLVIII (1948), pp. 585-90.

BORCHARDT, L. 'Ein Königserlass aus Dahshur', in *Z.Ä.S.*, XLII (1905), pp. 1-11.

BORCHARDT, L. *Die Entstehung der Pyramide an der Baugeschicte der Pyramide bei Mejdum nachgewiesen*. Berlin, 1928.

FAKHRY, A. '*The Southern Pyramid of Sneferu*', in *Ann. Serv.*, LI (1951), pp. 509-22.

FAKHRY, A. 'The Excavation of Sneferu's Monuments at Dahshur, Second Preliminary Report', in *Ann. Serv.*, LII (1954), pp. 563-94.

FAKHRY, A. *The Monuments of Sneferu at Dahshur*, Vol. I, *The Bent Pyramid*, Vol. II, *The Valley Temple*. Cairo, 1959-61.

GOEDICKE, H. 'The Pharaoh *Ny-Swth*', in *Z.Ä.S.*, 81 (1956), pp. 18-24.

GRIFFITH, F. Ll. 'The Inscriptions of the Pyramid of Medum', in Petrie, W.M.F. *Medum*. London, 1892.

HELCK, W., *see under* General.

JÉQUIER, G. 'Rapport préliminaire sur les fouilles exécutées en 1924-5 dans la partie méridionale de la nécropole memphite', in *Ann. Serv.*, XXV (1925), pp. 71-5.

Jéquier, G. *Douze and de fouilles dans la nécropole memphite*. Neuchâtel, 1940.

Lauer, J.-P. 'Sur la pyramide de Meïdoum et les deux pyramides du roi Snefrou a Dahchour', in *Orientalia*, 36 (1967), pp. 239–54.

Maragioglio, V. and Rinaldi, C. A. Parts III and VI, *see under* General.

Maspero, G. and Barsanti, A. 'Fouilles de Zaouiét el-Aryān (1904–5)', in *Ann. Serv.*, VII (1906), pp. 257–86.

Maystre, Ch. 'Les Dates des pyramides de Snefrou', in *Bull. Inst. fr.*, XXXV (1935), pp. 89–98.

Mustapha, H. 'The Surveying of the Bent Pyramid at Dahshur', in *Ann. Serv.*, LII (1954), pp. 595–601.

Petrie, W. M. F. *The Pyramids and Temples of Gizeh*. London, 1883.

Petrie, W. M. F. *A Season in Egypt, 1887*. London, 1888.

Petrie, W. M. F. *Medum*. London, 1892.

Petrie, W. M. F., Mackay, E. and Wainwright, G. A. *Meydum and Memphis (III)*. London, 1910.

Reisner, G. A. and Fisher, C. S. 'The Work of the Harvard University Museum', in *Bull. M.F.A.*, 9 (1911), pp. 54–9.

Reisner, G. A., *see under* Chapter I.

Ricke, H. 'Baugeschichtlicher Vorbericht über die Kultanlagen der südlichen Pyramide des Snofru in Dahschur', in *Ann. Serv.*, LII (1954), pp. 603–23.

Ricke, H., *see under* General.

Rowe, A. 'Excavations of the Eckley B. Coxe, Jr. Expedition at Meydum, Egypt, 1929–30', in the *Museum Journal*. Pennsylvania, March 1931.

Smith, W. S. 'Inscriptional Evidence for the History of the Fourth Dynasty', in *J.N.E.S.*, XI (1952), pp. 113–28.

Vandier, J., *see under* General.

Varille, A. *À propos des pyramides de Sneferu*. Cairo, 1947.

Vyse, H. and Perring, J. S., *see under* General.

Chapter Four

Badawi, A. 'The Stellar Destiny of Pharaoh and the So-called Air-Shafts of Cheops' Pyramid', in *Mitt. deutschen Akad. Berlin*, Band X, Heft 2/3 (1964), pp. 189–206.

Baikie, J. 'The Sphinx', in J. H. Hastings, *Encyclopaedia of Religion and Ethics*, Vol. XI, pp. 767–8. Edinburgh, 1920.

Baly, T. J. C. 'Notes on the Ritual of Opening the Mouth', in *J.E.A.*, 16 (1930), pp. 173–86.

Bergmann, E. v. 'Die Sphinx', in *Z.Ä.S.*, XVIII (1880), pp. 50–1.

Blackman, A. M. 'Some Notes on the Ancient Egyptian Practice of Washing the Dead', in *J.E.A.*, V (1918), pp. 117–24.

Blackman, A. M. 'The Rite of Opening the Mouth in Ancient Egypt and Babylonia', in *J.E.A.*, X (1924), pp. 47–59.

Borchardt, L. and Sethe, K. 'Zur Geschichte der Pyramiden', in *Z.Ä.S.*, 30 (1892), pp. 83–106.

Borchardt, L. *Gegen die Zahlenmystik an der grossen Pyramide bei Gise*. Berlin, 1922.

Borchardt, L. *Längen und Richtungen der vier Grundkanten der grossen Pyramide bei Gise*. Berlin, 1926.

Borchardt, L. *Einiges zur dritten Bauperiode der grossen Pyramide bei Gise*. Berlin, 1932.

Capart, J. and Werbrouck, Marcelle, *see under* General.

Černý, J. 'A Note on the Recently Discovered Boat of Cheops', in *J.E.A.*, 41 (1955), pp. 75–9.

Černý, J. 'Name of the King of the Unfinished Pyramid at Zawiyet el-Aryan', in *M.D.A.I.K.*, XVI (1958), pp. 25–9.

Clarke, S. and Engelbach, R. *Ancient Egyptian Masonry*. Oxford, 1930.

Cole, J. H. *The Determination of the Exact Size and Orientation of the Great Pyramid of Giza (Survey of Egypt, Paper No. 39)*. Cairo, 1925.

DERRY, D. E. 'Mummification', in *Ann. Serv.*, XLI (1942), pp. 240–65.

DRIOTON, É. review of Grdseloff, B. 'Das Reinigunszelt', in *Ann. Serv.*, XL (1940), pp. 1007–14.

FIRCHOW, O. 'Königsschiff and Sonnenbarke', in *W.Z.K.M.*, 54 (1957), pp. 34–42.

GOYON, G. 'La chaussée monumentale et la temple de la vallée de la pyramide de Khéops', in *Bull. Inst. fr.*, LXVII (1969), pp. 49–69.

GRDSELOFF, B. *Das ägyptische Reinigungszelt*. Cairo, 1941.

HASSAN, S. *Excavations at Giza*, 8 vols. Oxford and Cairo, 1932–53.

HELCK, W. 'Zur Entstehung des Westfriedhofs an der Cheops-Pyramide', in *Z.Ä.S.*, 81 (1956), pp. 62–5.

HELCK, W., *see under* General.

HÖLSCHER, U. *Das Grabdenkmal des Königs Chephren*. Leipzig, 1912.

JÉQUIER, G. *Manuel d'archéologie égyptienne*. Paris, 1924.

JÉQUIER, G. *Le Mastabat Faraoun*. Cairo, 1928.

JUNKER, H. 'Von der ägyptischen Baukunst des Alten Reiches', in *Z.Ä.S.*, 63 (1928), pp. 1–14.

JUNKER, H., *see under* Chapter I.

LAUER, J.-P. 'Le Temple funéraire de Khéops à la grande pyramide de Guizeh', in *Ann. Serv.*, XLVI (1947), pp. 245–59.

LAUER, J.-P. 'Note complémentaire sur le temple funéraire de Khéops', in *Ann. Serv.*, XLIX (1949), pp. 111–23.

LAUER, J.-P. 'Récentes dècouvertes dans la nécropole memphite', in *C.-R. Ac. Inscr. B.-L.*, October 1954, pp. 368–79.

LAUER, J.-P. 'Sur l'âge et l'attribution possible de l'excavation monumentale de Zaouiêt el-Aryân', in *Revue d'Égyptologie*, 14 (1962), pp. 21–36.

MARAGIOGLIO, V. and RINALDI, C. A. Parts IV, V and VI, *see under* General.

MOHAMMAD ZAKI NOUR, MOHAMMAD SALAH OSMAN, ZAKY ISKANDER and AHMAD YOUSSOF MOUSTAFA. *The Cheops Boats*, Part I. Cairo, 1960.

PETRIE, W. M. F. *The Pyramids and Temples of Gizeh*. London, 1883.

RAWLINSON, G. *History of Herodotus* (Everyman's Library, edited by E. H. Blakeney). London, 1912.

REISNER, G. A. 'The Tomb of Meresankh, a great-granddaughter of Queen Hetepheres I and Sneferu', in *Bull. M.F.A.*, XXV (1927), pp. 64–79.

REISNER, G. A. *Mycerinus, The Temples of the Third Pyramid at Giza*. Cambridge, Massachusetts, 1931.

REISNER, G. A. *A History of the Giza Necropolis*, Vol. I. Cambridge, Massachusetts, 1942.

REISNER, G. A. and SMITH, W. S. *A History of the Giza Necropolis*, Vol. II, *The Tomb of Hetep-heres, the Mother of Cheops*. Cambridge, Massachusetts, 1955.

RICKE, H., *see under* General.

ROWE, A. 'Some Facts concerning the Great Pyramids of el-Gîza and their Royal Constructors', in *Bull. of the John Rylands Library*, 44, No. 1 (1961), pp. 100–18.

SMITH, E. BALDWIN. *Egyptian Architecture as a Cultural Expression*. New York, 1938.

SMITH, W. STEVENSON. 'Old Kingdom Sculpture', in *A.J.A.*, XLV (1941), pp. 514–28.

SMITH, W. STEVENSON. *A History of Egyptian Sculpture and Painting in the Old Kingdom*. Oxford, 1946.

THOMAS, E. 'Air Channels in the Great Pyramid', in *J.E.A.*, 39 (1953), p. 113.

THOMAS, E. 'Solar Barks Prow to Prow', in *J.E.A.*, 42 (1956), pp. 65–79 and pp. 117–18.

TRIMBLE, VIRGINIA. 'Astronomical Investigation concerning the so-called Air Shafts of Cheops' Pyramid', in *Mitt. deutschen Akad. Berlin*, 10 (1964), pp. 183–7.

VANDIER, J., *see under* General.

VYSE, H. and Perring, J. S., *see under* General.

WADDELL, W. G. 'An Account of Egypt by Diodorus Siculus', in *Bull. F.A.C.*, I (1933), Parts 1 and 2.

Chapter Five   ALLEN, T. G. *Occurrences of Pyramid Texts with Cross Indexes of these and other Mortuary Texts*. Chicago, 1950.

BISSING, F. W. VON. *Das Re-Heiligtum des Königs Ne-woser-Re*, 3 vols. Berlin and Leipzig, 1905–28.

BORCHARDT, L. *Das Grabdenkmal des Königs Ne-user-Re*. Leipzig, 1907.

BORCHARDT, L. *Das Grabdenkmal des Königs Nefer-ir-ke-Re*. Leipzig, 1909.

BORCHARDT, L. *Das Grabdenkmal des Königs Sahu-Re*, 2 vols. Leipzig, 1910–13.

BORCHARDT, L. *Die Pyramiden, ihre Entstehung und Entwicklung*. Berlin, 1911.

DRIOTON, É. 'Une Représentation de la famine sur un bas-relief égyptien de la Vᵉ Dynastie', in *Bull. Inst. d'Ég.*, XXV (1942–3), pp. 45–54.

ERMAN, A. *The Literature of the Egyptians* (translated by A. M. Blackman). London, 1927.

FIRTH, C. M. and GUNN, B. *The Teti Pyramid Cemeteries*, 2 vols. Cairo, 1926.

FIRTH, C. M. 'Excavations of the Department of Antiquities at Sakkara (1928–9)', in *Ann. Serv.*, XXIX (1929), pp. 64–70.

GRDSELOFF, B. 'Deux inscriptions juridiques de l'Ancien Empire', in *Ann. Serv.*, XLII (1942), pp. 25–70.

HASSAN, S. 'Excavations at Sakkara (1937–8)', in *Ann. Serv.*, XXXVIII (1938), pp. 519–20.

HASSAN, S. 'The Causeway of Wnis at Sakkara', in *Z.Ä.S.*, 80 (1955), pp. 136–44.

JÉQUIER, G. *La pyramide d'Oudjebten*. Cairo, 1928.

JÉQUIER, G. *Les pyramides des reines Neit et Apouit*. Cairo, 1933.

JÉQUIER, G. *La pyramide d'Aba*. Cairo, 1935.

JÉQUIER, G. *Le monument funéraire de Pepi II*, 3 vols. Cairo, 1936–41.

KAISER, W. 'Zu den Sonnenheiligtümern der 5. Dynastie', in *M.D.A.I.K.*, 14 (1956), pp. 69–81.

LACAU, 'Suppressions et modifications de signes dans les textes funéraires', in *Z.Ä.S.*, 51 (1914), pp. 1–64.

LACAU, P. 'Suppressions des noms divins dans les textes de la chambre funéraire', in *Ann. Serv.*, XXVI (1926), pp. 69–81.

LAUER, J.-P. 'Le temple haut de la pyramide du roi Ouserkaf à Saqqarah', in *Ann. Serv.*, LIII (1955), pp. 119–33.

MARAGIOGLIO, V. and RINALDI, C. Parts VI and VII, *see under* General.

MERCER, S. A. B. *The Pyramid Texts in Translation and Commentary*. 4 vols. New York, 1952.

POSENER-KRIÉGER, P. and DE CENIVAL, J. L. *The Abu Sir Papyri* (Hieratic Papyri in the British Museum, Fifth Series). London, 1968.

RICKE, H. 'Erster Grabungsbericht über das Sonnenheiligtum des Königs Userkaf bei Abusir', in *Ann. Serv.*, LIV (1956–7), pp. 75–82.

RICKE, H. 'Zweiter Grabungsbericht über das Sonnenheiligtum des Königs Userkaf bei Abusir', in *Ann. Serv.*, LIV (1956–7), pp. 305–16.

RICKE, H. 'Dritter Grabungsbericht über das Sonnenheiligtum des Königs Userkaf bei Abusir', in *Ann. Serv.*, LV (1958), pp. 73–7.

RICKE, H. 'Das Sonnenheiligtum des Königs Userkaf', in *Beiträge zur ägyptischen Bauforschung und Altertumskunde*, Heft 8, Band 11. Wiesbaden, 1969.

SCHOTT, S., *see under* General.

SETHE, K. *Die altägyptischen Pyramidentexte*, 3 vols. Leipzig, 1908–22.

SETHE, K. *Übersetzung und Kommentar zu den altägyptischen Pyramidentexten*, 4 vols. Glückstadt.

SPELEERS, L. *Traduction, index et vocabulaire des textes des pyramides Égyptiennes*. Brussels, 1935.

WINTER, E. 'Zur Deutung der Sonnenheiligtümer der 5. Dynastie', in *W.Z.K.M.*, 54 (1957), pp. 222–33.

Chapter Six   ARNOLD, D. 'Bemerkungen zu den Königsgräbern der frühen 11. Dynastie von El-Târif', in *M.D.A.I.K.*, 23 (1968), pp. 26–37.

AYRTON, E. R., CURRELLY, C. T. and WEIGALL, A. E. P. *Abydos III*. London, 1904.

BRUNTON, G. *Lahun I, The Treasure*. London, 1920.

BRUYÈRE, B. *Fouilles de l'institut français du Caire*, Vol. VIII. Cairo, 1933.

CARTER, H. 'Report on the Tomb of Menthuhotep I', in *Ann. Serv.*, II (1901), pp. 201–5.

DAVIES, NINA M. 'Some Representations of Tombs from the Theban Necropolis', in *J.E.A.*, 24 (1938), pp. 25–40.

DUNHAM, D. *The Royal Cemeteries of Kush*, Vol. I, *El-Kurru*; Vol. II, *Nuri*; Vol. III, *Decorated Chapels of the Meroitic Pyramids at Meroe and Barkal*; Vol. IV, *Royal Tombs at Meroe and Barkal*. Boston, Massachusetts, 1950–7.

EDGERTON, W. F. 'Chronology of the Twelfth Dynasty', in *J.N.E.S.*, I (1942), pp. 307–14.

FIRCHOW, O. *Studien zu den Pyramidenlagen der 12. Dynastie*. Göttingen, 1942.

GARDINER, A. H. and BELL, H. I. 'The Name of Lake Moeris', in *J.E.A.*, 29 (1943), pp. 37–50.

GARNOT, J. S. F. 'Les fouilles de la nécropole de Soleb (1957–8)', in *Bull. Inst. fr.*, LVIII (1959), pp. 165–73.

GAUTIER, J. E. and JÉQUIER, G. *Fouilles de Licht*. Cairo, 1902.

GUNN, B. and GARDINER, A. H. 'The Expulsion of the Hyksos', in *J.E.A.*, V (1918), pp. 35–56.

GUNN, B. 'The Name of the Pyramid-Town of Sesostris II', in *J.E.A.*, 31 (1945), pp. 106–7.

HAYES, W. C. 'The Entrance Chapel of the Pyramid of Sen-Wosret I', in *Bull. M.M.A.*, XXIX (1934), Section 2, pp. 9–26.

HELCK, W., *see under* General.

JÉQUIER, G. *Deux pyramides du Moyen Empire*. Cairo, 1938.

LANSING, A. 'The Museum's Excavations at Lisht', in *Bull. M.M.A.*, XV (1920), pp. 3–11; XXI (1926), Section 2, pp. 33–40; XXIX (1934), Section 2, pp. 4–9.

LYTHGOE, A. M. 'Excavations at the South Pyramid of Lisht in 1914', in *Anc. Egypt*, 1915, pp. 145–53.

LYTHGOE, A. M. 'The Treasure of Lahun', in *Bull. M.M.A.*, December 1919, Part 2.

MACE, A. C. 'Excavations at Lisht', in *Bull. M.M.A.*, November 1921, Part 2, pp. 5–19 and December 1922, Part 2, pp. 4–18.

MARAGIOGLIO, V. and RINALDI, C. A. 'Note sulla piramide di Ameny 'Aamu', 'in *Orientalia* 37 (1968), pp. 325–38.

MORGAN, J. DE *Fouilles à Dahchour*, 2 vols. Vienna, 1895–1903.

NAVILLE, E. and HALL, H. R. *The XIth Dynasty Temple of Deir el-Bahari*, 3 vols. London, 1907–13.

NEWBERRY, P. E. 'The Co-regencies of Ammenemes III, IV and Sebeknofru', in *J.E.A.*, 29 (1943), pp. 74–5.

PETRIE, W. M. F. *Hawara, Biahmu and Arsinoe*. London, 1889.

PETRIE, W. M. F. *Illahun, Kahun and Gurob*. London, 1890.

PETRIE, W. M. F. *Kahun, Gurob and Hawara*. London, 1890.

PETRIE, W. M. F., WAINWRIGHT, G. A. and MACKAY, E. *The Labyrinth, Gerzeh and Mazghuneh*. London, 1912.

PETRIE, W. M. F., BRUNTON, G. and MURRAY, M. A. *Lahun II*. London, 1923.

RANDALL-MACIVER, D. and MACE, A. C. *El-Amrah and Abydos*. London, 1902.

RAPHAEL, M. 'Nouveau nom d'une pyramide d'un Amenemhēt', in *Ann. Serv.*, XXXVII (1937), pp. 79–80.

REISNER, G. A. 'Excavations at Napata, the Capital of Ethiopia', in *Bull. M.F.A.*, XV (1917), No. 89, pp. 25–34.

REISNER, G. A. 'Known and Unknown Kings of Ethiopia', in *Bull. M.F.A.*, XVI (1918), No. 97, pp. 67–81.

REISNER, G. A. 'The Royal Family of Ethiopia', in *Bull. M.F.A.*, XXI (1923), No. 124, pp. 12–27.

VANDIER, J. *La tombe de Nefer-Abou*. Cairo, 1935.

VANDIER, J., *see under* General.

WINLOCK, H. E. 'The Theban Necropolis in the Middle Kingdom', in *A.J.S.L.*, XXXII (1915), pp. 1–37.

WINLOCK, H. E. 'The Tombs of the Kings of the Seventeenth Dynasty at Thebes', in *J.E.A.*, X (1924), pp. 217–77.

WINLOCK, H. E. *The Treasure of El-Lahun*. New York, 1934.

WINLOCK, H. E. 'Neb-hepet-Re Mentu-hotep of the Eleventh Dynasty', in *J.E.A.*, 26 (1940), pp. 116–19.

WINLOCK, H. E. *Excavations at Deir el-Bahri, 1911–1931*. New York, 1942.

WINLOCK, H. E. 'The Eleventh Egyptian Dynasty', in *J.N.E.S.*, Vol. 2, No. 4 (1943), pp. 249–83.

WINLOCK, H. E. *The Rise and Fall of the Middle Kingdom in Thebes*. New York, 1947.

Chapter Seven   ANTONIADI, E. M. *L'Astronomie égyptienne depuis les temps les plus reculés jusqu'à la fin de l'époque alexandrine*. Paris, 1934.

BORCHARDT, L. 'Ein altägyptisches astronomisches Instrument', in *Z.Ä.S.*, 37 (1899), pp. 10–17.

BREASTED, J. H., *see under* Introduction.

CLARKE, S. and ENGELBACH, R., *see under* Chapter IV.

COLE, J. H., *see under* Chapter IV.

DUNHAM, D. 'Building an Egyptian Pyramid', in *Archaeology*, 9 (1956), No. 3, pp. 159–65.

FAULKNER, R. O. 'The King and the Star-Religion in the Pyramid Texts', in *J.N.E.S.*, XXV (1966), pp. 153–61.

GUNN, B. review of Peet, T. E. 'The Rhind Mathematical Papyrus', in *J.E.A.*, XII (1926), pp. 123–37.

LAUER, J.-P. 'Les grandes pyramides étaient-elles peintes?', in *Bull. Inst. d'Ég.*, XXXV (1953), pp. 377–96.

LAUER, J.-P. 'Comment furent construites les pyramides', in *Historia*, No. 86 (1954), pp. 57–66.

LAUER, J.-P. 'Sur le choix de l'angle de pente dans les pyramides d'Égypte', in *Bull. Inst. d'Ég.*, XXXVII (1956), pp. 57–66.

LAUER, J.-P. 'À propos de l'orientation des grandes pyramides', in *Bull. Inst. d'Ég.*, 1960, pp. 7–15.

LAUER, J.-P., *see under* General.

LUCAS, A. 'Were the Giza Pyramids Painted?', in *Antiquity*, XII (1938), pp. 26–30.

LUCAS, A. *Ancient Egyptian Materials and Industries*. 4th edition revised by J. R. Harris. London, 1962.

MACE, A. C. 'Excavations at the North Pyramid of Lisht', in *Bull. M.M.A.*, IX (1914), p. 220.

MASPERO, G. 'Note sur le pyramidion d'Amenemhait III à Dahchour', in *Ann. Serv.*, III (1902), pp. 206–8.

PETRIE, W. M. F. *The Pyramids and Temples of Gizeh*. London, 1883.

PETRIE, W. M. F. 'The Building of a Pyramid', in *Anc. Egypt*, 1930, Part II, pp. 33–9.

POCHAN, A. 'Observations relatives au revêtement des deux grandes pyramides de Giza', in *Bull. Inst. d'Ég.*, XVI (1934), pp. 214–20.

RAWLINSON, G. *see under* Chapter IV.

ROWE, A., *see under* Chapter IV.

SCHARFF, A. *Das Grab als Wohnhaus in der ägyptischen Frühzeit*. Munich, 1947.

SMITH, S. 'A Babylonian Fertility Cult', in *J.R.A.S.*, October 1928, pp. 849–75.

THAUSING, G. 'Zum Sinn der Pyramiden', in *Anzeiger der phil.-hist. Klasse der Österreichen Akademie der Wissenschaften*, No. 7 (1948), pp. 121–30.

WADDELL, W. G. *Herodotus*, Book II. London, 1939.

WHEELER, N. F. 'Pyramids and their Purpose', in *Antiquity*, IX (1935), pp. 172–85.

ZÁBA, Z. *L'orientation astronomique dans l'ancienne Égypte, et la précession de l'axe du monde*. Prague, 1953.

Notes on the Illustrations

Walters and the Rogers Fund, 1916. (bottom) The Metropolitan Museum of Art, New York. Contribution from Henry Walters and the Rogers Fund, 1916.

172 The Metropolitan Museum of Art, New York. Contribution from Henry Walters and the Rogers Fund, 1916.

175 Egyptian National Museum, Cairo. Photo: John Ross.

176–7 Deir el-Bahri. Photo: Hirmer Verlag München.

178 (top) Egyptian National Museum, Cairo. Photo: John Ross. (bottom) The Metropolitan Museum of Art, New York. Contribution from Henry Walters and the Rogers Fund, 1916.

183 Egyptian National Museum, Cairo. Photo: Hirmer Verlag München.

187 Egyptian National Museum, Cairo. Photo: John Ross.

188 Egyptian National Museum, Cairo. Photo: John Ross.

192–3 Meroe. Photo: Museum of Fine Arts, Boston.

199 Aswan. Photo: Alistair Duncan, Middle East Archive.

209 Egyptian National Museum, Cairo. Photo: John Ross.

211 Egyptian National Museum, Cairo. Photo: John Ross.

213 The Metropolitan Museum of Art, New York. Museum Excavations, 1913–14; Rogers Fund Supplemented by Contributions of Edward S. Harkness.

214–15 Saqqara. By courtesy of Ahmed Moussa. Photo: John Ross.

216 Egyptian National Museum, Cairo. Photo: John Ross.

220 Giza. Photo: John Ross.

Special thanks are due to John Ross for his valuable assistance in collecting the illustrations.

Notes on the Drawings

The drawings were adapted by J. C. Rose from the sources listed below. Page numbers from this book are followed in brackets by numbers indicating the volume, page or plate in the source material.

W. B. EMERY, *The Tomb of Hor-Aha*: 26 (Plate I)

W. B. EMERY, *Great Tombs of the First Dynasty*: 32 top (Vol. III, Plate 85), 32 bottom (Vol. I, Plates 21–6)

J.-P. LAUER, *La Pyramide à Degrés*: 40 (Vol. II, Plate IV), 42 top (Vol. III, Plate II), 42 bottom (Vol. III, Plate I), 44 (Vol. II, Plate LXXXIII), 45 (Vol. II, Plate LX), 46 (Vol. II, Plate LXX), 47 (Vol. II, Plate XLV)

M. Z. GONEIM, *Horus Sekhem-khet, The Unfinished Step Pyramid at Saqqara*: 57 top (Vol. I, Plate IV), 57 bottom (Vol. I, Plate III)

G. A. REISNER, *The Development of the Egyptian Tomb down to the Accession of Cheops*: 61 (fig. 57), 122 (fig. 71)

J. STIENON, 'El Kôlah' in *Chronique d'Égypte*: 63 (No. 49, fig. 10)

L. BORCHARDT, *Die Entstehung der Pyramide*: 65 (Plates 3 and 4)

W. M. FLINDERS PETRIE, *Medum*: 66 (Plate IV)

Col. H. VYSE, *Operations carried on at the Pyramids of Gizeh*: 69 (Vol. III, facing p. 66), 75 top (Vol. III, facing p. 69), 76 (Vol. III, figs. 1 and 2, facing p. 64), 86 (Vol. I, facing p. 3), 115 (Vol. II, facing pp. 72 and 80)

Annales du Service des Antiquités: 74 top (Vol. LII, p. 567, A. Fakhry), 74 bottom (Vol. LII, p. 611, fig. 4, H. Ricke), 75 bottom (Vol. LII, p. 607, fig. 1, H. Ricke), 96 (Vol. XLVI, p. 247, Plate LXVIII, J.-P. Lauer), 133 (Vol. LIII [1955], Plate 3, facing p. 134, J.-P. Lauer)

R. LEPSIUS, *Denkmäler aus Aegypten un Aethiopien*: 81 (Text Vol. II, p. 5)

J. CAPART and M. WERBROUCK, *Memphis à l'ombre des Pyramides*: 92 (figs. 53–4), and W. S. Smith, *The Art and Architecture of Ancient Egypt*: 92 (Plate 27a)

U. HÖLSCHER, *Das Grabdenkmal des Königs Chephren*: 104 (Plate III), 109 (Plates II and VII)

G. JÉQUIER, *Le Mastabat Faraoun*: 125 (fig. 2)

L. BORCHARDT, *Das Grabdenkmal des Königs Ne-user-Rē*: 127 (Plate I)

L. BORCHARDT, *Das Rē-Heiligtum des Königs Ne-woser-Rē*: 132 (Vol. I, Plate I)

L. BORCHARDT, *Das Grabdenkmal des Königs Sahu-Rē*: 134 (Vol. I, Plate 16), 135 (Vol. I, Plate 9), 136 (Vol. I, Plate 11), 204 (Vol. I, Plate 7)

K. SETHE, *Pyramidentexte*: 139 (Vol. III, p. 116)

G. JÉQUIER, *Le Monument funéraire de Pepi II*: 142 (Vol. III, Plate 1)

E. NAVILLE, *The XIth Dynasty Temple of Deir el-Bahari*: 159 (Vol. II, Plate XXIII)

'Preliminary Reports of the Excavations at Lisht' published in the *Bulletin of the Metropolitan Museum of Art*, Part II, July 1920, p. 4; Part II, March 1926, p. 37; Part II, November 1934, p. 23; and from a private communication from Lindsley F. Hall of the Metropolitan Museum of Art: 162

W. M. FLINDERS PETRIE, *Kahun, Gurob and Hawara*: 180 (Plate II), 181 top (Plate IV)

G. JÉQUIER, *Deux pyramides du Moyen Empire*: 181 bottom (Plates I and VIII), 184 (Plate VIII)

B. BRUYÈRE, *Rapport sur les fouilles de Deir el-Medineh* (1930): 191 (Plate XXXII)

Bulletin of the Boston Museum of Fine Arts: 195 (Vol. XVI, p. 70)

L. BORCHARDT, *Zeitschrift für ägyptische Sprache*: 198 and 200 (Vol. XXXVII, 1899, p. 10)

P. E. NEWBERRY, *El-Bersheh*: 202 (Part I, Plate XV)

Index

Page numbers in **bold** type refer to colour plates; page numbers in *italics*, to black-and-white illustrations.